LINES
ARGUMENT
FOR POLICY DEBATE

LINES OF ARGUMENT
FOR POLICY DEBATE

CAROL WINKLER

Georgia State University

WILLIAM NEWNAM

Emory University

DAVID BIRDSELL

City University of New York, Baruch College

Madison, Wisconsin • Dubuque, Iowa • Indianapolis, Indiana
Melbourne, Australia • Oxford, England

Book Team

Editor *Stan Stoga*
Developmental Editor *Mary E. Rossa*
Production Editor *Jayne Klein*
Visuals/Design Developmental Consultant *Marilyn A. Phelps*
Visuals/Design Freelance Specialist *Mary L. Christianson*
Publishing Services Specialist *Sherry Padden*
Marketing Manager *Carla J. Aspelmeier*
Advertising Manager *Jodi Rymer*

WCB Brown & Benchmark

A Division of Wm. C. Brown Communications, Inc.

Vice President and General Manager *Thomas E. Doran*
Editor in Chief *Edgar J. Laube*
Executive Editor *Ed Bartell*
Executive Editor *Stan Stoga*
National Sales Manager *Eric Ziegler*
Director of CourseResource *Kathy Law Laube*
Director of CourseSystems *Chris Rogers*
Director of Marketing *Sue Simon*
Director of Production *Vickie Putman Caughron*
Imaging Group Manager *Chuck Carpenter*
Manager of Visuals and Design *Faye M. Schilling*
Design Manager *Jac Tilton*
Art Manager *Janice Roerig*
Permissions/Records Manager *Connie Allendorf*

Wm. C. Brown Communications, Inc.

President and Chief Executive Officer *G. Franklin Lewis*
Corporate Vice President, President of WCB Manufacturing *Roger Meyer*
Vice President and Chief Financial Officer *Robert Chesterman*

Cover and interior design by Carol S. Joslin
Copyedited by Martha Morss

Contents

6 COUNTERPLANS 99

7 INTERACTION AMONG LINES OF ARGUMENT

8 ROLES OF THE SPEAKER

Preface

Lines of Argument for Policy Debate is a part of a three-part instructional series about argumentation and debate. It is designed to be used in conjunction with *Lines of Argument,* a core text which introduces the topical traditions of argumentation as they apply to general debate issues: invention, research, evidence, reasoning, delivery, cross-examination, flowcharting, and ethics. This companion text supplements the core volume by identifying the lines of argument specific to policy debate.

Lines of Argument for Policy Debate differs from most textbooks on the debate market. Rather than treating all of the stock issues in a single chapter as the components of a prima facie case, it devotes a full chapter to each of the general lines of argument in policy debate. Chapter Two, for example, explores the issue of significance in policy debate. The chapter begins by identifying the lines of argument useful for establishing that a significant problem exists, continues with lines of argument useful for denying the significance of a problem, and ends with the lines of argument that help debaters resolve conflicting claims of significance.

To help beginning debaters understand the far-reaching applicability of the general lines of argument in policy debate, we provide a variety of examples. In most of the chapters, a running argument between two characters illustrates each of the argumentative options. Additionally, we provide excerpts from National Debate Tournament Championship Rounds so beginning debaters can understand how the lines of argument are presented in actual intercollegiate debates. While these debates are generally strong examples of conventional debate practice, instructors should let students know that they frequently do not include complete citations. Final round transcripts have been edited slightly in some cases to make the tournament arguments more easily understood by beginning debaters. The authors would like to thank Jim Pratt, president of the American Forensics Association, for his willingness to grant permission to use the excerpts of the debates.

While each of the general lines of argument is considered independently, the policy text also includes a chapter that explores the interrelationships between the various arguments in a debate. By showing debaters ways to use argumentative interrelationships to minimize the impact of their opponent's arguments and maximize the impact of their own, the book develops an integrated perspective on the multitude of arguments that can occur in a single setting.

Having equipped the debater with the material to begin to debate, we move to a discussion of the format of contemporary debate. Chapter Eight explores the conventional practices regarding what sorts of arguments occur within each of the constructive and rebuttal speeches. Goals are established for each speech. Throughout the chapter, we use a single hypothetical debate to illustrate what each speaker is expected to do.

The policy text concludes with a consideration of how the lines of argument interact with different perspectives of debate evaluation. Prominent debate paradigms are presented, but the discussion is limited to how different perspectives on debate influence the interpretation of the general lines of argument in policy debate.

Instructors using this text should feel free to use whichever portions of the text are relevant for the skill and experience level of their debaters. As an introductory text, *Lines of Argument for Policy Debate* starts at the beginning, introducing the most basic aspects of the activity. It does not, however, stop with traditional introductory considerations; it explores the multiplicity of options available for arguing a point. As a result, some sections may not be appropriate for every classroom. The text has been designed to accommodate instructors who may want to drop some of the more complex material. No basic discussions in any one chapter depend on the advanced discussions in some other chapter.

For example, in Chapter Five, "Analyzing Topicality Through Lines of Argument," the first two sections of the chapter, "Identifying Key Terms" and "Sources of Definition," are relevant to all beginning debaters. However, the section "Standards for Evaluating Competing Definitions" may not be appropriate for the average debate class. This section might be more useful to debaters who plan to actually participate in interscholastic debate tournaments. Another example is our extensive treatment of counterplans. This is important information for advanced students, but introductory courses often omit material of this sort. Students need not have read the chapter on counterplans in order to comprehend subsequent chapters. Instructors should feel free to eliminate such self-contained sections from their reading assignments.

One of our primary goals in writing *Lines of Argument for Policy Debate* was to remove much of the mystery that surrounds competitive debate. By relying on the general topics of lines of argument in policy debate, we hope to attract many students who might have been intimidated by debate or thought it was an activity reserved exclusively for expert or talented speakers. Debaters at all levels will discover options for policy argument that they may never have considered or never have examined in a formal way.

Acknowledgments

Since beginning work on this book we have benefited from the wisdom of a great many colleagues working in the field of debate and argumentation. We are particularly thankful for the careful and insightful criticism from the review teams assembled by Brown & Benchmark: Steven R. Brydon, California State University, Chico; Nicholas Burnett, California State University, Sacramento; Alan Cirlin, St. Mary's University; Joseph M. Corcoran, California State University, Chico; Dale Hample, Western Illinois University; William Keith, University of Louisville; Michael Leigh, Orange Coast College; Scott Nobles, Macalaster College; Edward L. Schiappa, Purdue University; and Paul Scovell, Salisbury State College. In addition, Melissa Wade of Emory University, Judy Butler of Spelman College, and Star Muir of George Mason University provided advice and encouragement. Together, these critics challenged us to write a much better book than we could have on our own; any errors that remain are no fault of theirs.

We would like to thank Georgia State University, Emory University, and Baruch College for providing us with the necessary support to complete this project. In particular, the authors would like to thank Marsha Stanback for providing grant support for the project in her role as chairperson of the Communications Department at Georgia State. Kimberly Kline contributed hours of necessary computer assistance. Greg Huber of Emory provided much needed assistance with graphics. We would also like to thank James Pratt of the American Forensic Association for allowing us to use transcripts of championship debates.

The staff at Brown & Benchmark have made authorship of a three-volume text as uncomplicated as the task can be. Special thanks are due Stan Stoga, an editor who encouraged the project and strived to improve it from its original conception. Thanks also to copyeditors Martha Morss and Jeff Putnam who did wonders for our prose.

We owe a great deal to the faculty of the National High School Institute of Speech. The collegial atmosphere of Northwestern University's institute produced a body of debate knowledge that surfaces throughout this three-book series. Many of the ideas in this text were shaped by the outstanding teachers who have worked in that program. We would like to thank David Zarefsky, Erwin Chimerensky, and Edward Schiappa, all directors of the institute, for providing a rich and rewarding environment in which to explore the debate process.

Finally, we would like to thank friends and family for their understanding during a lengthy process. Jean Gallagher was kind and tolerant and even paused to rework some of the more infelicitous language.

1

The Nature of Policy Debate

Chapter Outline

Process of Policy Debate
General Lines of Argument and Policy Debate
Summary and Conclusions

Key Terms

policy debate
significance
inherency
solvency
topicality
burden of proof
presumption
affirmative
negative
judge
fiat
plan
case
stock issues
counterplan

Dad: Myron, take out the garbage!

Myron: I don't think it's fair that I always have to take out the garbage. Florie only has to do silly indoor things. I think we ought to develop new duties around here. I think I ought to get to wax the floors and she ought to be sent outside in forty degree temperatures.

Professor Coldheart: Remember, those term papers are due on Friday; I will give no extensions.

* * *

Shelley: Excuse me, Professor C.? I was wondering if the whole class could get an extension on that term paper? Remember how we kept telling you that all the books on our topic areas were missing from the shelves most of the semester? Well, they just found thousands of books locked up in the basement. Look, there's even an article in the school paper about it. Now that we have access to those books, maybe you should give us an extension. I'm sure our papers would be much better.

The Senator: As you know, I'm a strong advocate of law and order. I don't want to clutter my legislative agenda with television regulation.

* * *

The Lobbyist: Senator, I respect your record in fighting crime. That's why I think you should support this bill to regulate violence on children's television. Our study shows that watching Saturday morning cartoons increases violent behaviors in children later in life. Unfortunately, the television industry won't change their programming as long as it makes money. Knowing that you are an expert in crime tells me that you would support any proposal that can decrease crime.

What do Myron, Shelley, and the lobbyist have in common? Each is an advocate for a course of action. Myron wants to wax floors instead of take out the garbage. Shelley wants to postpone her deadline so that she can produce a better product. And the lobbyist wants Congress to regulate violence on television to save children from violence. Myron, Shelley, and the lobbyist are supporting policies. Engaging in **policy debate** is the process of advocating courses of action.

What kind of arguments are Myron, Shelley, and the lobbyist making? They are each arguing that there is a significant need for a new policy. Myron feels that he is being unfairly treated because he has to take out the garbage. Shelley claims that her education is being penalized because someone locked all of the books she needs in the library basement. The lobbyist thinks that violence on television turns innocent children into violent adults. **Significance** is the argument that identifies the problem occurring under existing policies.

Myron, Shelley, and the lobbyist also argue that present policies allow for the continued existence of the significant problem. Myron says that the current policy, requiring him to take out the garbage while Florie waxes the floors, creates an unfair condition. Shelley says that the policy of no late papers will lead to a bad educational experience. The lobbyist says the television industry will continue using violent cartoons without new legislation. Each advocate identifies a current policy that perpetuates the need for new policies. **Inherency** is the argument that the problem will continue unless the actions specified in the resolution are adopted.

Myron, Shelley, and the lobbyist also argue that a new policy would remedy the problem caused by the present policies. Myron believes that waxing the floors would restore fairness to his life (we never said that Myron was bright). Shelley believes that an extension will improve the quality of her paper (we believe she might be correct about that). The lobbyist believes that decreasing violence on Saturday morning cartoons will decrease violent crime someday (and that getting the regulation passed will enhance the senator's reputation). Each advocate argues that the new policy could solve the problem. **Solvency** is the argument that the problem can be reduced or eliminated by new policies.

Myron, Shelley, and the lobbyist address themselves to a narrow set of issues. Myron is asked to take out the garbage, and he complains only about that task. Shelley is asked to complete a paper in a given amount of time; her response is to argue about the relationship between the time limit and the paper's quality. The lobbyist is implicitly asked to justify television regulation in terms of crime prevention. He meets the senator's resistance by showing a relationship between viewing violent television and violence itself. None of the three advocates strays from the issue prompted by the person who raised the argument. **Topicality** is the argument that the policies advocated are the same policies recommended in the debate resolution.

Why do these arguments recur in policy debates? When you advocate a policy change, you have a responsibility to prove that there is a reason to alter the current course of action. Myron has to convince his parents that there is need to adopt the new course of action allowing Myron to wax the floors instead of take out the garbage. Shelley has to convince Professor Coldheart to postpone the deadline for the term paper. The lobbyist has to convince the senator to change the existing policy allowing the television industry to determine the content of children's shows. Advocates of change have to prove that a new policy is necessary, that the old policy cannot solve a need, that the new policy can, and that the appropriate authority can adopt new policies. **Burden of proof** is the requirement that those affirming changes in the course of action must demonstrate significance, inherency, solvency, and topicality.

If Myron, Shelley, and the lobbyist had not made these arguments (significance, inherency, solvency, and topicality), the parents, the professor, and the senator would not even be aware that new policies might be necessary. Would Myron's parents think about changing the household chores in the absence of Myron's complaint? Would the Professor consider delaying the deadline for the term paper if Shelley didn't make a case for it? Why would the senator care about children's cartoons if the lobbyist did not suggest the need for new regulations? We tend to presume that the current course of action is quite acceptable until an advocate convinces us otherwise. **Presumption** holds that the current course of action is justified until we are convinced otherwise. Without a reason to change policies, we continue with the present way of doing things.

Myron, Shelley, and the lobbyist can overcome the presumption resting with the present policy by fulfilling the burden of proof regarding the issues of significance, inherency, solvency, and topicality. When Myron, Shelley, and the lobbyist convince the parents, the professor, and the senator that a substantial problem exists under current policies and that new polices which these authorities can enact will solve the problem they overcome the presumption to stay with existing policy.

Myron, Shelley, and the lobbyist have introduced us to the fundamental concepts involved in advocating new policies. Formal academic debate shares these general arguments with informal discussions such as those about garbage and term paper deadlines. Academic debate, however, also has several important conventions to help ensure education and competitive fairness.

Process of Policy Debate

Academic debates involve two sides: an **affirmative** side, charged with defending a formal debate resolution, and a **negative** side is charged with denying the resolution. In most debates, the sides comprise two individuals, or a team, who each offer a constructive speech affirming or negating the resolution and a rebuttal speech to explain and summarize their arguments. The speeches are timed to ensure that both sides have equal time to defend their positions.

A **judge** compares each side's arguments and decides which side wins the debate. For the sake of argument, the judge assumes that the particular policy advocated by the affirmative would be put in place. This assumption is referred to as **fiat** in debates. The judge allows the affirmative to imagine that the new policy can be placed into effect to avoid debates about whether or not it would come into effect. If the policy is assumed to be in place, the debate can focus on the merits of the proposal and any competing policies offered by the negative.

The affirmative team in policy debate must determine which policy to support and provide a rationale for that policy. The proposal advocated by the affirmative is the **plan,** while the rationale for the policy is the **case** for change. You are already familiar with the types of arguments that make up an affirmative case. If you can show that a significant problem exists, that it is an inherent problem, that your plan would solve some of the problem, and that your policy falls within the scope of the debate resolution, you will succeed at presenting an appropriate case for change.

General Lines of Argument and Policy Debate

Policy debates include arguments that are predictable. This is fortunate for debaters because they can identify the recurrent arguments and be better prepared when they engage in policy debate. In Chapter Two of the core text, we identified two types of arguments. General lines of argument are broad themes of inquiry that occur across subject areas. Traditionally, these lines of argument have been referred to as the **stock issues.** In the field of policy debate, these general lines of argument are that there is a significant problem, that the problem will continue into the future, that an alternate policy offers a solution, and that an appropriate authority can undertake the new policy. Specific lines of argument, on the other hand, are dependent on the subject area under discussion. The reasons why Myron wants new chores would be completely irrelevant to the lobbyist wanting new television regulations.

We devote the remainder of this text to describing the general lines of argument that recur in policy debate in more detail. We use specific lines of argument that might occur in particular subject areas of debate to illustrate how the general lines of argument function. We focus each of the next four chapters of the book (Chapters Two through Five) on the general lines of argument in policy debate. We analyze each argument separately to identify further lines of argument that affirm significance, inherency, solvency, and topicality. Each chapter also analyzes lines of argument that negate significance, inherency, solvency, and topicality. Finally, we indicate the arguments useful in resolving conflicts between the two. This introduction to general lines of argument in policy debate should prepare you to succeed in the specific circumstances of any policy debate. By applying the general lines of argument to the particulars of an argumentative situation, you will be able to generate specific lines of argument for specific resolutions. Myron, Shelley, and the lobbyist phrased their arguments differently because each was addressing the core issues of their particular policy controversy.

In Chapter Six we identify a line of argument, known as the counterplan, that is useful for refuting the affirmative's entire defense of resolution. A **counterplan** is an alternative to the affirmative's plan for solving the significant problems perpetuated by present policies. Counterplans can be based on relatively small changes or may encompass radical departures from present practices. This line of argument is useful for debaters opposing the resolution because it interfaces with each of the four general lines of policy argument. The counterplan provides a nonresolutional means for solving a continuing problem in the present system. This unique integrated approach to the general lines of policy argument warrants a separate discussion.

We analyze each line of argument in a separate chapter, but the four lines of argument are connected and interdependent. Remember that the affirmative debater must overcome the presumption of a current policy by proving that a new policy is needed, solvent, and topical. It is important for you to learn these arguments in detail and to see that, combined, they form a complete rationale for the resolution. The individual arguments are important but so are the interrelationships.

In Chapter Seven we pay particular attention to the interaction among the four general lines of argument. We offer debaters an analytical view of the strategic opportunities they may discover in academic debate. Understanding interrelationships among arguments allows you to develop complete and coherent arguments of your own. Knowing how arguments interact also provides you with an opportunity to identify the inconsistencies and irrelevancies of your opponent's arguments.

In Chapter Eight we present the traditional roles of each speaker in a formal debate. We examine the conventional application of the four general lines of argument. We identify standard time limits, orders of speeches, and the conventional expectations for participating in a debate.

In Chapter Nine we explore how debate judges evaluate the general lines of argument in a debate. We offer an explanation of the different perspectives judges may bring into a debate. We also examine the potential biases of judges and provide guidance in identifying such biases. We also suggest ways in which you can appeal to different perspectives.

Summary and Conclusions

To be effective policy advocates, debaters must understand that four general lines of arguments recur in every policy debate. These include that a significant problem exists, that the problem is inherent, that a policy is available that can solve the problem, and that this policy falls within the topical scope of the resolution.

In policy debates, an affirmative team charged with defending the resolution and a negative team attempting to deny the resolution try to convince a judge that they should win the debate. To make this decision, the judge permits the affirmative to imagine that their proposal would be in effect. This assumption, known as fiat, allows the debaters to focus on the merits of their proposals rather than the probability that they will be adopted.

Affirmative debaters must present a plan and a rationale for that plan. The rationale consists of the four general lines of policy argument. These debaters also have the burden of proving the four general lines of argument. This argumentative burden stems from the presumption that the current course of action is desirable until the affirmative team convinces the judge otherwise. By overcoming the presumption against the resolution, the affirmative can persuade the judge to affirm the resolution. If the negative team disproves one of the four general lines of argument, the judge will negate the resolution.

You must remember that you are advocating these arguments in an environment of argumentative clash. The affirmative attempts to fulfill the burden of proof while the negative attempts to disprove the affirmative argument. The interaction of arguments complicates the situation, providing each team with opportunities to magnify their strengths and minimize their weaknesses.

Exercises

1. Choose a significance, inherency, and solvency argument that supports each of the following potential courses of action: mandatory boot camps for first-time drug offenders, introduction of a national lottery to support education, and the banning of nuclear power.
2. Assume that your resolution is, "Resolved: that the federal government should increase its foreign military commitments." Which of the following potential cases would be topical: increased arms sales to Saudi Arabia, increased pay for military personnel, a CIA mission designed to overthrow a foreign dictator, and increased

research dollars to industries engaged in the production of military weapons and supplies. Defend your answers.

3. Examine the level of presumption associated with each of the following policies: freedom to practice the religion of one's choice, the existing tax code, the current level of defense spending, and certification requirements for teachers. Do different courses of action have more presumption than others? What factors determine the weight of presumption for a particular course of action?

4. Assume that your resolution is, "Resolved: that the power of the presidency should be significantly curtailed." Imagine that you are concerned about the number of conflicts that have resulted in a U.S. military presence. Identify a plan that would fall within the boundaries of the resolution. Next, develop a counterplan that would also attack the problem. Which one of the alternatives would be superior? Why?

2

Analyzing Significance Through Lines of Argument

Chapter Outline

Key Terms

significance
scope
magnitude
social significance
traditional significance
moral imperative
disadvantage
link
uniqueness
impact
cost-benefit analysis
link turn
probability
impact turn

Tyrone: Over 3 million Americans are homeless today. These people have it bad: no place to live, no educational opportunity for their kids. They don't even know where their next meal will come from.

Julie: It's not as bad as all that. I read the other day that census data shows that only 200,000 people are homeless. And a lot of those can get a roof over their head and a hot meal from homeless shelters.

Tyrone: You believe the census?! The government didn't count the homeless because they don't want to pay to take care of them. Those shelters. Take a look around. Do you think the homeless would choose to sleep in boxes and under bridges if they could have a roof and a hot meal?

Julie: I'm not saying there are no homeless people. I just think its a problem that's been exaggerated.

Does a significant homelessness problem exist? Is it exaggerated? Is being homeless just a matter of having to stay in a shelter or do people continue to suffer at unacceptable levels? Issues such as these make up the first general line of argument of policy debate: **significance.**

Anyone attempting to argue for a change in policy must convincingly make the claim that a significant need exists to alter current policy. The costs of remaining committed to existing remedies should be unacceptable. Enough people must be suffering, either now or in the future, to warrant a change in policy.

As the advocates of change, affirmative debaters in policy debate have the responsibility to initiate the significance argument. They must convince the judge that a significant change is needed to overcome the presumption against affirming the resolution. Negative debaters may choose to challenge that a need for change exists or may choose to ignore the issue altogether, and focus instead on other issues they believe are more important.

In this chapter we present the lines of argument that revolve around significance in policy debate. Specifically, we outline the options for presenting lines of arguments that prove that a significant need exists for change, that deny that a significant need exists, and that are useful in resolving conflicts between the two.

Lines of Argument for Proving Significance

When making a case that a substantial problem exists under a current policy, affirmative debaters can use a variety of argumentative strategies. They can argue that the significance of the problem derives from the number of individuals affected, the amount of harm experienced by those individuals, the societal costs of not redressing the problem, the traditional values underlying the policy that would address the problem, or the moral responsibility of societies and individuals to address the problem.

Scope of the Problem

To argue that a problem is significant in **scope,** debaters provide a numerical assessment of the victims of current policies. The argument identifies the number of people affected adversely. If affirmative debaters want to advocate a need for the expansion of the United States food aid program, they could point to the significance of over 400 million people worldwide suffering from severe malnutrition. In our opening example, Tyrone demonstrates the scope of the homeless problem by stating that over three million people are homeless. Notice that Tyrone does not provide a precise figure for the number of homeless in America. At times, specific figures are not available to describe the precise extent of the problem. Faced with this situation, you can rely on estimates to indicate the scope of the problem.

In addition to raw numbers of people affected, the geographic dispersal of affected populations is sometimes a relevant test of the scope of the problem. If, for example, all homeless people in the United States lived in New York City, advocates might reasonably argue that the problem is of local, not national, significance. Tyrone could prove the problem to be of national scope by showing that it involves many localities across the country.

Magnitude of the Problem

Not all significance arguments require or are suited to a quantitative approach. A second line of argument for proving significance is the magnitude of the problem for the affected individuals. The **magnitude** of a problem is the degree to which individuals are adversely affected by the current policy. If the deprivation caused by existing policy substantially harms a few individuals, debaters can still make a case for change. The AIDS controversy provides an example. School officials have denied the right to attend school to relatively few children with AIDS. Despite the inability to prove that large numbers are being deprived of an education, advocates for changing this policy could argue that education is critical to the development of the child. Every child deserves the right to attend school.

Nothing precludes you from using lines of argument showing both the scope and the magnitude of the problem. Frequently, the two arguments are combined to make the most compelling case for change. Tyrone identifies the scope of the problem when he says that there are three million homeless people; he also identifies the magnitude of the problem for these three million people when he points out that they have little shelter, education, or food. The magnitude of the problem is so great, that the existence of even a few homeless individuals could justify changing existing policies.

ARGUMENT FOR SIGNIFICANCE

In the final round of the 1979 National Debate Tournament, Northwestern University (Don Dripps and Mark Cotham) affirmed the resolution, "Resolved: that the federal government should implement a program that guarantees employment opportunities for all United States citizens in the labor force." Harvard University (John Bredehoft and Mike King) negated the resolution. Mr. Dripps presented the following argument for Northwestern to prove that unemployment was a significant problem justifying the resolution. Mr. Bredehoft attempted to minimize the significance of the harm in the accompanying speech.

Mr. Dripps argued that unemployment is so harmful to individual worth that we have an ethical responsibility to minimize the harms of unemployment, that unemployment causes illness and death for a large number of persons, and that society suffers from criminal behavior and mental disorders created by large numbers of unemployed.

Mr. Bredehoft responded that there is no loss of individual dignity with unemployment and then proceeded to deny the arguments that unemployment causes illness, death, and social harms. He argued that the assumptions behind those claims are faulty, that the evidence that supports it is faulty, and that, therefore, the problem of unemployment is not as great as Northwestern claims.

Affirmative	Negative
Unemployment causes massive human suffering. (A) The grim toll of even marginal increases in unemployment was documented by the painstaking study of Dr. Harvey Brenner of Johns Hopkins University, undertaken for the Joint Economic Committee in 1976. That controlled epidemiological study revealed that for each 1 percent increase in unemployment, the nation suffered a 4.1 percent increase in suicides; a 1.9 percent increase in cardiovascular, renal, and cirrhosis mortality; and a 1.9 percent increase in overall mortality—that is, each 1 percent of unemployment results in 36,000 needless deaths.	(1) No general harm. Edwin Dale, 1970: "There is no direct connection between a rise in the national unemployment percentage and a rise in serious hardship." (2) It is a net benefit if you value your leisure time any certain amount. One, Fieldstone of Harvard in 1978: "The private cost of unemployment is very large for some of the unemployed, but it is quite small for others. The average private cost of unemployment is therefore much less relevant than the distribution of such costs." He continues, "If the individual values his leisure and nonmarket activities at even 50 cents an hour, there is no net private cost to unemployment.

Social Significance

A third line of argument for proving significance is that a given issue is important to society as a whole. Unrelated to a specific number of victims or the specific damage to a given individual, **social significance** implies that a problem affects the entire society.

> Tyrone: If we don't help these people now, their children will grow up homeless. Without proper education and nutrition, where do you think these children will end up? Unless we want to be footing the bill for these children in the future, and their children's children beyond that, we'd better start taking care of these folks now. That means a government program with lots of money.

Here, Tyrone is arguing that the societal benefit of stopping the cycle of homelessness justifies action now. While the nation's citizenry may not fully realize the costs of coping with the long-term problems of homelessness, society will eventually pay a steeper price than it would today. Many other problems can be considered significant problems for society. National security matters frequently fall into this category. While the need to intervene militarily in a foreign nation may not be obvious to the average citizen, many advocates of such matters insist that society's future is at stake if the nation's leadership does not act. The need to encourage increased investment in small businesses is another example. If a larger number of small businesses can flourish, the economy of the nation can expand.

Traditional Significance

The fourth line of argument for proving significance is that an issue has traditional importance. Appeals to **traditional significance** argue that some conventions of nations, cultures, and communities are valuable historically. These traditions carry importance in public policy debate.

> Tyrone: Our society has always helped the needy. The New Deal gave the nation the means to recover from the Great Depression. The War on Poverty provided millions of poor people with needed food and medical care. We shouldn't just abandon people when they need help the most.

In this appeal, Tyrone establishes the traditional importance of helping the homeless. He shows that throughout the twentieth century the nation has not turned its back on people facing desperate circumstances. Remaining consistent with important traditions heightens the value of Tyrone's claim that the United States government should help the homeless.

Debaters should not underestimate the value of tradition as a persuasive appeal. Legal authorities such as the Supreme Court rely on precedent—earlier cases of practices—as a basis for their legal interpretations of court cases. Likewise, debaters can use established practices to argue the significance of their cases. If you argued that state and local moves to institute waiting periods for gun purchases violate individual rights, you could magnify the significance of

SOCIAL SIGNIFICANCE

In the following excerpt, Northwestern University attempts to establish that unemployment is a socially significant problem by showing that it leads to crime and delinquency. Harvard University responds by indicating that Northwestern's evidence is biased and that better sources show unemployment does not increase crime, and in fact it may actually decrease the level of crime.

Affirmative

(3) Unemployment produces widespread crime and delinquency. Intuitively, young people with neither income to gratify their material needs nor employment to occupy their time are likely to solve both inadequacies through criminal activity. Empirically, this is the case. Dr. Brenner's study, for example, revealed that a 1 percent rise in unemployment produced a 4 percent increase in state prison admissions and a 5.7 percent increase in homicides—that is, 1,700 murders for each 1 percent of unemployment. In October of 1977, the Employment and Training Reporter indicated that according to Brenner's statistics "for every 1 percent increase in unemployment . . . robbery" increased "by 6,704 and burglary by 8,646." Representative Conyers noted the widespread consensus on this issue in 1977: "Even the most conservative crime theorists acknowledge the close relation between crime and unemployment. Data from Congressional Research Service, Congressional Budget Office, and Joint Economic Committee studies show a clear relationship between employment and imprisonment rates for both state and federal prison systems. A recent CBO study, for example,

Negative

(3) Now, on the crime part. Again, note that they quote Brenner. (a) They also quote Conners. Oh, of course he's a union hack. He's from Detroit, the home of the UAW. He depends on the union people for his votes and for his job. Of course he is going to say this.

(b) There is no link to crime. James Q. Wilson of Harvard in 1975: "Crime rose fastest in this country at a time where the number of people living in poverty or squalor was declining." Richard Brenner in 1976: "Existing estimates of the incidence of criminal behavior have been subject to extraordinarily severe, negative criticism in the academic and professional communities." He even recognizes it himself.

Now I would argue (c) [Unemployment actually reduces crime]. Block and Nold of Stanford in April of 1979 published a study. What did the study find? "Brenner indicates that a 1 percentage point decrease in unemployment would be associated with a decrease of .59 and .83 in homicide rates, respectively. These large differences are caused by Brenner's lack of recognition of the indirect effects of a proposed change in policy variables. The indirect effects of decreases in unemployment are of such a magnitude and direction that they would more than

(Continued)

Affirmative (Cont.)

documented a 94 percent positive
correlation between unemployment
and federal prison admissions.''

Negative (Cont.)

offset the beneficial effects of policy
change.'' What is the significance?
''We calculated the net effect,'' and
this is the study, not us, ''of a 1
percentage point decrease in
unemployment, taking into account
both the direct and indirect effects
to be an increase in the homicide
rate per 100,000 by .83 for the 15–
24 year age group and .94 in the
25–40 year age group.'' What do
you [get] when you multiply it out?
About 2,300 more deaths a year.

that threat by appealing to America's traditional adherence to the basic principles embodied in the Constitution. To risk infringing on these principles would undermine the value of the entire institution. Appeals to traditional values are by no means limited to the legal arena. Debaters can discover them in topics ranging from health care to the economy, from space exploration to education.

Moral Imperative

The final approach to establishing that a significant problem exists is the use of the moral imperative. **Moral imperatives** are ethical responsibilities that are fundamental to the human order. Typically, values such as justice, honesty, fairness, compassion, and family fall within this category.

> Tyrone: The government has an obligation to help the homeless. If the government is not compassionate to those citizens who are in trouble, there is no point in having an organized society. We might as well be fending for ourselves.

In his final argument, Tyrone fortifies his claim that we should support the homeless by appealing to a moral imperative. He argues that the government has a responsibility to protect those citizens who are unable to care for themselves; otherwise, there is no rationale for a centralized government. The responsibility is so fundamental that it goes to the very foundations of the role of government within a democratic society.

Moral imperatives can be a highly persuasive means of establishing the significance of a problem. Society is replete with examples of individuals who have endured extreme personal sacrifice to uphold their ethical responsibilities. Whistle-blowers regularly lose their jobs or have to tolerate continued harassment in the workplace for their insistence on the lawful operation of their organizations.

MORAL IMPERATIVE

In this excerpt, Northwestern University establishes that unemployment is a problem that society has a moral obligation to solve by showing how it degrades the self-worth of the individual. Harvard University responds by questioning the strength of Northwestern's evidence once again and by showing how unemployment may actually be good because it increases leisure time.

Affirmative

(I) Unemployment degrades the individual. In a modern industrial society employment is equated with dignity and self-worth. [Conversely], involuntary unemployment implies individual worthlessness and loss of dignity. The presumptive harm of such involuntary idleness was argued by Andrew Biemiller in 1976: "High and persistent joblessness condemns millions of Americans to the economic scrap heap. This is morally wrong, socially wrong, and economically wrong." Absent a compelling social rationale, it is the burden of those who would oppose full employment to overturn the presumption in favor of individual dignity. For those whose policy calculus focuses morbidly and mechanically on death, it might be remembered that American workers currently devote a third of their adult lives to their jobs—a rough suggestion of the significance bound up in losing such an important aspect of one's life.

Negative

(I) Unemployment persists. (A) It will exist. That's fine. (B) It's a problem. (1). It degrades the individual. Biemiller: (a) He's a union hack; he's from the AFL-CIO. What do you expect him to say? (b) Where is the economic scrap heap? What is this? This is no harm. (c) Why is it bad? Maybe they have fun on the scrap heap. (d) In terms of evidence that may come out later, I would suggest it's fine to be unemployed; have lots of leisure time.

Society allows the possibility that guilty defendants will go free to preserve the principle that each individual is presumed innocent until proven guilty beyond a reasonable doubt. Anita Hill, the woman who charged Supreme Court Justice Clarence Thomas with sexual harassment, risked public censure to fulfill what she testified were her ethical responsibilities as a citizen. Appeals to moral imperatives are based on the principle that upholding an ethical responsibility is more important than any harmful consequences that might result from acting in an ethical manner.

You should not feel limited to a single line of argument when establishing the significance of a problem. Frequently, two or more of the lines of argument work in conjunction with each other to produce the strongest possible persuasive appeal. At times, two means of establishing significance may overlap. By using a variety of these approaches, you can maximize the likelihood that you will convince the judge that a substantial problem exists—an issue you must win to have the judge vote to affirm the resolution.

Lines of Argument for Denying Significance

Once the affirmative team establishes that a significant problem exists, negative debaters usually attempt to reduce the importance of the claim. Like the affirmative debater, negative debaters have a variety of lines of argument they can use to achieve their goals. To deny significance, they can argue that no problem exists, that the problem is less important than the affirmative claims, or that the supposed problem has desirable consequences.

No Problem Exists

Using the first line of argument, negative debaters may choose to deny the existence of the problem. In the homeless debate, Julie cannot credibly deny the total scope or magnitude of the problem. She can, however, argue that the tradition claimed by Tyrone is nonexistent.

> Julie: There is no national tradition to provide government handouts for poor people. The New Deal and the War on Poverty were twentieth-century aberrations. This nation was built on the belief that people get ahead through their own hard work, not on government handouts.

By undermining the traditional foundation of the significance claim, Julie completely denies one of Tyrone's lines of argument for affirming significance. While this does not eliminate the harm associated with the homelessness problem, it does provide an alternate perspective on those who suffer.

The argument that the affirmative has no significance at all is rare in debate because, in most instances, affirmative debaters choose significance claims that have some merit. Occasionally, however, the negative team will be able to argue that there is no value traditionally to the significance claim. As an example, the affirmative could argue that keeping comedian George Carlin's seven dirty words off television violates free speech, a right guaranteed by the Bill of Rights. The negative could insist that these particular words have no value. As nothing more than obscenities they do not deserve the protections afforded to free expression.

Problem Is Exaggerated

Rather than claim that the affirmative lacks any significance, negative debaters might choose to use a second line of argument: that the affirmative is overclaiming the problem's significance. This line of argument attempts to persuade the judge that the effects of the problem are substantially less than the affirmative claims.

The exaggeration of significance can occur at a number of levels. You can claim, for example, that the affirmative team is inflating the scope of the problem. Here the goal is to reduce the number of individuals adversely affected by the problem.

> Julie: Tyrone, you are wrong about the number of homeless people. More accurate figures show that only about 200,000 people are homeless.

How could Julie reach the conclusion that Tyrone had exaggerated the scope of the homeless problem? She might know that the figures quoted by Tyrone came from social groups that work with the homeless. Julie reasons that these groups have every incentive to inflate the number of those affected. Higher numbers increase public and private spending for their cause. She might also realize that the homeless are very difficult to count. Such ambiguity gives the social groups every opportunity to inflate the figures. Finally, she might know that the definition of a homeless person varies depending on who is doing the counting. Is someone homeless who has lacked shelter for a week, or is it necessary to lack shelter for six months in order to be considered homeless? For all these reasons, the Census Bureau estimate of 200,000 might be more credible.

If you do not think that the affirmative exaggerates the scope of the problem, you might think that the affirmative exaggerates the magnitude of the problem. This line of argument attempts to persuade the judge that the effects of the problem on the victims are substantially less than what the affirmative claims.

> Julie: Shelters offer the homeless a place to stay when the weather is bad. Homeless children can get balanced meals through welfare programs and education in the public schools.

Here, Julie argues that the quality of life experienced by the homeless is not as bad as Tyrone claims. The present system does attempt to address the horrifying conditions currently associated with homelessness. Certainly, Julie is not going so far as to say the homeless have a good life, but she claims the magnitude of the consequences is easily exaggerated.

Affirmative debaters can also overclaim the societal arguments for significance. The actual impact on society, either presently or in the future, may not be as damaging as the affirmative would like the judge to believe.

> Julie: The entire budget for responding to the needs of the homeless is only a small percentage of what the government spends every year. Certainly, the cost per person for caring for the homeless is minimal.

With this argument, Julie attempts to reduce the societal significance of helping the homeless. As you recall, Tyrone suggested that the country will have to pay large amounts of money to care for the cycle of homelessness. Julie denies this claim by arguing that the total budget for homelessness is quite small. The societal impact of the problem, Julie reasons, is negligible.

The affirmative can also exaggerate claims of traditional significance. The question of what constitutes a tradition is a subject that is always open to debate. Is the tradition cited by the affirmative actually a stopgap measure employed to handle a particular set of circumstances? Is the tradition outdated? Have circumstances changed since the period of reliance on tradition, making it inapplicable in current circumstances?

> Julie: Giving handouts to the poor is wrong. If the Republican leadership in the 1980s taught us anything, it is that people have to learn to help themselves. Only when people help themselves can we break the cycle of homelessness.

Julie indicates with this example that Tyrone's tradition of helping the downtrodden is an outdated philosophy. Julie could argue that the poverty programs of the New Deal and the 1960s caused the current cycle of homelessness. Only by abandoning Tyrone's tradition will the goal of actually helping the homeless come to pass.

The final means for exaggerating the significance of a problem is to mislabel an obligation as a moral imperative. Some ethical responsibilities justify personal sacrifice, but others do not. Those that fall in this latter group warrant changes in action only when considered against other factors.

> Julie: The government cannot possibly take care of each citizen who has fallen on hard times. If I overspent my budget going shopping, does that mean the government should pay my rent? I don't think so.

Here, Julie demonstrates the weakness of a moral imperative that is defined too broadly. The results could easily become absurd, as her personal example of compulsive shopping illustrates. Be alert to sweeping claims of moral obligation. They rarely withstand careful analysis.

REFUTATION OF SIGNIFICANCE

In this excerpt, Northwestern University defends the use of the results of Brenner's unemployment study. Despite some problems, the debaters indicate that the study can be used to establish that unemployment does cause problems and that the study's weaknesses tend to underestimate the problems caused by unemployment. Harvard University disagrees. The team maintains that the method used by Brenner to conduct his study is so flawed that it renders the conclusions false. The team insists that the study is so poor that it cannot be taken as proof that unemployment causes problems.

Affirmative

(b) Like any good social scientist. Dr. Brenner had issued a number of basic caveats regarding the interpretation of his study. We would preface the discussion of Dr. Brenner's work by noting that these caveats in no way constitute indictments in the conventional sense of the word. The primary reservation regarding Brenner's work, as applies to all empirical research, is that his findings do not demonstrate causality, merely a strong correlation between unemployment and pathology. Yet as Mr. Garvin noted some years ago, while we can never in a metaphysical sense prove absolute causation, absent some alternative explanation for a strong correlation between events which are plausibly connected, we must assume for the purposes of policy that the relationship is indeed causal. As Brenner himself concludes, "Having stated the caution on causal interpretation, we should nevertheless point out that the statistical techniques used in this study are standard for the problems encountered, and do not necessarily involve greater error or bias than would be true in other research based on correlation or regression techniques."

Negative

Brenner is flawed because of the lag thesis. The lag thesis is flawed. (a) It accounts for his findings. Eyer in 1976: "Since the economic fluctuations that [Brenner] studies average about five to six years in length, it is easy to see that the use of a three-year lag can convert a relation that moves directly with unemployment to one that moves inversely with it."

(b) He gives no justification. The same source: "Brenner . . . ignores social causes of stress other than unemployment. His models predict heart attacks from the business cycle, for instance, by inserting a three-to four-year lag in the equations between the unemployment peak and the heart attack peak. His Keynesian policy recommendations for prolonging economic growth follow naturally . . . the insertion of a three-year lag in the equation:" however it "does not of course give it scientific validity."

(c) It is wrong. I will introduce a medical study. The same source continues: "Lagged pathological impact of life events is an order of magnitude shorter than the lag required to explain the major peak of the death rate with the business

(Continued)

Affirmative (Cont.)

(c) The other major reservation widely held regarding Professor Brenner's study is the accuracy of the basic statistical information fed into his computer model. Yet, such uncertainties tend to understate, rather than inflate, the true toll of unemployment. Professor Brenner explains : " These measurement problems would tend to significantly bias downward the size of the impact of unemployment on a given social problem as measured by the coefficient associated with it. This necessitates regarding the quantitative estimates of impact of the unemployment rate with caution and with the awareness of possible substantial underestimates."

Interestingly, an independent assessment of Brenner's research appeared by Draper and his colleagues of London's Guy's Medical School in a February 1979 issue of The Lancet. They conclude that "probably the largest and most statistically elaborate inquiries into the effect of unemployment on health and other social indicators in different countries (including the U.K.) have been carried out by an American medical sociologist, Dr. Brenner." Their rationale? "Three kinds of studies"—prospective inquiries which follow workers from the trauma of being told that they are to lose their jobs, studies of the psychological and physical effects of particularly stressful events, and evidence about the higher mortality levels of the poor—"lend support to his findings, and they strengthen the case for considering and combatting the adverse effects of unemployment.

Negative (Cont.)

booms." Cassal and Cobb's study, they continue, "is the only study which evaluates the possible lagged impact of unemployment per se." Cassal and Cobb's results suggest "that the lags between life events and illness are on the order of weeks and months, not several years" as Brenner assumes.

Now I would argue (d) there is not sufficient information. Kathleen Classen, economist at the Public Research Institute of Arlington, Virginia, in 1978: "We need more information than you find in the Brenner study." LA Times in 1978: "Although the originators of the Humphrey Hawkins bill have hailed Brenner's work, the question of how valid the new research is remains unanswered." Walter Oi, economist at the University of Rochester, in 1978, in specific reference to the Brenner study summed up the negative position: "Our problem these days is the low cost of computer time. We compute too much and think too little. If you put numbers through long enough, something statistically significant will eventually come out."

(e) It is not causal. And this is an important indictment, because even if they indicate that causality in some metaphysical sense is not true, they must still indicate a reasonable chance that if you adopt the plan you will in fact solve the problem, i.e., that the plan solves something that causes the problem. LA Times in 1978: Brenner issued "a disclaimer that the research did not show a cause-and-effect link." Brenner himself, 1976: "There has not been complete consensus among

(Continued)

REFUTATION OF SIGNIFICANCE—Continued

Negative (Cont.)

specialists as to the full causal linkages in a number of cases reviewed in this chapter." He continues: "More spoecific policy applications will require extensive research efforts that focus more precisely on the causal mechanism involved." Norman Beckman, the Director of the Congressional Research Service, in 1976: "Dr. Brenner . . . has provided a detailed analysis of other programmatic research in this area, which may suggest possible avenues for exploring causal linkages between unemployment and these various social ailments. However, at this stage of our knowledge, we cannot assert a causal relationship between unemployment and various forms of social pathology."

(f) He assumes his own conclusion. How does Brenner figure out that this stress effect is going to be deleterious? Well, he looks at old stress studies and says, hey, these people found stress was harmful. I, for the purposes of my study, will assume stress is harmful, and that is exactly what he does. Brenner himself: "In the multivariate equations described above, each of the sources of economic life stress—decreased income, inflation, and unemployment—are understood to be unidirectional in their impact on pathology. Their impact, in other words, is conceived as entirely deleterious." No wonder the study found that unemployment was harmful; it assumed that unemployment was harmful. No great wonder there.

(g) It is insufficient for policy. LA Times in 1978: "In addition to

(Continued)

```
┌────────────────────────────────────────────────────────┐
│          REFUTATION OF SIGNIFICANCE—Continued            │
│                                                          │
│                   Negative (Cont.)                       │
│                   methodological weakness, the Brenner   │
│                   study fails to provide any useful policy│
│                   guidance, according to Mark Moore,     │
│                   an associate professor of public policy│
│                   in the Kennedy School of Government    │
│                   at Harvard University." Of course      │
│                   this evidence is superior, indicating a│
│                   public policy expert finds it          │
│                   insufficient for taking action. LA     │
│                   Times in 1978: "Some social scientists │
│                   express skepticism and believe that    │
│                   Brenner's work needs more scrutiny     │
│                   and testing before it is used as a basic│
│                   for government policy."                 │
│                                                          │
└────────────────────────────────────────────────────────┘
```

Perpetuation of the Problem Has Desirable Consequences: Disadvantages

In some instances the negative may choose to forego any attempt to eliminate or reduce the significance of the problem cited by the affirmative. Instead, the team may employ the final line of argument for denying significance: that continued existence of the problem has desirable consequences. At first glance, this argument may seem counterintuitive. It says something bad is really something good. However, we make this kind of judgment every day. Tetanus shots hurt, but we suffer that sting because we feel that protection outweighs the pain. The immediate situation (an unpleasant sensation) seems like something to be avoided, but the long-term benefits (immunity) justify that situation. If someone were to argue that children should forego vaccination because of the pain it causes, we would not hesitate to argue that the benefits outweigh that comparatively minor drawback.

We can apply the same kind of argument to broader social circumstances. Suppose an affirmative team argued that current tax policies damage small business. That damage imposes certain clear social costs, but, on the other hand, keeping small businesses in decline may be necessary to protect the environment and endangered species. Many environmentalists make precisely this argument about small business activity in heavily forested areas.

Sometimes, this sort of analysis can seem cruel. For example, some demographers have argued that malnutrition—undeniably a personal calamity—has an important role to play in controlling human populations. They say that keeping women in certain populations malnourished keeps their fertility low, the number of babies they produce small, and the number of future victims of starvation exponentially lower. These demographers argue against many food assistance programs because they feel that occasional famines are natural methods of population control which prevent far greater loss of life in the future.

The important thing to note here is that debaters must not rely exclusively on their first instincts for dealing with society's problems. Our natural inclination is to alleviate suffering, and no one would argue that we should change that orientation. We must, however, take account of those cases where the effort to alleviate suffering in fact produces more suffering in its wake. Debaters who engage in arguments of this sort are in effect making different predictions about the relationship between an action and its effect.

In debate, this line of argument is called a disadvantage. A **disadvantage** identifies the costs associated with policy actions designed to remedy significant problems. A disadvantage answers the affirmative claim of significance by proving that the effect of solving the problem causes more significant harmful consequences. Thus, the net effect of the affirmative policy is to create more problems than benefits. In order to argue that a disadvantage is persuasive, negative debaters need to prove three points: that a link exists between the affirmative policies and the disadvantage, that the cause of the problem is unique to the affirmative proposal, and that a negative impact would occur as a result of affirming the resolutional policy.

Linking the Disadvantage

The first of these requirements, referred to as a **link**, argues that the affirmative policy will cause the disadvantage to occur. Policies can cause disadvantages in two ways. First, the policy's effect of reducing the problem can have negative consequences. The previous examples of disadvantages fall into this category. Negative speakers would argue that promoting the growth of small businesses and increasing the nutritional intake of women in less developed countries have negative effects that the judge should consider when deciding to affirm the resolution.

> Julie: If you throw patchwork solutions at homelessness, you'll only hurt the chances for people to really change the root causes of poverty. Charity begins in the home, not with government. If you merely give poor people a shelter, you never reach out and care for the needy. You only hide them in a government program.

Julie argues that reducing the homeless problem has negative consequences. By reducing the scope and magnitude of homelessness, Tyrone would undermine reforms that can really solve the problem of poverty. He also undermines the charitable instincts of society by hiding the poor in government shelters, leading us to believe that social problems can be fixed by government. All the while, the actual cycle of homelessness and poverty increases.

The second type of link to a disadvantage is based on how the affirmative policy will attempt to remedy the significant problem. Unlike each of the previous examples, which linked disadvantages to the solving of the problem, this type of link depends on the specifics of the affirmative's proposal.

Julie: If we try to house all the homeless, we won't have enough money left over to fund our schools. If we don't fund our schools, teachers will leave, kids won't be educated, and dropout rates will increase. Public education will become a nightmare.

Here, Julie argues that if the government increases housing for the homeless, it would cause a trade-off with spending for education. If Tyrone's policy had funded housing programs through cuts in the military budget rather than through the general revenues of the Congress, the disadvantage would not be connected to his proposal.

Uniqueness of a Disadvantage

A disadvantage has **uniqueness** if the affirmative proposal alone would cause the disadvantage to occur. If the problem would occur with or without the affirmative proposal, the negative arguments would be irrelevant. The situation with the plan would be no more or less disadvantageous than the situation without the plan. In order to show the relevance of their disadvantages, negative debaters must be able to show that the affirmative proposal and only the affirmative proposal would provoke the problem.

Consider the alleged disadvantage that increased funding for the homeless would undercut spending for education. To be persuasive, the negative would have to show that under the affirmative proposal education will receive less money than it would otherwise. If state and local governments in the present system are already spending more money for housing the homeless with no effect on educational spending, or if educational cuts are already occurring for reasons unrelated to homelessness, the disadvantage would occur regardless of affirmative policies. In either case, the negative would not be able to claim a unique link between the policy and to the disadvantage.

Impact of the Disadvantage

The final criterion for an effective disadvantage is that the argument must have impact. **Impact** of the disadvantage refers to the consequences of adopting the affirmative proposal. Negative debaters can establish the impact, or significance, of a disadvantage by showing that the scope of those affected would be large, that the magnitude of the harm would be great, that the social consequences would be intolerable, that traditions would be disrupted, or that an erosion of a moral imperative would result.

In the example above, Julie shows that cuts in educational budgets would have unacceptable consequences. She argues that the quality of education of the nation's youth would decline, that teachers would leave education for more financially rewarding ventures, and that dropout rates would increase. Taken together, she relies on scope, magnitude, and societal significance to establish the impact to the disadvantage.

Negative debaters should not feel limited to a single line of argument when answering the affirmative claim for significance. Frequently, debaters can use several arguments to help minimize or outweigh the affirmative claim for significance. By using a variety of these arguments in a coordinated approach the negative debaters maximize the likelihood that they will convince the judge that a substantial problem does not exist or that solving it would produce more problems than benefits. Winning this issue alone can persuade the judge to negate the resolution.

Lines of Argument for Resolving Significance Claims

When debaters attempt to resolve the lines of argument pertaining to significance, they engage in cost-benefit analysis. **Cost-benefit analysis** weighs the benefits of affirming the resolution against the costs of doing so. It is important for you to realize that while each argument requires individual attention to be won or lost, comparison of all the arguments in the debate is ultimately what will persuade the judge to affirm or negate the resolution.

The central issues involved in significance claims are similar for both affirmative and negative debaters. As a result, we do not focus on lines of argument from an affirmative or negative point of view in the remainder of this chapter. Instead, we ask a series of questions related to the benefits and costs of affirming the resolution. These questions provide lines of argument for both sides in a debate as they attempt to resolve the significance issue.

Does a Significant Problem Exist?

When assessing the benefits to be gained from affirming the resolution, three questions are central. First, *does a significant problem exist?* This question is primary because the affirmative team must be able to prove that the answer is yes to persuade a judge to affirm the resolution. If the negative team can create doubt as to whether any substantial problem exists, the judge will likely see no reason for affirming the change required by the resolution.

In our homeless debate, it should be clear that a significant problem does remain. While Julie may be able to demonstrate that government help for the homeless does not represent a traditional value for society or a moral imperative, she cannot deny that some people are suffering from homelessness. She offers some remedies under the present system for dealing with the consequences of homelessness, but she may not be able to show that every homeless person has access to her remedies.

How Important Is the Problem?

If a significant problem exists, the next question becomes how important is the problem? *What is the scope and magnitude of the problem?* The fact that millions of individuals suffer devastating consequences is more compelling than the fact that a smaller group is simply inconvenienced. Is the problem grounded in important societal, traditional, or ethical interests? In most instances, the affirmative team will want to maximize the problem, while the negative will want to minimize the significance claim.

DISADVANTAGES

In the final round of the 1983 National Debate Tournament, the University of Kansas (Roger Payne and Mark Gidley) affirmed the resolution, "Resolved: that all United States military intervention into the internal affairs of any foreign nation or nations in the western hemisphere should be prohibited." Dartmouth College (Robin Jacobsen and Tom Lyon) negated the resolution.

The University of Kansas argued that the United States should prohibit actions that are likely to result in a military invasion of Cuba. At that period of the cold war, Kansas argued, such an invasion would not only cost many lives but also incur a response from Cuba's benefactor, the Soviet Union. Ms. Jacobsen argued in response that an invasion is unlikely to occur, unlikely to prompt a Soviet response, and further that such an invasion would be preferable to the alternative, an invasion in a Middle Eastern country. Ms. Jacobsen's statement of the disadvantage is followed by Mr. Gidley's responses. Note that the last piece of evidence read by Ms. Jacobsen compares the probable impact of the interventions in both arenas.

Negative	Affirmative
[Intervention] would actually shift to the Middle East, if we don't go into Cuba. (a) Western Hemisphere precludes Middle East intervention. Leiken, CSIS, '81: "US military actions in Central America would . . . bog down the United States politically and perhaps militarily in the Caribbean Basin, thus robbing us of freedom and action elsewhere." Montgomery, Oklahoma State, in '80: "That study [by the Library of Congress] concluded that successful operation of ground forces in the Persian Gulf would depend on the absence of U.S. involvement anywhere else at the same time. . . . One consequent scenario far from the Gulf but affecting plans for forwarding supplies and manpower from the United States to those waters pits the United States against Russian interests in the Caribbean and Central America.	*First, attack equals nuclear war. Proven up above. Second a new Cuban missile crisis would be much worse. Anderson indicates in 1982 "If a similar situation did develop" [like the Cuban missile crisis], the risks of escalation would be much higher today because we do not have the military superiority that we enjoyed 20 years ago." [Second, refer to (b) Middle East War. We would have to draw down [forces in the] Middle East, as Leo Grande indicates in 1982: "To occupy the island of Cuba would require the United States to strip every other theatre of operations including Western Europe and the Persian Gulf." Third, [there is] no reason you could not increase forces through the draft. Fourth, [the negative] does not prove that Reagan wants to go in. Fifth, argument is, of course, the Soviets should stay out by her own evidence. Sixth argument: [The disadvantage is] empirically*

(Continued)

Affirmative (Cont.)

denied. [U.S. troops] should go in now. The seventh argument is [there's] no reason to go in. The Israelis are already winning, and [this] is not assumed by her evidence.

In terms of the Klare evidence, we would indicate, first argument: Turnaround. We would indicate we prevent Mideast war. National Security Record indicates in '81: "The Soviet Union had repeatedly threatened to seize West Berlin if the United States intervened in Cuba. Such a reaction could still take place against Berlin or in the Middle East." indicating Soviet response would be [unintelligible]. Second, in terms of the Klare evidence she reads down on the three subpoint, it [the negative] doesn't assume invasion of Cuba.

In some debates, the level of harm associated with a current policy may be of questionable significance. What is significant varies from debate to debate. Some debate judges have a preconceived notion of the minimal level of harm that the affirmative must prove to persuade them that the problem is significant. Other judges assume that any problem is significant as long as it outweighs the costs associated with affirming the resolution. In most instances, however, the debate judges rely on the debaters to convince them that a significant problem exists or does not exist.

In our debate between Tyrone and Julie, the problem of homelessness does appear to be important. Julie may be correct that Tyrone's figures exaggerate the number of homeless individuals, but the lowest number is 200,000. Two hundred thousand suffering individuals should constitute a sufficient number to justify a plan of action. But just how harmed are these people? Julie indicates that shelter, food, and education are readily available. Tyrone's initial statement, however, claims that many of the homeless are not being fed, educated, or housed. So, despite the availability of these resources, many homeless appear to be unable or unwilling to take advantage of them. While the total number of homeless without fundamental human resources may be smaller than Tyrone had originally thought, there are still a substantial number suffering significant consequences.

Julie effectively dismisses the societal, traditional, and ethical significance of the homeless problem. By showing what a small percentage of the budget the homeless problem affects, she demonstrates that the per capita cost of future care of the homeless is negligible. The claim of a tradition of helping the homeless is controversial at best. The tradition appears to be a governing philosophy of the dominant political party of the thirties and sixties, rather than a tradition that pervades the nation's history. Some ethical obligations of helping the homeless may be present, but they are too broadly defined by Tyrone to have meaning in the debate.

Remember that these arguments are not self-resolving. Tyrone cannot sit back and let the 200,000 figure do his arguing for him; he must tell the judge that the raw numbers are unimportant if both debaters can agree that *at least* 200,000 citizens suffer the horrors of homelessness. Julie cannot make her historical points clear without coming to terms with Tyrone's characterization of New Deal policies. Debaters are responsible for providing relevant analysis and showing how their claims respond to their opponents' arguments.

Do the Benefits of the Policy Outweigh the Costs?

In the previous two sections, we have indicated how debaters assess the potential benefits of changing a course of action. Once debaters consider the potential benefits of affirming the resolution, they should examine the costs of the affirmative's policy. Both affirmative and negative debaters should analyze the costs of altering current policies before comparing them to the benefits of a proposal. This involves assessing the disadvantages advanced by the negative. Six questions form the basis of arguments that relate to disadvantages.

The first question is whether the affirmative policy would cause the disadvantage to occur. In other words, *is there a link to the disadvantage?* Consider the disadvantage, advanced by Julie, that increased spending on the homeless will cause a decrease in spending for education. She argues that the link to the disadvantage is certain; education is the first social program to be cut whenever increases in spending in other areas are necessary. To prove her point she could indicate that historically cuts in educational budgets have been the response to increased spending in other areas. Affirmative debaters, by contrast, try to argue that no link exists to their proposals. Tyrone might point out that his proposal specifically prevents cuts in education budgets, or that his plan would not cost the government anything because it is funded by private donations. By the end of the debate the negative must persuade the judge that a link between the disadvantage and the affirmative policy does exist or the disadvantage becomes irrelevant in the debate.

A second question in evaluating a disadvantage is, *does the affirmative policy prevent the disadvantage's occurrence?* This line of argument is referred to as a **link turn** because it argues that instead of causing the disadvantage the affirmative policy actually prevents the disadvantage from occurring. An affirmative debater has a strong incentive to make this argument since prevention of the disadvantage would count as another reason for affirming the resolution. In our example,

Tyrone might be able to prove that if we wait to help the homeless costs will soar. Not attending to the plight of the homeless will lead to enormous expenditures in the areas of health care, crime prevention, and child support services. Spending a little money now to house the homeless, would actually prevent huge expenses later that would cut deeper into educational budgets. While it first appears that Tyrone's proposal would cause a disadvantage, he can maintain that it prevents a disadvantage from occurring. Julie would have to respond that costs would not increase in the future or that future funds would prevent cuts of educational budgets. By making such arguments, Julie would attempt to prevent her disadvantage from being turned against her.

The third question to ask about a disadvantage is, *would the disadvantage occur without the affirmative policy?* Previously described as the uniqueness of the disadvantage, this argument shows that only the affirmative proposal causes the disadvantage to occur. Negative debaters must convince the judge that their disadvantage is uniquely caused by the affirmative for the argument to enter into the assessment of the debate. Julie argues that the spending disadvantage on the homeless is unique because any increase in funding will result in cuts in the educational budgets. She insists that the increase in funding of Tyrone's proposal over and beyond existing levels of expenditures results in unique cuts to education. If other costly programs came along, the impact would also hurt the funding available for education. Affirmative debaters try to maintain that the disadvantages are not unique. Tyrone might point out that the Congress is already planning increased funding for social programs. As a result, the educational budget will tighten regardless of whether the judge affirms or negates the resolution.

The fourth question concerning disadvantages is, *what is the **probability** that the disadvantageous consequences will occur?* Even if Julie can show that increased spending on the homeless will result in cuts in the educational budget, the question remains whether those cuts will lead to serious consequences. Julie argues that educational cuts would result in cuts in teacher salaries, prompting further shortages of public school teachers. Tyrone can respond by indicating that the probability of cutting teacher salaries would be low. More likely, cuts would be made in administration or projected building projects. The importance of a steady supply of teachers would prevent cuts in teachers salaries from occurring.

The fifth question used to resolve a disadvantage is, *would the impact of the disadvantage, on balance, be positive or negative?* Certainly federal cuts in educational budgets might result in shortages in the supply of teachers, but they might also result in less involvement by the federal government in educational decision making. More local control, Tyrone could argue, enhances freedom of thought and expression, values embodied in the First Amendment. Such a line of argument is sometimes referred to as an **impact turn** because it argues that the impact of the disadvantage is positive rather than negative.

Affirmative debaters must be careful not to link-turn and impact-turn the same disadvantage. If they do, they in effect argue that their plan prevents some positive outcome. Tyrone would make this mistake if he had argued both that his plan prevents the occurrence of the disadvantage (that it would prevent even larger costs in the future) and that the impact of the disadvantage is actually positive (increased costs would lead to less governmental involvement, resulting in more freedom of expression). Julie would simply have to grant that both arguments were true to win the disadvantage.

The final question to be asked about a disadvantage is, *does the negative impact of the policy outweigh the benefits gained from affirming the resolution?* At some point, the debaters need to compare the costs and benefits of affirming the resolution. Are the benefits from housing the homeless greater than the costs of creating a teacher shortage in the nation's public schools? Tyrone must be prepared to argue that the benefits of affirming the resolution outweigh the cost of affirming the resolution. Julie must be prepared to do the opposite.

Debaters attempting to resolve significance claims must recognize that no one cost-benefit analysis is absolutely correct and irrefutable. As with all arguments in a debate, the cost-benefit claims that are argued more persuasively will result in a favorable judge's decision. This analysis involves a comparison of the lines of argument presented in this chapter and a comparison of the evidence used in support of these lines of argument. You should familiarize yourself with the lines of argument presented in this chapter so you know the options available for creating a case for and against significance. To complete the process, you should consult Chapter Five of the core text to refresh yourself on the lines of argument useful in resolving evidentiary conflicts that arise in comparing significance claims. Having mastered the lines of argument relevant to evidence and claims, you should feel confident addressing the first general line of argument in any policy debate: significance.

Summary and Conclusions

To overcome presumption against affirming the resolution, affirmative debaters must present the first general line of argument in policy debate: significance. A debater pursuing this line of argument maintains that a significant need exists to alter current policies. The option not to take action is intolerable because to do so would have substantial consequences.

To establish that a significant need exists to affirm the resolution, several lines of argument are available. The debater can argue that the scope of the current policy affects a large number of individuals adversely, that it results in great harm to any individual affected, that it creates societal costs that are too high, and that it violates valued traditions or moral imperatives. These lines of argument may be used in isolation or may be put together to fully portray the problems under the existing policy.

To deny the significance of the problem, you can argue that no significant problem exists, that the problem is exaggerated, and that the existence of the problem has desirable consequences. To be persuasive with this last form of argument, negative debaters must show that a disadvantage will result from the affirmative plan, that the link is unique, and that the disadvantage will have serious negative consequences or impact.

To resolve contradictory claims about significance, debaters engage in cost-benefit analysis. To determine the benefits of affirming the resolution, you should ask: Does a significant problem exist? If so, what is the magnitude or scope of the problem? Is the problem of social, traditional or ethical significance? Do the negative effects of the problem outweigh its positive effects?

To determine the costs of affirming the resolution, debaters should ask several questions about disadvantages present in a debate. Does the affirmative policy cause the disadvantage to occur? Does the affirmative policy prevent the disadvantage's occurrence? Would the disadvantage occur without the affirmative's policy? What is the probability that the disadvantage will occur? Will the impact of the disadvantage be, on balance, positive or negative? Does the impact of the disadvantage outweigh the costs of not affirming the resolution?

Debate judges resolve controversies about significance by comparing the claims that are made and the evidence used to support those claims. Remember that the affirmative's burden of proof is to show the benefits of affirming the resolution.

Exercises

1. Obtain a copy of popular news periodical such as *Time, Newsweek,* or *U.S. News and World Report.* Browse the issue for an article that discusses a significant problem. How does the article establish significance? Does the author use scope, magnitude, social significance, traditional significance, or moral imperatives? Are these strategies combined? What is the article's effect on you?

2. Construct a disadvantage against a plan that would allow women in combat roles during times of military conflict. What is the link between the plan and the disadvantage? Why is the disadvantage unique to this course of action? What is the impact of the disadvantage?

3. Give a five-minute speech advocating a policy of your choice. What would be the benefits of adopting your recommended policy? What would be the consequences? Do the benefits outweigh the consequences? Why?

4. Imagine that you are advocating lowering the national drinking age to eighteen. Your opponent argues that your plan would be disadvantageous because you would increase the number of deaths caused by drunk drivers. Using the lines of argument discussed under "Do the Benefits of the Policy Outweigh the Costs?" in this chapter, develop at least five reasons why the disadvantage does not constitute a reason to reject your plan.

5. Pair yourself with one of your classmates. Have a debate about the significance of a policy of your choosing. If you are the affirmative, try to prove that the problem you cite is substantial and that the benefits of your plan outweigh any possible disadvantages. If you are the negative, attempt to reduce the significance of the problem and show that the plan to solve the problem would be, on balance, a bad idea.

3

Analyzing Inherency Through Lines of Argument

Chapter Outline

Key Terms

inherency
existential inherency
structural inherency
attitudinal inherency
incrementalism
minor repair

Connie: I read in the newspaper the other day that the government is considering requiring anyone convicted of driving under the influence (DUI) to serve three years in prison.

Sean: That seems unnecessary. Mothers Against Drunk Driving (MADD) has pushed through a lot of laws that increase enforcement of DUI laws all around the country.

Connie: Maybe, but the death toll from drunk driving is too high. I think we need stronger penalties and increased enforcement to convince people to stop drinking and driving.

Sean: I think people are becoming a lot less tolerant of drunk driving. Once it becomes stigmatized, it will be like cigarette smoking. People will stop.

Are present laws sufficient to alleviate the problem of drunk driving? Will changing attitudes eliminate the need for enacting stiffer penalties? Or must further action be taken if there is to be any remedy for the problem? These are some of the questions that emerge in debates about the second general line of policy argument: inherency.

Inherency is the consideration of whether the significant harm will continue without the action proposed in the resolution. The affirmative team must show that the problem will persist in order to convince a debate judge that the resolution is necessary. If all people decide to stop drinking and driving, there is no reason to affirm a resolution calling for mandatory minimum sentences for DUI offenders.

As with significance, inherency is an issue that the affirmative must win in order to win a debate. The affirmative team has the burden of proving that the problem will continue into the future unless resolutional policies are enacted. Negative debaters can win the debate if they can show that the problem is resolving on its own or that actions falling outside the scope of the resolution can solve it.

In this chapter we outline the arguments revolving around the issue of inherency. Specifically, we detail the lines of argument useful for affirming the inherency of the problem, for denying that an inherent problem exists, and for resolving conflicts between the two.

Lines of Argument for Affirming Inherency

An affirmative team attempting to prove that a given problem is inherent generally has three options. They can maintain that the problem persists despite efforts to remedy it. They can identify a structural barrier to the resolution of the problem. Or they can show that attitudinal obstacles prevent the problem's elimination.

Existential Inherency

If you maintain that a problem is inherent because it will continue to exist despite efforts to remedy it, you would be basing your argument on existential inherency. **Existential inherency** argues that the existence of a problem is sufficient to prove that the harm will continue.

> Connie: The police cannot catch more than a few of the people driving under the influence. Even when police do make arrests, drunk drivers get off with probation or light prison sentences.

In this example, Connie points out that the problem of drunk driving will continue despite current law enforcement efforts. She makes no attempt to explain why current policies fail or why we might expect the inconsequential enforcement procedures to persist into the future.

Debaters ordinarily use existential inherency to describe problems that appear to be intractable in light of current efforts to address them. AIDs, the national deficit, and poverty are all examples of problems that lend themselves to claims of existential inherency. Despite the government's best efforts, it has not been able to alleviate these ills. Minimal reductions may occasionally occur, but the bulk of the problems remains.

Not all members of the debate community consider existential inherency a legitimate line of argument for proving that a problem is inherent. Those who oppose the use of existential inherency argue that it is impossible to know if a problem will persist unless some underlying cause for the problem can be identified. Only by knowing the reason for the problem's persistence, so the argument goes, can the affirmative draw reasonable conclusions about whether the resolution will be able to solve the inherent problem. Advocates of existential inherency respond that it is unnecessary to show why a problem will continue. Knowing that it will continue is sufficient to warrant an affirmation of the resolution.

Structural Inherency

When you argue that a structural problem in the present system prevents the elimination or reduction of a problem, you are offering the line of argument known as **structural inherency.** Structural barriers can be of many different types. The structural problem may reside in a shortage of resources, a bureaucratic or statutory limitation, or in legal obstacles to further action.

> Connie: Congress and judges won't require mandatory minimum sentences for drunk drivers. Prisons are so overcrowded; they would never even think about it.

In Connie's argument, the structural barrier to adopting the affirmative proposal is a physical limitation on available prison space. As long as the prisons remain overcrowded, no one can reasonably expect increased penalties for DUI offenders.

Many problems continue to exist because structures impede their elimination. The United States trade deficit with Japan is a prime example. As long as Japan has large amounts of investment dollars in U.S. real estate and businesses, as long as bilateral trade agreements exist between the two nations, and as long as current contracts remain in place between Japanese firms and groups within the

United States, structural barriers will prevent the present system from closing the door to Japanese products.

Air pollution is another problem that will continue because of structural barriers. Emission standards are too low to prevent the nation's automobiles from polluting the air. The federal government offers tax incentives for businesses to invest in some environmentally hazardous industries, such as fossil fuels. The pollution control standards of the Clean Air Act are too lenient to prevent large amounts of air pollutants from escaping into the environment. Taken together, structural obstacles mount with the result that degradation of the nation's air supply continues.

Attitudinal Inherency

If structures do not hinder efforts to change the status quo, attitudes may intervene to prevent a solution to the problem. Referred to as **attitudinal inherency,** this line of argument explains why opposition forces allow the problem to continue.

> Connie: People don't want stiffer penalties for DUI offenders. Drinking is socially acceptable, and people have to get home from happy hour somehow.

Connie is arguing that societal attitudes will impede efforts to decrease deaths from drunk driving in the present system. Like its structural counterpart, attitudinal inherency appears in a number of forms ranging from apathy to intense opposition. Competing interests, such as the desire to have one's friends or family avoid penalties, have a higher priority than the desire to remedy the problem.

In many instances, problems persist because some individual or group benefits from the continued existence of the problem. The lack of safety regulations on toys for small children exists in part because of the profit motive of the toy producers. Minimum competency tests are not required of teachers in part because of the opposition of the teachers' union to competency testing. Military interventions that result in deaths and injuries to the nation's soldiers recur in part because of the continuing need to justify the size of the military-industrial complex.

Some overlap exists between attitudinal and structural claims of inherency. Once an attitude has become entrenched over time and becomes institutionalized, it emerges as a bureaucratic structure. Take the example of civil rights. Following the Civil War, many citizens believed that the Fourteenth Amendment protected minorities from discrimination under the equal protection clause. Attitudes against equal rights for minorities nevertheless persisted, creating structures that required the adoption of Title VII of the Civil Rights Act of 1964 to remedy the problem. Some would argue that attitudes and structures opposing civil rights persist, necessitating further action to remove opposing structures. In cases such as these, the distinction between an attitude and a structure becomes blurred.

Both attitudinal and structural inherency provide a rationale for why the present system will allow the problem to continue. The depth of these explanations

STRUCTURAL INHERENCY

In the final round of the 1985 National Debate Tournament, the University of Iowa (Robert Garman and Karla Leeper) affirmed the resolution, "Resolved: that the United States government should significantly increase exploration and/or development of space beyond the earth's mesosphere." Harvard University (Ed Swaine and Jonathan Massey) negated the resolution.

The University of Iowa argued that the United States government was not doing a sufficient amount of exploration into the possibility of extraterrestrial intelligent life. Contacting extraterrestrial beings might enhance our knowledge and perhaps help us solve apparently intractable problems. In the following argument, Mr. Garman argued that the governmental structures block access to radio frequency which prove necessary to contacting extraterrestrial. Mr. Swaine argued that the current structures are adequate in the accompanying response.

Affirmative

Unfortunately, present SETI [Search for Extra-Terrestrial Intelligent Life] efforts are inadequate as we explain in contention I: radio frequency interference precludes SETI. While NASA has allocated 1.5 million dollars for a SETI listening program to begin operation in 1988, (A) radio frequency interference in the spectrum threatens to obstruct the efficacy of the search. The magnitude of the problem is explained by the Christian Science Monitor in 1982: "Earth's atmosphere is growing so clogged with man-made radio noise—from satellites to television signals—that within 10 to 20 years it may be nearly impossible for an earthbound receiver to detect radio signals from some other intelligent source in the galaxy. In fact, the interference is already so significant that scientists wonder whether their radiotelescopes already have received intelligent extraterrestrial signals that they failed to recognize as such."

(B) As the level of interference increases, the problem will steadily worsen. Scientists Edelson and Levy state in 1980 that "radio frequency

Negative

On the inherency, first argument, (1) you can cope with interference now. Morrison in 1983: "I suspect the techniques for discriminating the interference will get better. You'll lose five or ten percent of the sky, but the next year you'll regain ten percent. It's a shifting kind of barrier. It's like the appearance of clouds in a telescope. No astronomer desires it, but they can all cope with it. And I think it's much the same thing."

(2) Low power uses [are] compatible [with SETI search]. Cosmic Search in January 1979: "Many low power uses of the band are compatible with SETI provided the transmitters are not in satellites."

(3) [The] waterhole is clear. Futurist in 1979:— this is much more recent evidence: "[T]he water hole . . . is relatively free of obstructing emissions from Earth and outer space."

(4) Amateurs do not block now. Delta Vee in 1981: "Large existing

(Continued)

Affirmative (Cont.)

interference (RFI) will be an
important limitation on the search.
Because of the sensitivity required of
a SETI receiver, virtually any
radiation picked up in the receiver
bandwidth will make the conduct of
this search more difficult."

Even new technological advancements
will not be able to overcome the
interference problem. Library of
Congress science writer Marcia Smith
argues in 1977 that "if the present
pace continues, receivers may not be
able to distinguish between man-made
interference and a signal arriving from
space, regardless of how advanced
radio telescope technology becomes."

(C) Currently, no portion of the
microwave spectrum is reserved for
SETI listening. Scientists must utilize
the same limited frequency bands
reserved for radio astronomy. If the
waterhole band is not reserved for
SETI listening, a reliable search for
ETs will be impossible. Professors
Billingham and Pesek argue in 1982
that "SETI observers will use the
rather narrow frequency bands set
aside for radio astronomy, in which
there is no allocation for
transmissions; however, they really
need access to much broader protected
frequency bands for comprehensive
exploration of the spectrum."

Negative (Cont.)

systems were built to search a
definite range of frequencies. For
this reason, frequencies below about
1.2 GHz or 1.2 billion cycles per
second are little used and are largely
wide-open for amateur searches.
Earth has been leaking strong
electromagnetic transmissions in
these frequencies from TV and radar
into space for several decades. These
radiations, traveling at the speed of
light, have now reached several
hundred of the nearby stars. It is
very possible that the first
identifiable intelligent signals will be
in these frequencies."

prompts many debate judges to accept, if not prefer, these lines of argument. Existential claims of inherency lack an explanation for why the problem will continue. Some judges do not think that the affirmative can demonstrate that a problem will continue without giving a reason. To be safe, you should be prepared to provide a structural or attitudinal barrier preventing present efforts from solving the problem. Whatever combination of these lines of argument you choose, you must convince the judge that the problem will continue into the future unless the policy recommended in the resolution is enacted.

Lines of Argument for Denying Inherency

To refute the affirmative's claim of inherency, the negative must indicate that the problem will not continue into the future. You can accomplish this by showing that the present system has solved the problem, that the present system is incrementally solving the problem, or that minor repairs to the current system could solve the problem.

Problem Is Solved

The strongest line of argument against the affirmative's claim of inherency is that current policies have already solved the problem. The present system has either adopted the affirmative plan or eliminated the harm through some other means.

> Sean: Did you hear what Congress did? Last week, they required all states to have mandatory three-year terms for drunk drivers. If the states refuse, the feds keep their highway funds.

As you probably expect, this line of argument occurs infrequently in debate. On occasion, the Congress, the Executive branch, or the Supreme Court will make a decision adopting the specific mandates of the affirmative plan. In a few instances, the affirmative team may not realize that their recommended action is already in effect. In these cases, the negative can capitalize by making an argument that the plan is passed. This makes it virtually impossible for the affirmative to meet its burden of showing that the problem will continue. This line of argument highlights the need for both the affirmative and negative teams to be current in their research.

When using the argument that the present system has already solved the problem, negative teams should be careful to avoid arguing that the affirmative plan will produce undesirable consequences. The chances of presenting contradictory arguments here is quite high. If the way the present system has solved the problem is comparable to the plan advocated by the affirmative, both the affirmative plan and present policies are likely to produce the disadvantage. Both the affirmative and negative teams should examine the differences between present efforts and the plan. Capitalizing on the subtle differences will ultimately determine who wins and who loses the debate.

Incrementalism

Although the present system rarely adopts the entire proposal embodied in the affirmative's resolution, it frequently takes steps to partially remedy a nagging problem. **Incrementalism** is the process of gradually working toward the elimination of a problem, constantly evaluating each step of the process.

Sean: Due to efforts by MADD, states across the nation are increasing enforcement of DUI laws. Also, several states have strengthened penalties for driving under the influence.

In the above example, Sean demonstrates how the negative can use the line of argument that authorities in the current system are working to solve the problem. The negative can claim that a gradual approach to solving the problem is superior to any radical action aimed at eradicating the problem altogether.

Incrementalism allows for experimentation with a number of possible solutions, followed by a fine-tuning of the laws to ensure stronger remedies. The present system analyzes the costs and benefits of each option and refines the process to discover the optimal solution. Negative debaters can argue that an incremental approach is best because it minimizes the chances that large detrimental consequences will result. If one step appears to be causing a problem, policymakers can slightly alter the approach or eliminate it altogether. The ongoing nature of the process allows for continual revision of misguided approaches.

Incrementalism is also useful because it permits a consensus to develop around a given alternative. If a policy is changed too radically or too quickly, the general public or groups within the public may not accept the change. The result is likely to be a program that does not accomplish its objectives and may produce a large public outcry. The gradual phase-in of a policy allows the public time to see progress toward the elimination of the problem. Time is available for discussing the public's perceptions of difficulties with enactment of the changes. Slowly, the public can adjust to and accept the shift in policy.

Finally, incrementalism generally allows for a more balanced allocation of resources. A radical shift in policy regularly entails large expenditures and a change in budgetary priorities. Incrementalism, by contrast, usually minimizes abrupt shifts in budgetary decision making. Small steps are generally less expensive, allowing other priorities to remain in the forefront of expenditures. Further, incrementalism prevents spending on costly policies that may fail to solve the problem or produce disastrous results.

Negative debaters should think creatively about how the present system might be working to solve a problem incrementally and not limit themselves to the affirmative interpretation of how to remedy the situation. In the debate between Carrie and Sean, Sean can argue that some states are increasing penalties for DUI, but he can also show that others are instituting alcohol programs on job sites. The latter program attempts to prevent the problem of drunk driving from occurring in the first place, not punish the offenders after the fact. The problem of DUI can be attacked from several directions, with all avenues providing potentially fruitful argumentative ground for the negative.

Minor Repairs

One option that the negative team has to demonstrate that current policies can work to solve the problem is to offer a minor repair. **Minor repairs** are small

INCREMENTALISM

In the final round of the 1974 National Debate Tournament, Harvard University (Greg Rosenbaum and Charles Garvin) affirmed the resolution, "Resolved: that the federal government should control the supply and utilization of energy in the United States." Augustana College of Illinois (Richard Godfrey and Mark Feldhake) negated the resolution.

Harvard argued that fossil fuel power plants were emitting too many pollutants and that current regulations did not provide sufficient financial incentive to encourage the energy industries to decrease pollution. Mr. Godfrey argued in his response that follows, that current structures were incrementally increasing pollution controls, that federal regulations keep escalating the costs of clean fuels, and that current pollution technologies are effective and increasing.

Negative

(A) The Clean Air Act established standards. (1) It sets standards the same as the affirmative. By definition now, there is no difference between the status quo and the affirmative team. Business Week, November 17, 1973: "Under the 1970 Clean Air Act, the EPA established primary air quality standards to protect public health by 1975 and secondary standards to protect property by a reasonable time later." Now, to the extent that people are still being killed, the only reason is because the standards don't come into effect until next year.

(2) The EPA is pushing the application of technology. Business Week, August, 1973: "Even so the EPA is pushing utilities to install scrubbers, hoping to keep the rapid advances in scrubber technology rolling. . . ."

(3) The EPA is enforcing [regulations] through courts. Business Week, September 22, 1973: "The court decision is bad news for power companies. Last week in one of his first acts as the EPA administrator, Russel Train, cited three power plants for violating air standards, and he scheduled general hearings on compliance starting next month." So constructive position number one indicates to you that the federal government already has the commitment towards controlling pollution and is indeed doing so through several mechanisms. . . .

Constructive position (B): There is no economic inherency . . . : (1) Pollution standards require the use of clean fuels. . . . Factors Affecting the Use of Coal in Present and Future Coal Markets, 1973: "In order to meet the standards, utilities will have to burn low sulfur fuel or utilize some form of desulfurization." But, as we all know, low sulfur fuels are in short supply. And, therefore, (2) as the price goes up for that fuel, it will become cheaper to install pollution control equipment. The Potential for Energy Conservation, January, 1973: "Assuming a premium for clean fuels of 45 to 50 cents per million BTU in the year 1980, stack gas cleanup is distinctly less expensive for at least 40 per cent of generating capacity." Please realize now there is an independent market mechanism which will stimulate the application of pollution control technology.

I will indicate constructive position (C): incentives for abatement are effective. Realize: (1) In 1969 a great deal of money was spent on [pollution] abatement equipment. Anthony,

(Continued)

adjustments to current policies designed to reduce the significance of an existing problem. If the present system is basically on the right track in attempting to resolve a problem, the negative might offer slight changes that could render the present system superior to the affirmative's plan of action.

> Sean: I don't think we need mandatory sentences. I think you could require everyone to take a two-hour class on the dangers of drunk driving and most people would be too scared to drive drunk. You could show those horrible accident scenes in driver's ed.

With this recommendation, Sean offers a minor repair to solve the problem of deaths from DUIs. Through a minor adjustment in the educational system, he hopes to alleviate the need for adopting a more radical change to address the problem of drunk driving.

To understand the concept of a minor repair, it may be useful to think of the term metaphorically. Say that your car will not start. You might suspect the starter and dread the cost of having to replace it. A minor repair, however, might be sufficient to remedy the problem. Perhaps the cause of your problem is not a worn-out starter, but a dead fuse in your electrical system. With a couple of dollars, you could remedy the problem with a minor repair.

Debaters rely on a number of minor repairs to maximize the benefits of remaining with present policies. One common approach is simply to increase enforcement of current laws. Since penalties already exist for drunk driving, the negative could simply advocate stronger enforcement of DUI laws by the police force. More frequent checkpoints, more surveillance of establishments that permit the consumption of alcohol, and a stronger willingness to write tickets for those caught drinking and driving might be sufficient to reduce the number of deaths from these drivers. If the potential drinkers are more afraid that they will be caught driving under the influence of alcohol, they may be reluctant to disobey the law.

Another popular minor repair that negatives propose is to increase funding for existing efforts. Here the negative argues that the present system has the proper approach but as yet has failed to provide ample funding for the effort. Increased pay for police to work extra hours might significantly curb the number of drunk drivers on the nation's highways. More money for prisons to lock up DUI offenders would send a message to those who might be thinking of drinking and driving.

Sometimes, small procedural changes can result in a large decrease of a problem. Suppose that one problem leading to increased DUI offenses is that no records are kept of repeat violations. A simple computerized system to track repeat offenses could alert the judge to the most chronic offenders and lead to harsher penalties for guilty defendants.

This list of potential minor repairs is not exhaustive. You should be creative in thinking of small adjustments that might lead to a significant reduction in the problem area. Targeted appropriately, a small change can oftentimes prevent the need for a more radical alteration in policy. If you plan to use the strategy of the minor repair, you have the burden to prove four lines of argument.

> *Minor repairs must be nontopical.* The minor repair needs to be an
> alternative to the resolution defended by the affirmative. If the minor
> repair falls within the scope of the resolution, it arguably becomes
> another justification to affirm the resolution. Since the curriculum of a
> driver's education course has little to do with the criminal justice
> system's enforcement of DUI laws, Sean should be able to persuade
> the judge that this particular minor repair is nontopical.
>
> *Minor repairs should be relatively minor changes.* If the minor repair requires
> a radical change, the change would fall outside the present system's
> capacity for modification as we reasonably know it. The negative can
> defend major shifts from the present system (see Chapter Six of this
> text for a discussion of counterplans) but not under the pretense of it
> being a minor repair. Sean's minor repair is simply a small curriculum
> change. It should require no new classes or teachers. Thus, he can
> defensibly characterize it as a minor repair.
>
> *Minor repairs must have adequate funding.* If no resources are available to
> carry out the minor repair, its effectiveness remains uncertain. Proper
> levels of funding are essential to the efficacy of most minor repairs.
> Negative debaters should specify the source of their funding if dollars
> are needed. Will the funding come from general revenues, with the
> result that some other program will have to be cut? Or will it come
> from some specific source, such as eliminating waste in government
> spending, a reduction of legislative salaries, or a defense cut? The
> negative can choose to be specific or general, but they must be
> prepared to defend the source of the minor repair's funding. Sean
> should be able to argue that his minor repair needs little to no
> funding. Requiring no new classrooms, no new teachers, no new
> textbooks, or no new classes, such a small change would simply be a
> more beneficial use of existing resources.

Minor repairs must solve or reduce the affirmative's harm. If the minor repair has no effect on the problem, its usefulness in the context of the debate is questionable. While minor repairs do not have to completely eliminate the existence of a problem, some reduction in the harm is necessary for the argument to have any impact. Negative debaters should be prepared to prove how much of the problem will be alleviated by the existence of the minor repair. On occasion, this calculation depends on how close the minor repair comes to solving the cause of the problem. At other times, the negative team will have specific evidence supporting the effects of their proposed change. While Sean will probably not be able to prove that education would eliminate all drunk driving fatalities, he should be able to show that the proposal would reduce the number of injuries and deaths. If people know the potential consequences of being involved in a DUI accident, some of them would likely alter their behavior.

With a minor repair, then, the negative has the burden to prove that the change is nontopical, minor, fundable, and solvent. The reason why the negative now has the burden of proof is that the minor repair represents a new policy over and beyond present programs. At least for some judges, such a change would entail risk that must be overcome by proof of the proposal's positive effects.

Lines of Argument for Resolving Inherency Claims

When deciding whether a problem will continue into the future, both affirmative and negative debaters should consider four lines of argument. Are negative options sufficient to solve the problem? Are they compatible with the affirmative proposal? Are they desirable as alternatives to the affirmative proposal? And, finally, do the negative options actually fall within the scope of the resolution?

Sufficiency

Debaters cannot assess whether a problem will continue without a consideration of whether negative options are sufficient to solve the problem. *Will present policies eliminate or simply reduce the likelihood that the problem will continue to exist?* Both affirmative and negative debaters must realize that the present system can make inroads into the affirmative's problem area without rendering the affirmative not inherent. In most instances, a portion of the harm will continue into the future. In the debate on drunk driving, Sean is able to show that several states have enacted laws to stiffen penalties for DUI offenders. But what of the states that are not pursuing stiffer penalties? What about states that are decreasing penalties for DUI? The problem is clearly going to persist in these areas, leaving Connie with the ability to claim that an inherent problem still exists. Only in the rare instances where the negative can show that the present system has passed the affirmative plan can it prove that present policies are sufficient to solve the problem.

MINOR REPAIR

In the final round of the 1977 National Debate Tournament, Georgetown University (David Ottoson and John Walker) affirmed the resolution, "Resolved: that the federal government should significantly strengthen the guarantees of consumer product safety required of manufacturers." The University of Southern California (Leslie Sherman and Steve Combs) negated the resolution.

Mr. Ottoson argued that federal policy was unlikely to require automobile manufacturers to install airbags in the near future. If the government were to impose such regulations, the automobile industry would delay them in court. Mr. Ottoson's speech and Mr. Sherman's defense of a minor repair follow.

Affirmative

Finally, we must recognize (C) that even if administrative-legislative discretion could somehow be overcome, current judicial structures block rapid employment of airbags; [the problem is] court delay. As Business Week recently noted: "If airbags ever are mandated, there is little doubt that the auto manufacturers will take the DOT to court. Thus, whatever the Department of Transportation decides about passive restraints, years of litigation may well be ahead before any real action is taken."

Negative

[The affirmative] . . . argue[s] that the courts [would] delay [the requirement of airbags]. (1) This [evidence from Business Week] is conclusionary. It does not say [auto companies] will take [regulators] to court. It just says . . ."might" and "may be". It does not give the reason. (2) The affirmative evidence says that [the courts] will delay, not that they will overturn the decision [to mandate airbags]. (3) This is an independent negative inherency. If it is true that they take them to court and the [DOT] is delayed, then people can sue the DOT for not [requiring] airbags. I'll argue (4) a minor repair . . . eliminating injunction relief [that is, if the court cannot grant injunctive relief while the DOT is in court, the auto industry will still have to put airbags in cars]. (5) I'll argue a minor repair in terms of prioritizing decision. [That is, simply make an airbags suit a high priority on the court docket]. . . . If you and I can decide in an hour and a half that airbags are feasible, there is no reason why we can't put this [issue] in the courts tomorrow and, in the span of one week, we can determine this and [resolve the issue in the

(Continued)

Sufficiency becomes a particularly relevant concern in debates about incrementalism. Will the present system that is committed to an incremental approach move quickly enough to solve the problem? If disadvantages emerge, will such a system move away from remedies to the problem? Will incrementalism lead to an alternative set of priorities? Without showing a commitment to alleviating the harm identified by the affirmative, the negative may have some difficulty showing that the current approach will be a sufficient solution to the problem.

Placed in the position of defending a present system that is rarely committed to eliminating the affirmative's harm, many negative debaters will rely on minor repairs to deny the affirmative's claim of inherency. Regardless of which strategy the negative chooses, however, the question of sufficiency remains. Will the minor repair solve the problem or merely reduce its presence? Sean's proposed curriculum change in driver's education may diminish a few deaths from drunk drivers, but it is unlikely to prevent all fatal accidents. Both affirmative and negative debaters should make realistic assessments of the effects of these alternatives so that they can weigh remaining harms against the other issues in the debate.

Compatibility

A second line of argument for resolving conflicting inherency claims is compatibility. *Are negative alternatives compatible or competitive with affirmative proposals?* This question is central to resolving issues of inherency because it helps decide which issues clash in the debate. If the affirmative and negative proposals are compatible, both may be adopted together without critique of either one. If the two proposals compete, acceptance of one forces rejection of the other. Sean's plan to change the curriculum of driver's education courses arguably supplements Connie's plan for mandatory sentences. Connie could indicate that the revised driver's education course could educate guilty defendants about the importance of their crime. A guaranteed prison term would reinforce that message.

As the previous example illustrates, affirmative debaters benefit strategically from the compatibility of affirmative and negative proposals. They can accept negative proposals as worthwhile suggestions that should be adopted in concert with affirmative proposals. Incrementalism, for example, might be a worthwhile approach for resolving any undesirable consequences that result from the plan. The time to commit to incrementalism, the affirmative would argue, is after the major change has been implemented. At the very least, the affirmative can insist that a compatible proposal in no way undermines the rationale for affirming the resolution. The value of increased enforcement of DUI laws arguably does nothing to undermine the wisdom of implementing mandatory sentences for guilty defendants.

Negative debaters, in contrast, seek to point out how the affirmative plan and the negative options compete. Whether the negative chooses to defend present policies or offer minor repairs, they benefit from proposing competitive alternatives to the affirmative's plan. If the negative's proposals somehow preclude adoption of the affirmative plan, the judge must choose the preferable alternative. In our example, Sean might argue that the budget could not sustain both the increase in defendants from increased enforcement and the adoption of mandatory minimum sentences. To do both would bankrupt the criminal justice system. By arguing that the plans are competitive, the negative shifts the focus of the debate away from the affirmative's plan to a comparison of the affirmative and negative proposals. To determine whether two policies are compatible or competitive, debaters should ask whether the two proposals could, should, or would exist together. If so, the policies are compatible; if not, they compete. Debaters should ask these questions in the broadest possible way to encourage creative ways of seeing the interaction between the two policies.

Desirability

The third line of argument for resolving competing inherency claims is the desirability of the alternative approaches. *Is the affirmative plan, with its advantages and disadvantages, more desirable than the present system with minor adjustments?* Or are the costs and benefits of the negative alternatives superior? Resolving conflicting inherency claims in this manner requires both affirmative and negative debaters to examine the debate from a broad perspective. The question is no longer whether a specific argument is stronger than another specific argument. This step requires the debaters to sum up the strengths and weaknesses of all the arguments that revolve around a particular proposal and weigh them against all the arguments revolving around an alternative.

In the debate between Connie and Sean, both debaters would need to do a cost-benefit assessment of the affirmative and negative alternatives. What are the advantages and disadvantages of having three-year mandatory minimum sentences? What are the advantages and disadvantages of depending on increased enforcement and education (minor repairs) to solve the problem? When the two alternatives are compared, which is superior?

Connie would argue that the benefits of adopting mandatory minimum sentences would outweigh those of adopting the minor repairs. In all likelihood she would conclude that increased enforcement of existing laws would be ineffective if the defendants knew that the judges would not impose harsh sentences. She would indicate that education would not help the large number of drunk drivers who are older than the average school population. She would minimize any problems resulting from mandatory minimum sentences, concluding overall that the additional benefits of her approach are sufficient to warrant a change in policy.

Sean would see the debate differently. He would stress both the predictable and unpredictable consequences of relying on mandatory sentences. He would argue that present laws coupled with increased enforcement of those laws would lead to a sharp reduction in DUI fatalities. Having the educational system reinforce the message that individuals should not drink and drive would further alleviate any remaining harm. Sean would focus on the benefits of taking small steps, such as time to garner public consensus for the policy and an opportunity for fine-tuning of the proposal if intolerable effects emerge. The more gradual approach, Sean would maintain, represents the most prudent action given the circumstances.

Topicality

The final line of argument for resolving conflicting inherency claims is *do the negative alternatives fall within the scope of the resolution?* The negative may defend an incremental system or offer minor repairs, claiming that these approaches are nonresolutional alternatives. Nevertheless, the affirmative always has the opportunity to explain why the resolution actually encompasses these proposals. If the affirmative succeeds, they may be able to convince the judge that the alternatives presented by the negative are merely further justifications for affirming the resolution.

Suppose that the resolution in the debate between Connie and Sean had been worded as follows: "Resolved: that the federal government should alter criminal justice procedures in the nation's courts." This wording is broad enough to include Connie's plan and may be broad enough to include Sean's minor repairs as well. Had Sean relied on increased enforcement of DUI offenders as a minor repair, Connie might argue that the shift in enforcement practices constitutes an alteration of criminal justice procedures in the court. With more cases coming to the docket, the judges might have been forced to alter their regular routines.

Sean, on the other hand, would probably prevail in the debate about the topicality of his educational minor repair. Shifting the content of a high school course seems remotely related to criminal court procedures at best. Connie would have a great deal of difficulty making a convincing argument to the contrary.

The question of topicality frequently emerges in debates about incremental approaches to solving problems. In short, many affirmative debaters argue that an incremental approach could be topical. If disadvantages to early steps in the process do not emerge, the present incremental system might move to alter criminal justice procedures in the nation's courts. Since many problems cited by affirmative debaters are quite convincing, the affirmative might conclude that in all likelihood the incremental system would have a tendency to take the actions called for by the resolution. The negative, on the other hand, could respond that the incremental approach does not necessarily fall within the bounds of the resolution. Such a system is likely to identify alternative actors or actions than those called for by the resolution. If there is no guarantee that the incremental approach would be topical, the negative would argue, then it cannot serve as another justification for the adoption of the resolution.

Inherency debates revolve around comparisons of the affirmative's mandates and the negative defense of current policy, with slight modifications in some cases. If the present system is not sufficient to solve the problem, if it is compatible with affirmative proposal, if it is undesirable, or if it is advantageous but falls within the bounds of the resolution, the affirmative will win the argument. On the other hand, a present system that is sufficient to alleviate the bulk of the harm claimed by the affirmative's case can prevent the need for adopting the affirmative plan. As long as that system is competitive with the affirmative proposal, desirable on its own merits, and falls outside the specifications of the resolution, the affirmative will not meet their burden on proof on the inherency issue.

Summary and Conclusions

The second general line of argument in policy debate is inherency. Inherency is the issue of whether the problem will continue without the action proposed in the resolution. The affirmative has the burden of proving that the problem will continue without the resolution, as they are the advocates of the resolution.

When attempting to claim that the problem will continue into the future, debaters have three options: they can maintain that the problem persists despite efforts to remedy it, they can argue that structural barriers (e.g. laws, bureaucratic structures, or court decisions) prevent the problem from being solved, or they can indicate that attitudinal obstacles (from apathy to intense hatred for a proposal) will prevent the current policy from remedying the problem.

When attempting to deny that the problem will continue into the future, negative debaters can show that the problem has been solved, that the present system will incrementally solve the problem, or that minor repairs to the current system will solve the problem. The negative has the option to advocate minor repairs to present structures if they can show that the minor repairs are actually small, nontopical changes that have adequate funding and will solve the problem identified by the affirmative.

In order to resolve competing claims for inherency, debaters should focus on four central questions. Are negative alternatives to the resolution sufficient to solve the problem? Are these alternatives compatible with resolutional options? What is the comparative desirability of competing alternatives for solving the problem? And, finally, do the alternatives fall within the scope of the resolution?

Exercises

1. The following is a list of problems that seem persistent given present policies. Find a cause for why each of the problems will continue. Afterwards, label your arguments as examples of existential, attitudinal, or structural inherency.

breast cancer	budget deficit
ozone depletion	AIDS
world hunger	small business collapses

2. Should we take a sweeping approach to solving the problem of discrimination? For example, should criminal penalties be set for failure to enact affirmative action? Or is an incremental approach better? What are the advantages and disadvantages of each approach? Which method would ultimately lead to less discrimination? Why?

3. Examine an issue of the *Congressional Record*. Find an example of a member of Congress who advocates a minor repair and one who advocates an incremental solution to a problem. How do the members justify their choices? Can you apply their arguments in your own debates?

4. Assume you were debating against a resolution that states, "Resolved: that the United States should provide employment opportunities for all American citizens between the ages of 18 and 65." The affirmative argues that jobs are needed to keep the crime rate low. Can you offer a minor repair? Would your minor repair be topical? Where would you get the funds? Would it solve the affirmative's advantage? Is your approach really a minor change?

5. Identify at least three intractable problems that you believe would be strong candidates for existential claims of inherency. How long have the problems been in existence? Has the present system truly made an attempt to decrease or eliminate the problem? Are current approaches for solving the problem currently under review by policymakers?

4

Analyzing Solvency Through Lines of Argument

Key Terms

solvency
fiat
should-would argument
comparative advantage
goal maximization
pilot project
plan-meet-need
plan-meet-advantage
attitudinal plan-meet-need
structural plan-meet-need
circumvention

Marie: Schools should offer sex education classes. If kids don't learn about contraception and sexually transmitted diseases, they are going to continue to have unwanted babies and dangerous illnesses.

Daniel: Sex education classes won't make any difference. Kids are going to have sex whether a class tells them to or not. And just how many teens do you know who have both the money and the guts to buy contraceptives?

Marie: Maybe sex education classes wouldn't stop all teen pregnancies. But if schools were willing to provide free contraceptives to all students, there would be a lot less misery in the world.

Will sex education courses eliminate the problem of teen pregnancy? Will they reduce or increase the problem? The conversation between Marie and Daniel addresses the question of whether a specific proposal will have an impact on the problem at hand. In debate, the line of argument that examines the effectiveness of a policy to reduce or eliminate significant problems is called **solvency.**

In Chapter One, we indicated that the affirmative team can imagine that the new policy they advocate will be put into effect. This process, known as **fiat,** sets the stage for debates about the plan's solvency, because fiat allows the advocate to assume the plan would exist. The affirmative presents a specific plan that they believe will remedy existing problems. (See Chapter Eight for recommendations for how to write plans effectively.) Rather than debate about whether the plan would come into being, all debaters assume the existence of the plan and focus on the impact of having the plan in place.

In our debate between Marie and Daniel, fiat allows Marie to assume that sex education classes would be implemented by all public schools. While Daniel cannot legitimately question whether the legislature would permit the existence of sex education classes, he can debate whether the classes, once in place, would have an impact on the problem of teenage pregnancy. He could point out that many teachers oppose the notion of sex education in the schools. If Marie's plan allows these teachers to teach the courses, Daniel could argue that they would not present the material in a manner that would allow the students to learn enough to affect the teenage pregnancy problem. While Marie could mandate that teachers have to go through training to learn how to teach the class, she cannot fiat that the teachers will change attitudes that they hold strongly.

Fiat, then, allows the affirmative to imagine that their plan is put in place without argument from negative debaters. If the negative presses the issue, arguing that the President would veto such legislation or the Congress would not realistically consider it in the first place, they would be making a should-would argument. A **should-would argument** is a line of argument that confuses the issue of whether a plan should exist with whether or not it would exist. Most debate judges consider should-would arguments an illegitimate form of argument because such arguments prevent the debaters from focusing on what should be public policy.

Since should-would arguments have little hope of success, the negative should concentrate their attacks on the solvency of the affirmative proposal. The question of solvency allows the negative to argue that the plan will not have an effect on the significant problem, or that it will not eliminate the existential, attitudinal, or structural barriers identified in the inherency argument. The affirmative must be able to convince the judge that its plan would have an impact on the inherent problems they previously identified in the debate.

Like the other two general lines of argument discussed so far, solvency is an issue that affirmative debaters must prove to overcome the presumption against affirming the resolution. No problem is a sufficient cause for change unless it has an effective remedy. To prove that they can indeed reduce or eliminate problems with current policy, the affirmative needs evidence that maintains that the specifics of the affirmative plan will be sufficient to have an impact on the problem. The remainder of the chapter will identify the lines of argument useful for affirming, denying, and comparing solvency claims. More detail on how debaters can prove and disprove solvency arguments will also be provided.

Lines of Argument for Affirming Solvency

To make the case that a specific plan would solve significant needs, you have three options. You can agree that your plan completely eliminates a problem, that your plan offers a better remedy than the existing policy, or that your plan is more likely to achieve desirable goals.

Elimination of the Problem

The first line of argument, that the plan will rid the present system of the problem entirely, has only limited application in most debates. Most problems have serious complications that make them difficult to completely remedy with any single plan.

> Marie: High schools and junior high schools should require all students to enroll in a sex education class. Teens aren't going to stop having unsafe sex unless they know the risks of their behavior.

While this statement is partially true, Marie would have some trouble proving that sex education classes would completely eliminate the teenage pregnancy problem. Most of us believe that some students are going to engage in sexual activity even when they are aware of the possible harmful consequences of their actions.

Some problems do have direct and complete solutions. For example, if you wanted to solve the problem of state executions of innocent citizens, you could ban the death penalty. If you wanted to solve the problem of excessive malpractice claims against doctors, you could cap the maximum jury award allowed in any malpractice trial. If you wanted to solve cost overruns for the stealth bomber, you could cancel any further expenditures on such projects.

Comparative Advantage

If a plan cannot entirely eliminate a problem, it may still be preferable to existing efforts to remedy the situation. To establish that a plan has a **comparative advantage** over existing remedies, the affirmative need only show that the plan would reduce the problem or prevent expected increases of the problem in the future. Because this line of argument does not require the affirmative to completely eliminate nagging problems associated with current proposals, it is the most frequently used approach for establishing solvency of the affirmative plan.

> Marie: High schools and junior high schools should require all students to take a sex education course. Many students would use birth control if they knew about it and knew how to get it.

In this example, Marie is making a much stronger case. Even if sex education classes do not convince all students to abstain from sex or practice safe sex, it would be hard to deny that some students would alter their behavior. Most affirmative debaters opt to argue solvency by claiming the policy is advantageous compared to existing policies. It is much easier to sustain the argument that the plan would reduce the problem than it is to maintain that a proposal will completely eliminate the problem.

Maximizing Goals

The third line of argument for affirming solvency is that the affirmative's policy maximizes beneficial goals of existing structures. When engaging in **goal maximization,** affirmative debaters examine the ways in which their policies can help achieve existing goals or objectives that present policies deem desirable.

> Marie: The AIDS epidemic is out of control. If we don't start telling kids about the risks of casual sex, they are going to get this disease and die. We need sex education classes.

Here, Marie offers eradication of the AIDS epidemic as a goal of the present system. Tying her plan to the goal, she stresses how sex education courses would convince some teenagers that they risk their health when they practice unsafe sex. This example of AIDS might give you the impression that affirmative debaters must be able to quantify how much closer the plan can come to achieving the desired goal. This is not necessarily the case.

Many of us, for example, would acknowledge that in a democratic society, voter participation is a desirable goal. An affirmative team might argue that a policy to register all citizens when they renew their driver's licenses would diminish registration barriers to voter participation. Even if the affirmative could not prove that a greater percentage of the American electorate would actually cast their ballots under this policy, they could claim that it is more in line with the goals and objectives of a democratic society than the current policy of voluntary registration.

In summary, when affirmative debaters make arguments to show that their plan will solve, they rely on the lines of argument that show the policy will eliminate the entire problem, that it will reduce the problem, or that it will encourage the achievement of desirable goals. Regardless of which of these options debaters choose, the burden of proving that the policy will solve the identified problem rests with the affirmative debaters. At first glance, proving such a claim may seem difficult. After all, how can you do more than speculate about the outcome of a proposal not yet in existence?

Proving Solvency Claims

You have several options for proving your solvency claims. You can argue that experts believe the plan would solve the problem, that a consensus of the experts supports the plan, that pilot projects point to the success of the plan, and that historical uses of the plan have yielded beneficial results.

In most cases the affirmative chooses a plan that is supported by experts, pilot project results, or empirical events. The negative can also use experts, pilot projects, or historical examples to deny that the affirmative plan will solve the problem. We will first examine the lines of argument to defend these means of supporting solvency. In the next section, we will examine the lines of argument to undermine these supporting materials. You should, however, feel free to use whichever arguments are appropriate to the particular circumstances of your debate.

Saying that an expert in the field believes that the plan would solve the problem gives authoritative support to the affirmative's claim of solvency. Some proposals have never been put into effect; they are merely ideas for how someone believes the problem could be remedied. When the individual is highly knowledgeable about the problem and its causes, the affirmative's case gains credibility. Just as the President or the Congress relies on experts to devise plans for remedying the nation's ills, you can argue that an expert's viewpoint should carry strong weight in a debate.

Even stronger than the recommendation of a single expert is the consensus of an entire community of experts. If all, or even a majority, of those knowledgeable on the subject support that a particular action would reduce or eliminate harmful conditions, the affirmative is in a good position to claim that their plan would solve the problem. When the American Medical Association agreed that cigarette smoking caused cancer and supported a ban of all smoking on airline flights, pressure mounted for the United States Congress to take action.

In addition to attracting expert support, some proposals have proven track records that you can examine to determine if a policy will succeed or fail. Known as **pilot projects,** these programs are designed and implemented to test the implications of a potential policy. If government officials are considering the adoption of a policy nationwide, they will sometimes try out the project in a smaller area. In some states, for example, law enforcement officials placed bracelets on criminals convicted of minor crimes. These bracelets alerted police when offenders left a designated area (usually their homes). Projects such as these are referred to by advocates and opponents who can draw upon a proven record of experience. Pilot programs need not be sponsored by government. On a smaller scale, many universities experimented with coeducational dormitories to determine the effect on student life. Only later did universities decide to retain gender segregated dorms or expand integrated dorms. In these cases, and thousands others like them, debaters have empirical data concerning the effectiveness of the program in reducing a particular problem. (See Chapter Six of the core text, under "Analogies," to assess whether a particular pilot project would warrant the implementation of a broader proposal.)

If the program does not currently exist as a pilot project, it may have been in operation at some point in the past. Debaters can examine these historical situations to help determine how a policy would affect a given problem. Affirmative debaters considering a ban on alcohol to reduce drunk driving fatalities, for example, should investigate the Prohibition era to determine if such a legal remedy actually reduced the number of deaths. Debaters should not feel constrained to look only at policies in the distant past. A recent Supreme Court decision or law passed by Congress allows you to compare situations where the plan was in existence and where it was not. Other countries may have adopted similar policies; these may indicate whether the proposed plan would succeed in the United States. (See Chapter Six of the core text, under "Analogies" to assess whether historical or other examples would warrant the adoption of the current proposal.)

Each of these options for proving that a plan would solve a significant problem is useful in conjunction with each of the three lines of argument for proving solvency. A pilot project might indicate that a plan would eliminate a problem, reduce a problem, or simply bring the system more in line with its own goals. Expert testimony and past use of a policy have similar flexibility across the lines of argument. Affirmative debaters must choose one of the lines of argument at a minimum, finding support for the argument to persuade the judge that affirming their policy would solve the problem.

Lines of Argument for Denying Solvency

Negative debaters have the option of arguing that the affirmative policy will not solve the identified problem. These negative attacks on solvency are called plan-meet-needs (PMNs) or plan-meet-advantages (PMAs). **Plan-meet-needs** are solvency challenges raised against the claim that the affirmative plan will eliminate a problem. **Plan-meet-advantages** are similar attacks made against proposals that are allegedly advantageous compared to the present system. In order to argue a plan-meet-need or a plan-meet-advantage, three lines of argument will prove useful: attitudinal barriers will prevent the successful solution of the problem, structural barriers will undermine the policy's effectiveness, and groups of individuals will circumvent the proposal rendering it ineffectual. As with each of the other general lines of argument in policy debate, negative debaters will win the debate if they can convince the judge that the affirmative will not solve existing problems.

Attitudinal Barriers

The first line of argument to deny solvency is that attitudinal barriers will prevent the policy from solving the problem. An **attitudinal plan-meet-need** is an argument that individuals have such strong attitudes against the proposal that they will likely diminish the positive effects expected from the plan.

> Daniel: Sex education classes will not increase the number of kids who use contraceptives. Parents won't let birth control be available at school, and kids are too embarrassed to buy it at the drug store.

Daniel argues that existing attitudes prevent sex education classes from affecting the teenage pregnancy rate. Even if teenagers understand the value of contraceptives, their embarrassment at having to purchase them from a drug store would offset any positive benefits of the education. Or parental backlash might prevent contraceptives from becoming available in high school settings. Taken together, these attitudes would impede the potential effects of any educational program, no matter how properly constructed.

Structural Barriers

The second line of argument to deny solvency is that structural barriers would preclude effective policies. **Structural plan-meet-needs** point to codified characteristics of the present system that impede the affirmative's ability to solve the problem. Prohibitive costs, legal barriers, bureaucratic structures, material shortages or defects, and constitutional questions can all undermine the success of a policy.

> Daniel: Knowing about contraception isn't going to help. Birth control is too expensive for most teens. And even if they can afford it, contraceptives are not 100 percent effective.

In this instance, Daniel is arguing that prohibitive costs and material defects will structurally undermine the ability of sex education classes to reduce teen pregnancies. He could have easily highlighted legal barriers such as possible future laws outlawing birth control access to minors, bureaucratic structures such as a school board bent on banning related textbooks, or constitutional questions such as the federal government's lack of control over curriculum matters. Any of these arguments could offset much of the advantage that Marie might claim.

Circumvention

The final line of argument to deny solvency is that individuals or groups of individuals will circumvent the proposal. **Circumvention,** as the name implies, occurs when individuals with selfish or perverse motives "go around" the plan to avoid complying with the intent of the proposal. To sustain this line of argument, debaters must prove three things: that the individuals have a motive for wanting the plan to fail, that the individuals have the means to undermine the success of the proposal,

ATTITUDINAL PLAN-MEET-NEEDS

In the final round of the 1982 National Debate Tournament, the University of Redlands (Jeff Wagner and William Isaacson) affirmed the resolution, "Resolved: that the federal government should significantly curtail the power of labor unions." The University of Louisville (Dan Sutherland and Dave Sutherland) negated the resolution.

Redlands affirmed the resolution by arguing that labor unions should be required to actively represent minority members who are suffering employment discrimination. In response, Mr. Dan Sutherland argued, as follows, that societal attitudes concerning race are so entrenched that legal requirements can never solve discrimination.

Negative

(2) Discrimination tradeoffs. [Discrimination is so embedded in our society that when the law attempts to stop discrimination in one place it merely shifts to another.] (a) Discrimination is inherent. Robert Blauner says in '72: "The values that people seek are never distributed equally: in the struggle for subsistence and social rewards there are always obstacles that impede some groups more than others. Thus systematic inequality and systematic injustice are built into the very nature of stratified societies." He [Blauner] goes on: "Social privilege is not unique to racist societies. Like hierarchy and exploitation, it is a universal feature of all class societies, including those in which ethics and racial division are insignificant."

(b) It's especially true in the labor market. The [affirmative arguments] certainly indicate that [racism infiltrates the labor market]. . . . Blauner goes on: "The collective mobility of the racial minorities is reduced because of discrimination in the labor market and at the work place."

(c) The discrimination will trade off. Although [the affirmative deals] with a specific form of discrimination, it will simply reappear in worse areas. As Hesburgh says in '69: "Prejudice puts out roots in all directions. Destroy one; another is already burgeoning. Blauner goes on: "The specific constellation of the colored man's place in society undergoes change, generally in a less restrictive direction, but the underlying themes reappear in new and unexpected ways."

(d) Alternative policies. (1) What we should do is, first of all, change attitudes and then laws and not the other way around as Samuels says: "Taking the bread-and-butter steps to improve conditions and complying with laws, while essential, are not enough. Changes in attitudes are as urgent as changes in overt behavior, for they lay the groundwork for any deep and lasting attempt to expunge prejudice."

(2) You must look at the big picture. We must stop discrimination in large sweeping ways, not one small policy at a time. As Segalman says in '77: "In defense of the rights of individuals and groups, the social objective and effects of such interventions have been generally ignored. The problems of design of social policy derive from one-sided or parochial views of multidimensional issues, based upon divergent value and social system orientation." [The affirmative does not] attack discrimination in the proper way, and it will trade off in worse areas, and that's simply our point as far as discrimination goes. We don't like discrimination either, but we think [the affirmative] is morally reprehensible, because [they] deal with the union movement which is even worse.

STRUCTURAL PLAN-MEET-NEEDS

In the final round of the 1976 National Debate Tournament, Georgetown University (Charles Chafer and David Ottoson) affirmed the resolution, "Resolved: that the federal government should adopt a comprehensive program to control land use in the United States." The University of Kansas (Robin Rowland and Frank Cross) negated the resolution.

Georgetown argued that the United States should increase the production of food for distribution overseas in the form of food aid to solve both malnutrition and hunger. Mr. Rowland offered the following series of arguments to prove that existing structures would not be able to fulfill the additional requirements of food aid distribution.

Negative

Insolvency would create doubt as to whether [the affirmative] could achieve their plan. That is justification for a negative ballot. I would argue (1) inadequate transportation. Proceedings of the American University Symposium, World Food, in 1974: "Food aid is in a holding pattern because of the logistics of having to move large amounts of aid are overwhelming. The U.S. now has fifty ships backed into Bombay harbor while people starve in Kerala". Time, November 11, 1974: It is also unlikely that "the world has enough ships, trains and trucks to move such quantities of grain."

I would argue (2) storage losses. Dr. George Borgstrom in 1975: "The most neglected aspect of the food issue is in the areas of food waste, spoilage and utilization . . . . One third to one half and even as much as 80 percent of the food in some countries is lost . . . ."

I would argue (3) corruption. Turn to Harry Toland of the North American Newspaper Alliance, 1975: "From all sides, the visitor hears that corruption, graft, black marketing . . . eat away at much of India . . . . It all bears directly on how well Indians eat-whether some of them eat at all." Kansas City Sun in August of 1975: "We must face up to the fact that many government leaders really don't care if their own people starve."

I would argue (4) specifically a lack of distribution capability. Robert Lewis in May, 1975: "The governments of poor countries with little capability to govern couldn't use the food effectively to feed their people, even if they wanted to."

I would argue (5) maldistribution . . . . Community Nutrition Institute, December of 1974: "Food aid tends to be distributed to where it can be delivered most easily. That tends to be the school systems. Then came the question on whether these kids were the most vulnerable. Research pointed to pregnant mothers and preschoolers. But the voluntary agencies prefer to stay in school feeding." Newsweek in November, 1974: "Existing stocks tend to be funneled into the politically volatile cities while the countryside supplies can fall to Scroogian levels."

CIRCUMVENTION

In the final round of the 1978 National Debate Tournament, the University of Southern California (John Cassanelli and Steve Combs) affirmed the resolution, "Resolved: that law enforcement agencies should have significantly increased freedom in the investigation and/or prosecution of felony crimes." Northwestern University (Stuart Singer and Mark Cotham) negated the resolution.

In defense of the resolution, Southern California argued that the Environmental Protection Agency could only prosecute water polluters with misdemeanor crimes. Raising these crimes to felonies and establishing more avenues of enforcement would allow the EPA to crack down on water polluters and deter others. In response, Northwestern argued that some agencies are vulnerable to circumvention if they are "captured" by anti-enforcement interests. Mr. Singer presented the circumvention argument.

Negative

(A) Agencies will be captured. Please note (1) the motive. (a) We argue the present inherency is the economic regulation. Economic impact statements are considered at present. Hence, industry has its input now. They are able and secure that their own economic interests will be considered. This is a direct, undeniable link within the affirmative case structure, too, [and explains] why agencies will be against the plan. (b) Of course, cost is going to be first borne by consumers. We'll have to pay for it on the water bill, hence decreasing the industries' ability there. Note (c) regulation in general is unpredictable; hence, you have a disincentive at that level.

I will argue (2) regulation agency capture is inevitable. Anthony D'Amato argues in 1970: "Members of a government agency are in daily contact with the businessmen whom they should watch over, and eventually the regulators adopt the perspectives and attitudes of those businessmen." Goldberg in 1974: "The so-called independent regulatory agencies, with some notable exceptions, are not always free from political influence, and . . . some tend to become captive to the interests . . . they are [bound by law] to regulate."

I would argue (3) that you will have an increased effort to capture them now that you adopt the affirmative plan. Jerry Cohen, counsel, explains in Senate Anti-trust Subcommittee in 1972: "Each time a regulatory operation becomes effective in the public interest, it generates a larger and opposite counterreaction."

I would argue (4) the means are there. (a) Contact, that is the first card. [I read from] (IIB2) D'Amato. (b) Contributions. Dr. Weidenbaum in 1976: "Illegal contributions [were] usually a response, often reluctant, to the demands from representatives of a powerful government which is in a position to do great harm to the company." (c) [Corporations] can simply hold open job offers. Hazel Henderson in 1970: "Corporations hold pervasive influence on . . . regulatory agencies by . . . holding out prize industry jobs to sympathetic officials on their retirement from government." Please note (d) enforcement is preempted. To the extent that the [affirmative] plan [allows] discretion, industries can simply capture [enforcement agencies] and prevent [enforcement].

and that attempts to circumvent the plan will have an impact that would reduce the affirmative's claim of solvency.

> Daniel: Parents would prevent any sex education course from working. Many parents think sex education leads to sexual experimentation. Do you think these parents would let their kids go to these classes? Or even to the school that offers them? Unlikely!

With this position, Daniel demonstrates each component required in a circumvention argument. Many parents have a motive to circumvent sex education classes because they believe that such classes encourage children to experiment with sex. The means to circumvent are that the parents will make their children skip the classes or remove them from the offending school system altogether. The weakest part of Daniel's argument is its impact. How many parents oppose the classes? Of these, how many will feel so strongly that they will pull their children out of school or out of the classes? A negative debater should explain to what extent the circumvention argument reduces solvency. If public opinion polls show that 60 percent of the parents oppose a sex education class, and Daniel can prove that many of these parents will shift their children to private schools, he might be able to estimate that between twenty and forty percent of the parents would circumvent the proposal.

Disproving Solvency Claims

You can use any one or any combination of the previous three lines of argument to deny the affirmative's solvency. Additionally, you may want to undermine the strength of the evidence used by the affirmative to make the claim of solvency. The negative has lines of argument available to contest each type of evidence used by affirmative debaters to demonstrate solvency (experts, consensus of experts, pilot projects, and historical examples). Chapter Five of the core text presents lines of argument for attacking evidence. This chapter will add evidentiary lines of argument specific to claims for solvency. Chapter Six of the core text, under "Analogies," presents lines of argument for deciding the relevance of pilot projects and historical examples.

Experts

When arguing against a policy recommendation made by a single expert or a group of experts, negative debaters can maintain that the expert is not recommending the specific policy advocated by the affirmative, the expert does not have expertise in the area of policy recommendation, the expert would benefit from the adoption of the policy, and the expert did not consider new data in his or her policy recommendation.

The first of these lines of argument, that the expert is not recommending the specific affirmative policy, is potentially the most damaging argument the negative can make. Affirmative debaters have the responsibility to show that their specific policy will solve the significant problem they describe. Frequently, experts will recommend only a portion of the affirmative's policy or will recommend general actions in the same subject area as the affirmative. In both instances, the expert falls short of providing authoritative support for the affirmative policy. If the affirmative advocates a mandatory sex education program and the expert cited identifies the benefits of a voluntary program, the affirmative has not met the burden of solvency. If the resolution requires that the policy be adopted at the federal level and the expert recommends that local school boards implement the program, the affirmative again has not fulfilled the solvency burden.

Even if experts are advocating the specific affirmative policy, they may lack a broad enough base of knowledge to qualify as a policy advocate. Many experts have a narrow frame of reference for evaluating any given policy. Doctors, for example, might recommend a sex education program because they see it as instrumental in reducing sexually transmitted diseases—a health concern. Those same doctors, however, may not have an understanding of the educational issues involved. What subjects will have to be eliminated from the curriculum to free up the time to teach the sex education course? What sort of training will be necessary to ensure proper instruction? In short, experts on health issues may not be sufficiently qualified to make general policy recommendations. Negative debaters should therefore point out when the overall cost-benefit analysis of a policy exceeds the expert's education and experience.

If the experts are qualified to recommend the specific affirmative proposal, the negative may discover that the expert would benefit personally from the policy. The likelihood of personal gain from the policy biases the expert, leading to questions about credibility. An expert from a pharmaceutical company, for example, might receive financial gain from any increase in teenagers' use of birth control devices. An educational expert might gain national recognition for originating the concept of the affirmative's plan. If negative debaters can prove that the expert would gain from the policy's adoption, they cast doubt on the believability of the expert's statement.

In some instances, affirmative experts may have both expertise and trustworthiness. On these occasions, the negative should seek recent data the expert may not be aware of or studies that contradict the assumptions or conclusions of the experts. This line of argument grants that when the expert made the original statement the conclusion had validity. Since that time, however, new facts place doubt on whether the policy will solve the problem. Imagine a situation where a recent pilot study testing the effects of sex education released preliminary findings that the program increased the teenage pregnancy rate. If these findings appeared after an expert claimed that sex education programs would decrease teen pregnancies, the negative could argue that the expert lacked the most up-to-date information on the subject.

None of the lines of argument used to question expert testimony on policy recommendations prevents the negative from using the others in the same debate. Cumulatively, they represent a strong attack on whether a given policy will solve significant problems.

Pilot Projects

Many affirmative debaters base their claims of solvency on the success of pilot projects which implement the policy on a small scale. In these cases, the negative can argue that the pilot project differs from the affirmative proposal, that the project will not generalize to the total population covered by the affirmative, that the participants in the affirmative plan would behave differently than those in the project, and that the overseers of the affirmative plan would behave differently than those associated with the project.

As with lines of argument denying expert testimony, the first concern of the negative is to test whether the pilot project matches the affirmative policy in its specifics. The negative should examine the pilot project to determine whether any additions or deletions from the model occurred in the construction of the affirmative plan. If so, the affirmative has failed to meet their burden of proving the solvency of their proposal. The argument is even more persuasive if the negative can show that differences between the pilot project and the affirmative plan would produce differing results. If a pilot project, for example, paid individuals to participate, an affirmative plan that required voluntary participation would be unlikely to generate comparable levels of enthusiasm for the project which would help to ensure its success.

If the pilot project and the plan are identical, the negative might argue that the population served by the small project might not be representative of those who would be affected by the affirmative plan. What policymakers observe to be the results of a pilot project for sex education conducted in a rural county in a southern state might not be relevant to the same project operated in a northern, metropolitan area. Negative debaters should always make sure that the affirmative carefully generalizes the results of a pilot project to a broader population.

One reason that the results might not be relevant to a broader population is that the subjects in the study may not have been selected from a nationwide sample. Individuals serving in pilot projects face unique conditions that may not be present under wide adoption of the policy. The mere fact that the subjects are under study can enhance their motivation to perform. If they received monetary compensation or some other form of payment to participate in the project, their behaviors may differ from those who do not receive such perks. Their willingness to participate in the study alone makes the group substantially different from individuals who might refuse or be reluctant to do so. In any case, the negative is frequently able to argue that the unique nature of the participants in a pilot project leads to overestimates of the benefits expected from nationwide adoption of the plan.

The participants, however, are not the only ones in the setting of a pilot project who might differ from those involved in the affirmative plan. The directors of the project are also likely to behave differently. When a pilot project is operating, the program directors have a number of motives for ensuring the success of the project. They may have originated the concept of the project, and would thus have a vested interest in seeing that it succeeds. Further, pilot projects are frequently the subject of reports in the media, which will generally cover the success or failure of these projects. Wanting to avoid an unfavorable press report, the directors of the projects may go to great lengths to see that the project is working. Finally, the groups funding pilot projects regularly scrutinize the practices and procedures of the projects to make recommendations for improvement. When the plans are adopted nationwide, such careful evaluation may be absent.

Negative debaters may find it useful to think of pilot projects as analogies to affirmative policies. While some similarities exist, the differences between the two should become the focus of the negative attack. The four lines of argument presented here represent general options for identifying what those differences are likely to be.

Past Policies

When affirmative debaters do not depend on expert testimony or pilot projects, they refer to policies that existed in the past to prove that their proposal will solve the problem. When attempting to deny a historical example, negative debaters can argue that the past policy was ineffective in solving the problem. If the policy did work, they can maintain that the past policy is not applicable today. The negative can insist that attitudes and structures currently in existence were not present when the previous policy was in effect. As a result, the negative would claim, the results of the two policies would be quite different.

The most direct attack on historical examples is to argue that the previous policy had little to no effect on the problem. Take, for example, sex education classes during the 1970s. Those classes taught the risks of contracting sexually transmitted diseases. Negative debaters, facing this example, could readily argue that the classes were a horrible failure. Today, sexually transmitted diseases, including AIDS, are at an all-time high.

If the affirmative can sustain that previous policies have had a positive effect, the negative should attempt to argue that past policies are irrelevant to present circumstances. Differences between past and present policies might be attitudinal or structural in nature. If the sex education classes of the 1970s arguably reduced the number of cases of syphilis, the negative should look for differences between the context of the 1970s and 1990s in which the classes were operating. With respect to attitude, the negative could maintain that the country's sociopolitical beliefs have shifted to the right. With rising concern about private morality, there is stronger opposition to sex education courses today than in the 1970s. The result, the negative could reason, is that the affirmative should not be able to assert that the positive benefits of the past will recur.

Structurally, circumstances have also changed since the 1970s. Debaters could point to the drops in federal funding for education. Prior to the cuts in the 1970s, the federal government might have been able to persuade schools to implement sex education courses. The schools would not want to lose federal funds. By the 1990s, localities could be willing to forego small amounts of federal funding to preserve their autonomy over curriculum matters. Like attitudinal shifts,

SOLVENCY

In the final round of the 1988 National Debate Tournament, Dartmouth College (Shawn Martin and Rob Wick) affirmed the resolution, "Resolved: that the United States should reduce substantially its military commitments to NATO member states." Baylor University (Danny Plants and Marty Loeber) negated the resolution.

Dartmouth argued that the United States was planning to sell nuclear submarines to fellow NATO member Canada, which would violate the nuclear Non-Proliferation Treaty (NPT), a global agreement designed to minimize the spread of nuclear weapons. To prevent a breakdown of the NPT agreement, Dartmouth argued the United States should not sell nuclear submarines to Canada. Mr. Martin explained how the structures of diplomacy and the NPT can prevent the global proliferation of nuclear weapons. Mr. Plants argued that other structures can circumvent the plan to provide Canada with the submarines and that the NPT is not a sufficient structure to solve the problem of proliferation.

Affirmative

(D) Solvency. Diplomatic actions will solve [the problem of nuclear proliferation]. The efficacy of this approach was demonstrated by VMI professor Wayne Thompson in '88: "Ties with the United States restrain and complicate the making of Canadian defense policy. Canadians must always ask themselves what their partners want them to do."

Technical means involve control of technology transfer. The plan would not allow Canada the means to build the subs. The ability to control technology was reported by the Financial Post in '87: "U.S. Navy clearance is essential for these firms [such as General Dynamics and Newport News Shipbuilding, to assist Canada in construction of submarines] because the navy owns some of the rights to all submarines it orders."

Such control would be complete, since Canadian subs would inevitably require U.S. technology. For example, the Alberta Report reported in June '87: "An American-designed pressurized water reactor . . . is the

Negative

Down below on the (D) subpoint, solvency. The first argument here is a [circumvention]. [Canada] could get it in other ways. Britain and France and the U.S. already have these kinds of submarines. [There is] no indication that they couldn't get them [from France and Britain].

The next [argument] is nuclear power plants provide enriched plutonium. Thus, [Canada] could [develop] it [through nuclear production facilities]. Donnally in 1987: "Development of uranium enrichment capabilities continues in several countries, including some with less industrial standing. The development of laser isotope separation is also becoming more prominent. If this should succeed, and there seems little reason to expect otherwise, the ability to produce weapons-grade uranium could spread quickly."

The next argument here is reactor-grade plutonium makes these weapons. Wilmhurst says in '84:

(Continued)

SOLVENCY—*Continued*

Affirmative (Cont.)

most likely power source for the Canadian submarine fleet.''

Additionally, it should be noted that Canada had to seek U.S. permission to obtain nuclear technology, regardless of the source. The Christian Science Monitor made this clear in February of '88: ''Canada is currently negotiating with both the British and French government a 'memorandum of understanding' which will permit transfer of technology needed to build the subs in Canada . . . . Under a Canadian-American treaty of 1959, though, the U.S. Congress must approve the sale to Canada of any 'military nuclear reactors and/or parts.''

Thus, through diplomatic and technical means the plan avoids Canadian development and weakens the nonproliferation regime. The importance of Canada's role in the nonproliferation regime was noted by Weiss in '86: ''Effective persuasion is more likely to come from non-nuclear-weapons nations (such as Canada . . .) that had the obvious capability to become military nuclear powers but elected not to do so. It is in the context of active diplomacy that Europe and the United States must collaborate in engaging such third-party persuaders in this endeavor.''

The Council on Foreign Relations concluded in '86: [It] is . . . essential to preserve and extend the international consensus against proliferation that now exists among most states capable of acquiring

Negative (Cont.)

''Another source of concern was the acceptance by expert opinion in 1974 that the distinction hitherto made between 'weapons-grade' and 'reactor-grade' plutonium, though still a valid technical distinction in terms of isotopic content, was no longer a valid distinction in terms of proliferation risk.''

The next argument here is that the NPT fails us. Marin-Bosh in 1985: ''The present state of affairs regarding the NPT can be described as a distressing example of unfulfilled promise.''

The next argument here is that new proliferants threaten the treaty. Goldblat says in '86: ''Accession to the Non-Proliferations Treaty by the most critical threshold states is doubtful for the foreseeable future,'' indicating that the NPT doesn't apply to the countries that are the greatest risk.

The next argument here is threshold states are not members. This is from Wilmhurst in 1984: ''If no new gestures can be devised to bring the potential weapon states into the non-proliferation system, there is not only the risk of another weapon state appearing but an equal danger that the non-proliferation community may split.''

The next argument here is that the superpowers will thwart it in other ways. McGrew in 1984: ''In 1980, the NPT Review Conference was unable to agree [on] a final

(Continued)

Affirmative (Cont.)

nuclear weapons or helping others do so, and the international commitments reflecting and reinforcing that consensus.''

Negative (Cont.)

communique partly as a result of assertions that the superpowers had abandoned any serious commitment to restraints on their own actions as implied in Article VI(5).''

. . . The [next] argument here is that proliferation is inevitable. This is from Wilmhurst in 1984: ''The most essential component of a nuclear military program is not the nuclear material nor the nuclear technology, but the political will, supported by a minimum of scientific and industrial capacity. If the political will is there, any country will, sooner or later, succeed in producing and creating the necessary nuclear material and technologies.''

Also, . . . all the [affirmative] evidence says that [the states] would be able to keep them in check, but this evidence indicates that there are other factors driving people to proliferate. They can get the weapons.

Next is nuclear power plants are a mechanism. I read evidence on that [earlier].

The next argument here is [that there is] no barrier [to countries obtaining nuclear weapons after the plan]. This is from Schwartz and Derber in 1986: ''This process has now advanced so far that it can only be a matter of time before the capacity to make or steal nuclear warheads becomes available to any nation or major organization that seeks it.''

structural changes prevent the affirmative from assuming that past successes will translate into future successes.

Lines of Argument for Comparing Solvency Claims

At this point, it may be obvious to you that some overlap exists among the solvency lines of argument. You may have noticed that attitudinal barriers appear strikingly similar to the motives cited in a circumvention argument. Structural barriers are similar to the means in a circumvention argument. Here we will examine arguments that closely resemble each other to assess how best to resolve conflicting solvency claims.

Attitudinal Barriers/Motives for Circumvention

When you attempt to resolve whether opposition to the plan will weaken its effectiveness, three lines of argument are useful. *Have attitudes already changed towards the proposal? Can the resolution or plan incentives overcome opposition? What impact will attitudinal opposition have on the plan's solvency?*

Have attitudes already changed towards the proposal? In some cases, the negative will identify attitudes that are outmoded. Public attitudes toward a policy can be quite variable; even a single event can alter public opinion. Presidential campaigns offer perhaps the most striking examples. The public will not care about an issue or even oppose a given proposal until the candidate of their choice offers the plan as part of their campaign. The public may support the insanity defense as an option for mentally ill defendants until a John Hinkley attempts to assassinate the President. Since attitudes can change so quickly, negative claims of attitudinal opposition and affirmative claims of public support are thus very tenuous.

In the debate between Daniel and Marie, Daniel argues that parents will never accept the availability of free contraceptives in educational settings. These attitudes may exist at the moment, but they could quickly shift to support such a proposal if the AIDS epidemic begins to spread throughout teenage populations. Even if the public remains opposed to schools giving out free contraceptives, the strength of that opposition could wane. Parents might reject the proposal on principle but fail to respond with actions that would undermine the success of the sex education program.

Will resolution or plan incentives overcome opposition? Anticipating that the negative will attempt to reduce solvency by showing attitudinal opposition, the affirmative can preemptively include inducements in the plan to magnify the chances that the public will comply. In resolving competing claims of solvency, both teams need to assess whether the incentives to accept the plan are sufficient to overcome anger or apathy towards the proposal. Is opposition so strong that the inducements would not work? Does the public care more about receiving the benefits offered in the affirmative proposal than they do about an objectionable policy?

On a general level, this debate focuses on the issue of whether people will comply with laws. The affirmative tends to enforce its plan with penalties sufficiently high to frighten would-be violators, but not so high that the Supreme Court would conclude that the penalty is cruel and unusual punishment. These penalties can be effective in preventing the most obvious actions that would undermine the plan's intent. Further, the sheer existence of a law may compel many members of the public to reconsider their opposition and decide to support the plan. An issue of great dispute is whether laws change attitudes or whether attitudes must change before the introduction of laws.

In the debate between Marie and Daniel, Daniel maintains that parents oppose sex education courses because they fear that the classes encourage sexual experimentation. To attempt to reduce this opposition, Marie could specify precisely what topics would make up the course. If the subjects all focused on the risks of engaging in sex, many parents originally opposed to the idea might welcome the introduction of the courses. If Marie made this argument, Daniel would need to be able to explain why the resolutional alternative could not overcome the opposition. He might argue that parents would never trust the teachers to present the topics of a sex education class in a suitable manner. In any event, both sides need to assess the impact of resolutional or plan inducements for plan compliance.

What level of impact will opposition have on the affirmative's claim of solvency? Having determined the present state of attitudes and whether these attitudes can be changed, the remaining issue is the potential impact of the opposition. Will the attitudinal barrier be sufficient to prevent the affirmative's plan from completely solving the problem? Or will the plan still be able to reduce the problem to some extent? How much solvency can be expected from the proposal?

Parental opposition is clearly an obstacle to full compliance with sex education classes. However, fear of the spread of AIDS and reassurances that the teachers will only teach topics that emphasize the risks of sexual activity will reduce parent opposition to the proposal. Both Marie and Daniel have a responsibility to determine the extent of the teenage pregnancy problem that will remain after all these factors come into play. How many of the parents object to the proposal, and how deep is their opposition to the plan?

Structural Barriers/Means for Circumvention

Structural barriers to solvency and means for circumvention are not identical concepts. Some structural problems, such as material shortages, affect the plan's success even if every individual supports the plan. More frequently than not, however, structural barriers become the tools of those individuals who oppose the plan and hope to circumvent it. Several questions need to be addressed to determine the ability of individuals to avoid the plan directives.

Are the avenues of circumvention and structural barriers sufficient to undermine the proposal? Negative debaters must show that these will have an important impact on the overall solvency claimed by the affirmative. A group angered by a proposal may simply not be powerful enough to keep it from reaching its goals. If Daniel's means for circumventing Marie's sex education policy is for parents to keep children home on days when the course is taught, the means may not be sufficient to have a dramatic impact. Marie could indicate that most school districts require students to attend classes a certain number of days. Failure to follow this policy results in students having to repeat the same grade the next year. In effect, then, the parents refusal to allow their teenagers to attend sex education courses this year would merely postpone attending those same classes next year.

Debaters should examine structural barriers in the same manner. *Is the structural barrier sufficient to prevent the affirmative from solving a significant proportion of the problem?* In our debate, Daniel can point out that birth control is not 100 percent effective. However, this does not mean that if students use the contraceptives they would not have fewer pregnancies. Marie could point out that the effectiveness of contraceptives ranges from 70 to 99 percent depending on the type of birth control used. Certainly, an advantage would still remain despite the structural problems of contraceptives.

Can the resolution or the affirmative plan eliminate structural problems and avenues of circumvention? In many instances, affirmative debaters can anticipate possible means of circumvention as they write up the specifics of their proposal. They may attempt to preempt these arguments by including prescriptions that undercut the possibility of circumvention. If Marie wanted to reduce the impact of parents refusing to allow their teenagers to attend sex education classes, she might mandate increased enforcement of the compulsory attendance laws. If students do not attend, truant officers could aggressively cite the teenagers for delinquency violations. Certainly Daniel could argue that such actions would not undermine the parents' resolve. Political pressure on judges and prosecutors might prevent the effective enforcement of the compulsory attendance laws.

Are the avenues of circumvention available to those motivated to undermine the proposal? Unlike the previous two lines of argument, this issue applies only to resolving circumvention arguments. It is not relevant to structural barriers because such arguments do not depend on a linkage between attitudes and structures for their success. When presenting a circumvention argument, negative debaters will sometimes present ways in which groups could undermine a plan's intent but fail to show that those capable of circumventing the proposal have the desire to do so.

Daniel claimed that the means for circumventing sex education classes would be for the parents to remove their children from the public school system. If Marie could show that those capable of affording private school had already removed their children from public school, or that attitudes against sex education increase as socioeconomic status decreases, she would successfully undercut the connection between the motive and the means in Daniel's circumvention argument.

Impact

Having determined whether the means and the motives of the circumvention argument exist, the debaters should examine the most important component of the argument: its impact. *How strong is the opposition after incentives to comply with the plan have been taken into account? Are the means for circumvention substantial enough to undermine the solvency of the affirmative proposal? What level of solvency remains after the circumvention occurs?*

Generally, the affirmative team will attempt to minimize the impact of the circumvention argument. Particularly in cases where the negative cannot offer specifics as to the impact of their arguments, the affirmative can assert that it will have little to no impact at all. The affirmative will stress the large part of the population that is not opposed to the proposal, the insufficiency of the means to have any detrimental effect on solvency, and the inability of the groups opposed to the plan to take meaningful action. In the final analysis, the affirmative will argue that sufficient solvency remains to be cost-beneficial over current policies.

The negative, by contrast, will attempt to maximize the impact of the circumvention argument. Negative debaters stress the breadth and the depth of the opposition to the proposal. They reveal the ease of circumventing the affirmative proposal. They indicate that the net effect will be a substantial, if not total, reduction of the affirmative's claim of solvency. Ultimately, the negative argues that the amount of solvency remaining makes it cost-beneficial to stay committed to existing structures. No need exists for the resolution as defined by the affirmative proposal.

Comparing Evidence

Frequently, debaters may find themselves in a stalemate when comparing lines of argument related to solvency. One team claims that attitudes will prevent the plan from solving the problem, while the other team maintains they will not. In these cases debaters must be able to compare the evidence used to demonstrate their solvency claims. All debaters need to convince the judge that their evidence is superior so that their claims will be more persuasive.

When comparing evidence, debaters will either be evaluating material that has similar strengths and weaknesses or that has differing strengths and weaknesses. When comparing similar evidence, the question becomes one of degree. Which expert gives testimony most specific to the affirmative plan? Which expert is most trustworthy? Which pilot project is most representative of the nation as a whole? Which past policy occurred most recently? Debaters on both the affirmative and the negative teams strive to demonstrate that their sources are comparatively stronger along the dimensions shared by both pieces of supporting material.

More often than not, however, two competing pieces of evidence will not share comparable dimensions. One team's expert is biased, while the other team's expert lacks experience in making policy judgments. One team's pilot project uses representative subjects, but the other uses a more representative setting. In these instances and others like them, debaters will have to explain why the strength of their evidence is more important in a given set of circumstances than the strength of the competing evidence. As an example, a debater could argue that a lack of policy-making experience would not ensure that an expert's conclusion is off-base, but a bias virtually assures that the expert will distort the claim.

In assessing evidence that has differing strengths and weaknesses, debaters should focus particularly on the context of the claim. What is the nature of the claim? What evidence is necessary to sustain the claim? How strong must the evidence be? The fact that the subjects of a pilot project are volunteers may be irrelevant or of marginal concern if everyone approves of the affirmative proposal.

Both the claims of solvency and the evidence used to support them should be analyzed. By the end of the debate, the affirmative must provide sufficient proof to show that the plan it advocates will provide at least a preferable alternative to present policies. If the negative can defeat either the evidence the affirmative uses to support the claim or the claim itself, the negative will win the debate.

Summary and Conclusions

Solvency is one of the four general lines of argument that an affirmative team must prove to overcome the presumption against the resolution. Solvency arguments are claims about whether a new policy will be capable of reducing or eliminating a significant problem. They are not disagreements about whether a plan would be likely to come into existence in the context of current structures.

To argue that a policy would be solvent, affirmative debaters rely on three lines of argument: that the plan will eliminate the problem, that the plan has greater solvency than existing policies, and that it comes closer to meeting desirable goals. Affirmative debaters will use expert testimony, pilot projects, or historical examples to prove that a particular policy will solve the identified problem.

In response, negative debaters have the option of arguing that attitudinal barriers will prevent a successful remedy to the problem, that structural barriers will undermine the policy's effectiveness, or that individuals will circumvent the proposal. With this final argument, negative debaters must be able to show that a motive exists to circumvent the plan, that the means exist to undermine its effectiveness, and that these elements will combine to actually make the plan less effective.

The negative also has options for undermining the persuasiveness of the evidence used to support the claim of solvency. To invalidate expert testimony, the negative can argue that the experts are not speaking specifically about the affirmative proposal, that they lack expertise in the policy arena, that they would benefit from the proposal's adoption, and that they made the recommendation before new, vital information became available. Pilot projects may not be specific or representative of the policy as it would be adopted nationwide. Previous policies may not have been effective or may be irrelevant to present circumstances.

When comparing the claims made to support or deny solvency, both affirmative and negative debaters must weigh competing claims and evidence. Debaters should examine attitudinal barriers and motives for circumvention to see if attitudes have or could be changed, and what level of solvency will occur given opposition to the plan. Debaters should assess the structural barriers and the means for circumvention to determine if they are available to those who oppose the plan, if they remain after the plan's adoption, and whether they are sufficient to have a significant impact on the affirmative's claim of solvency. Finally, all debaters need to evaluate the impact of any solvency arguments.

When comparing the evidence used to demonstrate solvency, debaters should attempt to distinguish support that has similar strengths and weaknesses and support that has different strengths and weaknesses. Evidence that is similar requires debaters to make judgments of degree, while evidence that is different requires an evaluation of opposing strengths.

Exercises

1. Assume that you are debating against a plan that passes a law requiring consumers to recycle all their glass and aluminum products. Which of the following arguments would be legitimate solvency attacks and which would be should-would arguments? Defend your reasoning.

    —With its pro-business bias, the Congress would block this legislation. It would not have a chance to pass.

    —Consumers would just litter the nation's roads with their glass and aluminum. They would think that recycling requires too much effort.

    —The Supreme Court would throw out the recycling plan. The federal government has no business in environmental regulations that should fall under state's rights.

    —This recycling plan could never be enforced. What are you going to do? Have the city garbage collectors inspect every can of garbage? People would know they would never get caught.

2. Assume you are interested in preserving species of wildlife that are about to become extinct. Find a plan that allows you to eliminate a problem in the topic area. Find one that you can defend as comparatively advantageous over current policies. Find one that you can show is closer to the goals of present system than the current policy.

3. In the early 1990s, the state of Georgia received federal funds to set up a pilot project that would establish boot camps for first-time drug offenders. Would such a pilot project be sufficiently

representative to draw conclusions about a similar nationwide project? Why or why not? You may want to refer to the section on analogies in Chapter Six of the core text to stimulate your thinking about potential similarities and differences.

4. Develop a circumvention argument against a plan that would require state governments to spend at least 50 percent of their highway funds on mass transit systems. What would be the motive of state governments to circumvent the plan? How would they do it? What impact would circumvention have on the federal plan's ability to improve the nationwide mass transit system?

5. Watch a congressional debate on C-SPAN. Do the representatives discuss whether a particular plan would solve a problem? Do opposing legislators offer plan-meet-needs or plan-meet-advantages that suggest the solution would not work? Do they cite attitudinal barriers, structural barriers, or circumvention as the reason the plan would not work? What type of support do they use to back up their claims?

5

Analyzing Topicality Through Lines of Argument

Key Terms

topicality
implicit definition
topicality standard
grammatical context
better definition
extratopicality

Anyone advocating the affirmative in a policy debate must be able to make the claim that the policies advanced in the plan are the same ones included in the debate resolution. Affirmative debaters have the responsibility to make this argument, known as **topicality.** They must define, implicitly or explicitly, the key terms of the debate resolution. If they can defend that their definitions are acceptable and demonstrate that their policy meets these definitions, they are topical. The negative may elect to argue that the affirmative is not topical by indicating that the affirmative definitions are not acceptable or by arguing that the policy does not meet the definitions.

When you debate, you will discover that both affirmative and negative debaters need to understand the importance of definitions, the process of defining terms, and the standards for evaluating definitions in debate. In the first section of this chapter we outline these issues, which can be used by either the affirmative or the negative in any given debate. Next, we examine the lines of argument available for arguing that the affirmative is topical and for denying that the affirmative is topical. We conclude by identifying the lines of argument you can use to resolve competing topicality claims.

Identifying Key Terms

There is no standard rule for determining which resolutional terms debaters must define. Nevertheless, you should be able to identify potentially controversial terms in any debate resolution. In making that determination, you should expect to always define certain terms that recur in policy resolutions. Many terms are likely to be controversial. Controversial terms frequently include the agent designated to implement the policy, the policy recommendation, the method or direction of implementation, and any modifying terms that qualify the policy or method of action.

Some terms in a resolution are rarely controversial. Noncontroversial terms, which you usually do not need to define, include articles (such as *a, an,* and *the*), the initial terms of all resolutions (i.e. *Resolved: that*), and other terms that do not relate to the core of the policy debate. However, occasionally, even seemingly noncontroversial terms may play an important role in a debate about definitions. In the resolution, "Resolved: that the federal government should significantly curtail the power of labor unions in the United States," you would generally think "labor union" means collective bargaining units such as the Teamsters Union, the United Auto Workers, and so on. However, does the term *labor union* include professional organizations such as the American Medical Association or the American Bar Association? Does a resolution that recommends curtailing the power of labor unions include these particular organizations? These questions would be open to debate despite the apparent meaning of the term.

Affirmative debaters must defend their interpretation of the resolution. Since any word has the potential to affect that interpretation, it is vital that you prepare to defend a definition of all resolutional terms. Since all definitions have the potential to disprove that a particular case supports the debate topic, the negative debater should investigate the potential definitions of all words in the debate topic.

Definitions: Implicit or Explicit

Some controversy exists regarding when and how the affirmative debater is to define the terms of the resolution. Traditionally, judges have expected affirmative debaters to define terms explicitly at the beginning of the debate. More recently, debaters have tended to define terms implicitly and defend their interpretations only when the negative attacks them. An affirmative debater may give an **implicit definition** of a term by giving an example of it in the plan. For the labor union resolution, an affirmative that included curtailing the power of the AMA in its plan would be operationally defining labor unions to include professional organizations. Operational definitions demonstrate, rather than state, how the affirmative understands the resolution.

In the resolution, "Resolved: that the United States should significantly increase its foreign military commitments," the affirmative could mandate that the United States rigorously enforce the Nuclear Nonproliferation Treaty. Such a plan implies that the affirmative defines foreign military commitments as commitments to curtail the spread of nuclear weapons. Affirmative debaters would still have to defend this definition if challenged, but they might not define the words of the resolution explicitly until the negative has attacked or questioned their interpretation of the resolution.

Importance of Definitions

Regardless of whether the affirmative explicitly or implicitly defines the terms of the resolution, all debaters need to realize the importance of the definitions. Definitions regularly determine whether arguments and debates are won or lost. Definitions of terms are important in the ultimate outcome of a large number of legislative, executive, and judicial decisions. Many contract negotiations are devoted to determining a fair and reasonable interpretation of the terms of agreement.

In one of the most notable Supreme Court decisions in the twentieth century, definitions were critical to determining the outcome. From 1972 to 1974, the Watergate scandal besieged the presidency of Richard M. Nixon. Several operatives of the Committee to Re-elect the President were caught breaking into the Democratic National Committee Headquarters at the Watergate Hotel in Washington, D.C. During the reelection campaign and subsequent months, the Nixon Administration engaged in a massive cover-up to keep the FBI, Congress, and the Office of the Special Prosecutor from uncovering the link between the burglary at the Democratic headquarters and the Committee to Re-elect the President.

Eventually, Congress discovered that President Nixon had been taping all conversations that occurred in the Oval Office. This practice afforded Congress and the Office of the Special Prosecutor the opportunity to examine the allegations of a cover-up. When the Office of the Special Prosecutor attempted to obtain the tapes, the President argued that executive privilege and national security gave the executive branch the power to withhold the tapes.

The case eventually came before the Supreme Court. At that point the Office of the Special Prosecutor argued that "national security" could not be defined in such a way that the executive branch had the authority to elude justice. National security cannot include subjects of a purely political nature. The administration's interpretation of national security was so broad that it would include any item, including political accountability, that could cast doubt on the integrity of the president. The Supreme Court, with Justice William Rehnquist abstaining, ruled 8 to 0 that the President was defining national security too broadly and ordered Nixon to turn the tapes over to the Office of the Special Prosecutor. Shortly after the ruling, Nixon resigned his office in disgrace. Unable to sustain his definition of national security in court, his powerful administration fell.

In addition to political controversy, matters of public policy are frequently influenced by the definition of terms. The meaning of the term *poverty* is frequently contested in the halls of Congress and within administrative agencies. The federal government has defined poverty by establishing a maximum annual income for a family of four. This definition is important because it determines eligibility for federal assistance programs. An individual unable to meet this definition would not qualify for food stamps, Aid for Families with Dependent Children, programs for Women with Infant Children, and other similar programs designed to help the needy. This low-income definition has at least two important implications. First, it means fewer people are eligible for poverty programs than would be if the limit was higher. Second, the government can argue that fewer people are in poverty and, hence poverty programs need not be extensive. The definition of poverty influences who receives assistance, how much money is spent on assistance, and estimates of the poor population.

In academic debate, definitions can also influence the decisions reached by judges. Debating definitions is important for three reasons. First, it is necessary to divide argumentative ground predictably and fairly; second, it is necessary to determine if the resolution is probably true or probably false; and, third, it is necessary to ascertain whether the affirmative case and plan support the resolution.

The Toulmin model of argumentation illustrates why a critic dismisses arguments that do not support the resolution. In the examples below, you can see very clearly how relevant arguments support the claim. The negative effects on the image of the United States from covert involvement with right-wing dictators support the claim that the United States should ban covert involvement in Central America to protect the credibility of our foreign policy. In the second example, the data and warrant are irrelevant to the claim because attacks on countries, even if they are small, are not examples of "covert involvement." The affirmative argument in the second example is nontopical.

Sample Topical Affirmative

Data: U.S. covert involvement in Central America supports right-wing dictators.
Warrant: Supporting right-wing dictators undermines the credibility of U.S. foreign policy.
Claim: The United States should ban covert involvement in Central America to maintain a credible foreign policy.

Sample Nontopical Affirmative

Data: The United States has publicly announced a plan to attack a Central American country.
Warrant: Attacks on small countries undermine the credibility of U.S. foreign policy.
Claim: The United States should ban covert involvement in Central America to maintain a credible foreign policy.

Definitions are important in academic debate because debaters can define terms, in a way that directs the discussion toward arguments favorable to their side. Debaters sometimes also define terms in a way that maximizes their strategic options in a given debate round. It has been said that the person who controls the terms of the debate controls the debate. This explains why many debate rounds focus on the definition of terms rather than on issues related to the subject matter of the debate.

Affirmative debaters may sometimes define terms very broadly in order to debate an issue that is on the periphery of the debate topic. For example, on a recent debate topic, "Resolved: that the United States should significantly increase its foreign military commitments," affirmative debaters predicted that negative debaters would have many arguments about why increased military commitments would be disastrous. The negative could have argued that increased commitments lead to more interventions, embolden adventuristic foreign policy, and undermine the economy. Affirmative debaters attempting to avoid these arguments maintained that "United States military commitments" included policies such as U.S. government compensation for victims of Agent Orange, U.S.-sponsored relocation of citizens of other countries displaced by atomic bomb tests, construction of additional civil defense shelters, and even guarantees that U.S. service personnel would have the freedom to marry a citizen of a foreign country without the interference of the military base commander. In these instances, defining the resolution broadly allowed the affirmative to control the argumentative ground by excluding many negative arguments.

Sometimes the negative attempts to severely restrict the interpretation of the resolution. They do so in order to narrow the range of possible affirmative defenses of the resolution. Discussing the resolution, "Resolved: that all military intervention in the internal affairs of any foreign nation or nations in the Western

Hemisphere should be prohibited," many affirmative debaters elected to ban military intervention in specific countries in the Western Hemisphere such as El Salvador or Nicaragua. Some negative teams were able to win the argument that such cases did not meet the requirements of the debate topic. According to these negative debaters, the topic meant that *all* intervention should be prohibited in the Western Hemisphere. This restrictive definition of the resolution narrowed the range of possible arguments requiring negative preparation.

Competitive control of the argumentative ground is not the only reason why topicality is important. Accurate definitions are also necessary to determine the probable truth of the resolution. If you define terms in such a way that it becomes unclear what the resolution means, then it is difficult for a judge to know if the resolution is probably true. The meaning of the proposition itself has to be clear to convince a judge to affirm the resolution. For example, in "Resolved: that more rigorous academic standards should be established for all public elementary and/or secondary schools in the United States," the meaning of the phrase "rigorous academic standards" is very debatable. Would rigorous academic standards include comprehensive standardized testing, graduation requirements, and specific classroom materials? The affirmative would need to define what this phrase means for a judge to decide if public schools should establish them.

Arguments about definitions also are necessary because they confine the debate to issues that are relevant to the resolution. If, for example, a judge determines that rigorous academic standards do not include requiring specific classroom materials, the judge would probably dismiss any arguments that prove that students had to read certain materials in some classrooms. A judge would only affirm the resolution if the affirmative debater proves that more rigorous academic requirements for graduation or standardized testing should be established. Judges will dismiss arguments not related to the topic; they will listen to all relevant arguments.

Sources of Definition

Many sources exist for defining the terms of the resolution. There are dictionaries, articles and academic papers, legislative codes and legislative histories, and legal interpretations of terms. When you begin researching a topic, you should examine all the various ways the term has been defined.

Even the number of dictionaries can be surprising. General language dictionaries define terms according to their everyday usage. Some dictionaries include notes on the usage of words. Other dictionaries use historical analysis of the language to define words. Still other dictionaries are specific to a field of study such as politics and law.

General Dictionaries

Many people assume that all general dictionaries are the same. However, this is not the case. For example, Merriam-Webster Dictionaries use citations from printed sources to derive their definitions. Random House dictionaries define terms based on how people use words in daily conversation as well as on the words' usage in print. The *Oxford English Dictionary (OED)* provides a detailed history of each term including examples of its use in print. Each of these dictionaries will offer the debater differing interpretations of some terms because they rely on different sources of definition. Debaters should examine all of them carefully for possible interpretations of the terms of the resolution.

Specialty Dictionaries

Once debaters know what topic they will be debating, they should attempt to discover any dictionaries that might be specific to that field of study. Many academic disciplines have dictionaries specific to their field of study. Additionally, some field-specific dictionaries cross academic disciplines. Several specialty dictionaries which are very useful for policy debaters include:

> *Black's Law Dictionary (BLD).* This is a dictionary of terms derived from legal opinion and court decisions. Designed to assist attorneys, this dictionary defines technical legal terms. Debaters can use *Black's* to read about both obscure and common terms. *Black's* also serves as a bibliographic reference for court cases and legislation relevant to the definitions of terms.

> *Words and Phrases (W&P).* This reference is a compilation of words and phrases that the United States court system uses. While technical legal terms are included in these volumes, *Words and Phrases* also include a large number of nontechnical terms found in legislation, contracts, and legal opinion. While *Words and Phrases* identifies and interprets terms, it also cites legal precedent and opinion to justify its interpretations. Debaters should use the citations in *Words and Phrases* to research the Supreme Court's written explanation of why a case was decided in a particular way. Debaters can use the reasoning of the court to justify their interpretation of terms in the debate round.

> *Corpus Juris Secundum (CJS).* This is a compilation of court opinions in particular subject areas. Much like *Words and Phrases, CJS* includes definitions used by the court. *CJS* also updates their legal interpretations with supplements included at the back of each volume. Debaters should examine *Black's Law Dictionary, Words and Phrases, CJS,* and other legal references because the cases and definitions cited in each source may be different. Each resource offers a variety of definitions which debaters should explore.

> *Dictionary of Political Science.* This dictionary is one of many dictionaries specific to the field of political science. Since many debate topics center on important political conflicts, political science dictionaries are frequently a useful resource for debaters. The *Dictionary of Political*

Science derives its definitions from articles, textbooks, and published papers developed in the field of political science.

There are many sources of definition available in almost every field of study. These specialized dictionaries are frequently a rich resource for the debater. They provide a contextual framework for understanding the interpretation of a term in a given field. You should attempt to familiarize yourself with any dictionaries that could provide definitions of controversial terms contained in debate topics.

Legislation and Legislative History

Legislators regularly find it necessary to define the terms of their legislation. These definitions are recorded in congressional hearings, transcripts of floor debates, and public laws, such as the *Code of Federal Regulations*. To find these resources, you should locate government depository libraries in your area. In these libraries, you can find transcripts of congressional hearings, which report the activity of congressional committees and subcommittees, *Congressional Record*, which includes debates on the floor of Congress, and all federal laws and regulations. All United States citizens are permitted access to such documents.

Academic Articles and Books

Academic authors frequently narrow their research to a particular area of study. Their works can be fruitful sources of definition for debate. When you research books and articles specific to the topic area, you should remain alert for definitions of resolutional terms that may appear in the material. Academic articles, research books, and textbooks all offer definitions of terms usable in debate rounds.

In sum, debaters have a large number of areas in which to seek definitions of resolutional terms. Differing definitions create a large number of interpretations of debate resolutions. Some of the interpretations presented will undoubtedly be contradictory. When debaters present contradictory definitions in a single debate round, debaters need to be able to defend the appropriateness of their definitions.

Standards for Evaluating Competing Definitions

When attempting to resolve conflicts between competing definitions, debaters can offer standards for selecting the most appropriate definition for the debate. **Topicality standards** are criteria used to resolve the conflicts between competing definitions. Standards provide a method for governing how the judge should interpret specific words in the context of a debate. Without standards for evaluating definitions and topicality arguments, the judge cannot determine which definition should govern the interpretation of the resolution. Many standards are available. Here we will discuss a few prominent arguments that recur in competitive collegiate and secondary school debate.

Grammatical Context

One of the most commonly used standards for topicality is **grammatical context.** This standard holds that the grammatical function of a word within a sentence should help govern the word's meaning. Many words have such variable interpretations that it is only through their relationship to other words that we can understand their meaning. The resolution, "Resolved: that the United States should significantly increase exploration and/or development of space," provides an excellent example of how a word must be considered in the grammatical context of the sentence. Debaters could define "space" as outerspace, which is the apparent meaning of the topic. But space is also a geometric concept that applies to a variety of other endeavors. The term could refer to the space beneath the ocean, space as part of the space-time continuum, or the space between your ears. A creative affirmative debate team could conceivably argue that the federal government should increase exploration of the ocean, time travel, or psychology. Space is a very general term which can be understood only in relationship to other terms. Without a grammatical standard, debaters could define space so broadly that the topic would be meaningless and would not offer a predictable ground for debate.

It is far better for you to define words in their context than to distort their meaning into another context. However, debaters occasionally argue that judges should not interpret resolutions according to grammatical standards. First, debaters can argue that strict adherence to grammar restricts the development of language. Language depends on the creativity and inventions of authors. Past conventions should not arbitrarily restrict creative thought and invention. Second, debaters can argue that grammar itself evolves. Thus a strict interpretation of terms and phrases might be an out-of-date interpretation. Third, debaters can argue that the strict grammatical standard has its origins in an oppressive language system. Many sociologists argue that the upper classes have used strict rules of grammar to reinforce their control and access to societal institutions. Many, for example, argue that standardized academic testing represents this approach today because the test-taker must apply the strict rules of grammar to perform well on tests such as the Scholastic Achievement Test and the Graduate Record Examination. Reinforcing the power of the grammatical standard might reinforce the oppression some believe such rules impose. Fourth, the debater can argue that strict adherence to grammar does not improve communication. Some argue that people communicate without grammar. As long as everyone understands what the debate means, grammar should not be a valid criteria for evaluating topicality.

Arguments opposed to the grammatical standard are highly problematic. While there is evidence to support each reason that undermines grammar, it may be difficult to convince a judge that strict adherence to grammar decreases creativity, hinders the evolution of language, serves an oppressive elite, or is necessary for effective communication. Academia and other social institutions remain committed to the importance of grammar. Many judges have trouble accepting arguments that indicate that grammar is unimportant to communication and understanding. As a result, you should be certain that your interpretation of the debate topic is consistent with grammatical standards of definition.

Each Word Should Have Meaning

This standard requires debaters to define each word in a way that contributes to the interpretation of the resolution. Sometimes it is possible to define a term of the resolution so that other words in the resolution are devoid of meaning and do not serve an important function in the debate. In the resolution, "Resolved: that the federal government should significantly strengthen the regulation of mass media communication in the United States," an affirmative debater could propose to increase regulations on the telephone industry. However, such an interpretation ignores that the telephone, while an electronic medium, is not a mass medium. The telephone is a medium for communication between individuals, not for communicating to the masses. By defending such a proposal, the affirmative makes the word "mass" a meaningless term in the resolution. A judge would probably conclude that the affirmative proposal is not topical because it ignores the meaning of this word. If debaters define terms in such a way that words become meaningless, they alter the fundamental grounds of the debate and judges usually reject such definitions.

There are reasons why each word in a resolution should not have its own independent meaning. In some resolutions there may be words that provide no unique meaning. For example, in the resolution, "Resolved: that any and all injury resulting from the disposal of hazardous waste should be the legal responsibility of the producer of the waste," some might maintain that the phrase "any and all" has one meaning. Each word only reinforces the meaning of the other; if a producer is responsible for any injury, the producer is responsible for all injuries.

While "any" and "all" are not synonymous, their combined effect is to underline a single purpose. If a professor tells you, "You are responsible for all material because any and all subjects could be included on the test," the phrase "any and all" only reinforces the teacher's message that you are responsible for "all" material. The combination of terms allows for emphasis, but robs "any" of its ability to designate a particular area of study. As a student you need to be ready to answer any questions on any subject since all subjects can be tested.

Reasonability

Another standard debaters frequently employ to determine the appropriate definition of a term is whether or not the definition sets a reasonable limit on argumentative ground. If debaters define the resolutional terms too broadly, the negative will not be able to predict possible affirmative cases. Such an interpretation would be unreasonable. In defense of the resolution, "Resolved: that the federal government should adopt a comprehensive program to control land use in the United States," an affirmative debater could argue that the federal government should protect land from environmental hazards such as strip-mining and pesticide use. All of these regulations appear to be reasonable interpretations of land use policy. However, the legal community considers land to include buildings, and agricultural experts consider land to include plants. Within the framework of these definitions, affirmative debaters could argue that the federal government could enact building codes, control hospitals, build prisons, and release prisoners since these activities relate to buildings, or they could argue that the federal government could regulate the consumption of tobacco, impose safety requirements on food, and regulate alcohol since these substances come from plants. These interpretations, while supportable with evidence, make the resolution very broad and unpredictable. Such definitions are probably unreasonable.

If a definition imposes an extremely narrow interpretation that results in only a few possible cases, it would also be unreasonable. Under the land use resolution, debaters could argue that land use only refers to zoning regulations. In the field of land use and land use planning, many experts argue that the only way the government controls land use is through zoning regulations. By narrowing the ground for the debate to such a small handful of cases, a debater would be defining the term too narrowly to be reasonable.

Better Definition

It is very difficult for a debate judge to determine what is a reasonable interpretation of a debate resolution. Some debate judges and some debaters argue that a better-definition standard is preferable to the reasonableness standard. Those advocating the better-definition standard argue that the reasonableness standard is vague and does not provide a guideline for choosing a particular definition. Instead, they argue that the **better definition** defended in the debate should be the accepted definition.

There is no consistently applied standard for what constitutes a better definition. Debaters can argue that the more limiting definition is better because it ensures in-depth discussion. Debaters could argue that the broader definition is better because debaters learn about more subjects through an expanded topic. Debaters could argue that the better definition is the one that has the most authoritative support. Debaters can conceive of many arguments to urge that one definition is better than another definition.

Debatability

Many debaters and judges also find the better-definition standard problematic. Some argue that there is no difference between the better definition and the reasonable definition. A more reasonable interpretation, after all, would be better in most debates. Others argue that if the better-definition standard is taken to its extreme, it will overly restrict the subject matter of the debate. Rejecting the vague reasonableness standard and the restrictive better-definition standard, some argue that the acceptable definition is one that results in a fair and focused debate.

Debaters can level the same criticism against the debatability standard that they do against all other standards. The meaning of the standard is open to discussion and may be difficult to determine objectively. What is a fair and focused debate? How can a judge use such a standard to evaluate the appropriateness of definitions for terms in the resolution?

Having established potential sources of definitions and standards to assess those definitions, we will next identify the lines of argument used to affirm the topicality of a proposal, to deny the topicality of a proposal, and to resolve conflicts between the two. In developing these lines of argument, both affirmative and negative debaters should turn to the sources and standards we have already discussed. Depending on the argumentative circumstances of each debate, teams may use the same or different standards and sources of definition to enhance the persuasive force of their positions.

Lines of Argument for Affirming Topicality Claims

To defend that their proposal is a topical interpretation of the resolution, affirmative debaters must be prepared to make three arguments. First, they must define terms; second, they must prove that their plan falls within the definitions they provide; and third, they must defend their definitions of terms according to defensible standards.

Defining Terms

Relying on the sources described earlier, debaters should research definitions that are consistent with their defense of the resolution. Debaters can implicitly define the terms through their plan, but if their implicit definitions are challenged, they need to be prepared with defensible definitions. You can define the terms of your resolution in two ways: by explaining what the definition includes and by specifying what the definition excludes.

When you identify what a term includes, you begin the process of setting definitional boundaries. You show what qualities or attributes must be present. In the resolution, "Resolved: that the United States should change its trade policy toward Pacific Rim nations," the phrase "Pacific Rim nations" would include all sovereign states that border on the Pacific Ocean. The affirmative could provide examples such as China, Hong Kong, Japan, South Korea, and Taiwan.

While explaining what is included in a definition is useful, sometimes indicating what is not included in the definition is necessary for a full understanding of the concept. By eliminating similar concepts that might easily be confused with a term, definition by exclusion adds precision to a term's meaning. Despite the fact that Siberia borders on the Pacific Ocean, affirmative debaters might argue it should be excluded from discussion because it is not a nation. Instead, it is merely a member of the Commonwealth of Independent States, formerly known as the Soviet Union. By excluding non-nation states from the list of possible cases that fall within the resolution, debaters effectively limit the meaning of the sentence as a whole.

Meeting the Definitions

Because there are many definitions for resolutional terms, the affirmative debater must decide which definitions are most consistent with the affirmative plan. Affirmatives should be able to prove that the affirmative policy is consistent with the definitions they are willing and able to defend. At times, debaters may offer a plan to affirm the resolution that does not fulfill their own definition of terms. For example, in the resolution, "Resolved: that the federal government should significantly strengthen the guarantee of consumer product safety required of manufacturers," an affirmative team might define "consumer products" as goods that can be consumed (such as food, drugs, and alcohol). If the affirmative proceeds to offer a plan that requires automobile manufacturers to provide safe child seats on new cars, the negative debaters could easily argue that car seats are not consumer products by the affirmative definition because they are used repeatedly and never consumed.

However unlikely it may seem, poorly prepared affirmative debaters can make the mistake of failing to meet their own definition of terms. Affirmatives can prevent this mistake by being thorough in their preparation and making certain that they can meet their own definitions. You can do this by using definitions from the primary articles in the affirmative case area, finding examples of the definition that are similar to or cover the affirmative case area, and finding evidence that discusses the affirmative proposal in the same language as the debate topic.

Standards for Comparing Competing Definitions

Regardless of what definitions affirmative debaters choose to use, they need to be able to defend the appropriateness of their definitions. To accomplish this objective, affirmatives can defend a standard for evaluating the definitions and prove that their definitions meet this standard. Affirmative debaters are well advised to construct their case around the core issues of the debate topic if they want to maximize the argument that their interpretation is appropriate.

Affirmatives improve their chances of persuading the judge that their interpretation of the debate topic is correct if they are able to meet restrictive standards. By arguing that their definitions are rigorous, they qualify their case under very strict interpretive rules. Affirmatives do not automatically lose when they cannot meet the strictest standards, but they do forfeit an important persuasive point. Suppose, for example, that an affirmative team were unable to meet the common standards of grammatical context and each word having meaning. Lacking these standards, they could only argue that grammar is unimportant or that each word does not have to have its own meaning. Because most judges think that grammatical context and the independent meaning of words are important standards, affirmative definitions that meet these two standards are likely to be more persuasive than arguments that indicate these standards are inappropriate for the debate. Affirmative debaters might also argue that their interpretation of the resolution meets one or more of the limitation standards listed above: that it sets a reasonable limit on the argumentative ground, that it allows for a debatable topic, and that it offers better definitions of resolutional terms.

If the affirmative interpretation of the resolution is grammatically correct, provides meaning for all words in the debate topic, and narrows the ground of argument more appropriately than the definition offered by the negative debaters, then the affirmative debaters can argue that their definition is better than the negative definition. Affirmative debaters should always remember that if the definition they elect to defend meets the standards demanded by the negative topicality argument, they have no reason to establish standards of their own for the topicality argument. If the affirmative plan falls within the definitions defended by the negative debater, then the affirmative can argue that their plan is topical by the negative's definition. The affirmative can efficiently answer their opponent's topicality argument by accepting the standards and definitions offered by the negative and proceeding to meet them.

Lines of Argument for Denying Topicality Claims

To show that the affirmative plan does not fall within the boundaries established by the resolution, negative debaters have two options. Initially, they can show how the affirmative plan fails to meet the definitions posited by the affirmative. Failing this, they can also argue that the affirmative plan fails to meet alternative definitions that represent a superior interpretation of the resolution. On occasion, portions of the affirmative plan clearly meet a reasonable interpretation of the resolution, while other parts are clearly beyond the scope of the topic, or extra-topical.

Failure to Meet Affirmative Definitions

Usually the simplest means for showing that the affirmative is not topical is proving that the plan does not fall within the affirmative's definitions. Here, the negative concedes that the affirmative team has properly defined the terms of the resolution. No standards for definitions are needed, as both teams agree that the affirmative definitions are appropriate. The argument occurs when the negative shows how the specifics of the affirmative proposal do not fall within the limits established by the affirmative definitions.

Assume that the resolution stated, "Resolved: that the United States should provide guaranteed employment opportunities for all American citizens between the ages of eighteen and sixty-five. An affirmative team might advocate a transportation and public works bill that would create ten million jobs. The same team might define *employment opportunity* as "the ability to get a job." The

TOPICALITY

In the final round of the 1990 National Debate Tournament, Harvard University (David Coale and Alex Lennon), affirmed the resolution, "Resolved: that the federal government should adopt a national energy policy which substantially reduces the nonmilitary consumption of fossil fuels in the United States." The University of Redlands (Rodger Cole and Marc Rubenstein) negated the resolution. In their defense of the resolution, Harvard argued that the federal government should fund the production of small nuclear power plants called high-temperature gas-cooled reactors (HTGRs) as a replacement for light-water reactors (LWRs). Harvard argued that the HTGR is safer and more reliable than current nuclear reactors. Redlands elected to argue that the affirmative plan was not topical since it did not show how HTGRS reduce fossil fuel consumption more than LWRs. Mr. Cole of Redlands presented the topicality argument. Mr. Lennon responded in the accompanying speech.

Negative

[My] first observation is [that the affirmative does not] substantially reduce [the consumption of fossil fuels]. The A subpoint [is] the definition. First, "substantially" must have meaning. Random House in '87: "Substantial: of ample or considerable amount, quantity, or size." Second, the burden is [on the affirmative] to compare [reductions between their plan and the present system]. Words and Phrases in 1966: "The word substantially is a relative term and should be interpreted in accordance with the context of the claim in which it is used."

(B) [The] affirmative violates [the meaning of the resolution]. In comparison to the status quo there is no net reduction in the consumption of fossil fuels. Contention one [of the affirmative case] claims that it is the status quo policy to reduce fossil fuels using light-water reactors. HTGRs may be claimed to be safer, but they do not reduce fossil consumption more than light waters.

Affirmative

The substantially debate. First, the plan mandates a substantial decrease. Second [the affirmative] can pick a subset [of fossil fuel consumption] like electricity. No case [argued this year] covers all fossil fuels. . . . [Third,] [the negative definition] overlimits. . . . No case could ever meet their interpretation. No case could be substantial if nuclear power isn't. [Fourth, the negative definition] is not in context. [In the context of energy policy] what is a substantial reduction? We will define [in the context of energy policy]. [Fifth,] substantial changes in [fossil fuel consumptions] are tiny. Yergin, Cambridge Energy Association in '78: "After all, in 1973, the countries that embargoed the United States were supplying only about five percent of total U.S. energy demand." [Sixth,] you don't have to compare [the reduction] to the status quo. Even if the status quo is topical, so are we. The status quo is one policy of reducing fossil fuels

(Continued)

Negative (Cont.)

(C) [The negative offers a] superior interpretation. First the affirmative destroys negative ground. The basis of the negative position on this topic is that reducing fossil is disadvantageous. None of these disadvantages [to reducing fossil fuel consumption] would be unique according to the affirmative case [because they argue that the present system will decrease fossil fuel consumption with LWRs]. Second, the negative provides clear meaning to the term substantial. It will be the negative position that the affirmative must prove some way in which the status quo consumes fossil fuels and reduce that consumption.

Affirmative (Cont.)

through light-water reactors. We are a different policy [of reducing fossil fuel consumption] by using HTGRs. [Seventh, measuring the] effects is crazy. . . . If the status quo ran out of fossil fuels at [the point you began using nuclear power], the plan would not be topical [by the negative definition]. . . . Next, our standard [is that] reasonable technological inputs [which substitute for fossil fuels] should be allowed. . . . Next, we [reduce consumption because LWRs] shut down [more frequently and need to be replaced by fossil fuels]. The case evidence [proves] we solve because HTGRs do not shut down as frequently.

affirmative could argue that the plan is topical because every American between the ages of eighteen and sixty-five could compete for those ten million jobs.

In this situation, negative debaters might well grant the affirmative definition of an employment opportunity as the ability to get a job. The negative could then show that more than ten million Americans between the ages of eighteen and sixty-five are out of work. Thus, not all the citizens would have the ability to get a job. They might be able to compete for the jobs, but they could not be assured of getting them. Negative debaters should always be alert to see if the affirmative plan meets the affirmative's own definitions.

Failure to Meet Negative Definitions

Since many affirmative debaters elect to define terms implicitly rather than explicitly, it is frequently necessary for the negative debater to initiate the argument that the affirmative plan does not fall within the definitional boundaries of the resolution. Even if the negative does not have to initiate the topicality argument, they may think that the affirmative definitions do not define the topic properly. In either case, negative debaters need to use three lines of argument to show that the affirmative is nontopical. First, negatives should offer their own definitions of the key terms of the resolution. Second, they should establish standards for evaluating the competing definitions that allow them to show the superiority of negative definitions. Finally, they should prove that the affirmative plan does not fall within the negative's definition of the topic.

Alternative Definitions

The negative can win the topicality argument by successfully maintaining that the affirmative interpretation of the resolution is unacceptable. The negative can argue that the affirmative's interpretation is too broad or too narrow. However, it is far more persuasive for the negative debater to maintain that not only is the affirmative definition unacceptable but that a more acceptable definition is available. If the affirmative definition is the only definition in the debate, a judge may be persuaded to accept that definition even if it is unreasonably broad or narrow. By offering an alternative definition, the negative provides the judge with a rationale for dismissing an unreasonable affirmative interpretation.

The lines of argument useful for defining terms have already been discussed. Debaters should feel free to discuss both what the definition includes and what it excludes. Examples can be useful for helping the audience understand the debater's interpretation of the topic.

Establishing Standards

Having defined the terms of the resolution, the negative debater needs to identify standards for how the judge should evaluate competing definitions. The most common standards (grammatical context, each word has meaning, reasonable limits, better definition, and debatability) have already been discussed. The negative debater should choose to defend the standard that provides the strongest rationale for rejecting the affirmative's interpretation of the resolution. Does the affirmative's interpretation ignore grammatical rules? If so, the negative can encourage the judge to consider grammatical concerns when assessing the affirmative's interpretation.

Choosing the appropriate standard is critical to the negative's ability to convince the judge that an affirmative's plan falls outside the scope of the resolution. Consider the resolution, "Resolved: that all military intervention in the internal affairs of any foreign nation or nations in the Western Hemisphere should be prohibited." In debates on this resolution, many negative teams chose to employ the grammatical standards for assessing topicality. These debaters argued that the use of the words "any" and "all" in conjunction with a negative statement such as "should be prohibited" could only be interpreted to mean that *all* military intervention into the affairs of *any* Western Hemisphere country should be prohibited. By emphasizing the grammatical standard in these debates, many negative debaters were able to convince judges that affirmative teams who only prohibited intervention in one or two countries did not fulfill the terms of the resolution.

If these same debaters had relied on the reasonable limits standard instead, their chance for success would have diminished. Would it be unreasonable for affirmatives to expect negative debaters to prepare for the finite number of countries in the Western Hemisphere? Probably not. There are fewer than twenty nations in the Western Hemisphere. Even if the affirmative could make a case that military intervention should be prohibited in each of the countries in the Western Hemisphere, the negative could easily anticipate the range of possible interpretations. A debater who relied on the reasonable limits standard, then, would have a difficult time convincing a judge that the affirmative was not topical.

If negative debaters believe the affirmative is violating the standard that each word should have meaning, they should argue that the standard is necessary for debate. The debater should illustrate how the affirmative renders a term of the resolution meaningless, offer an alternative definition that gives each word meaning, and explain how the definition meets the standard.

If the negative believes the affirmative unfairly broadens the debate topic, it should pick one of the three limitation standards for debate: reasonability, better definition, and debatability. Having selected a standard, the negative should explain how the affirmative violates the standard, and offer to explain how an alternative definition meets the standard. Through this process, the negative explains to the judge the proper interpretation of the resolution.

Establishing Nontopicality of the Affirmative Proposal

By offering alternative definitions and defending standards that provide a rationale for accepting those definitions, the negative persuasively offers its own interpretation of the resolution. The remaining step for showing that the affirmative is nontopical is to explain why the affirmative's plan falls outside of this interpretation. If the resolution calls for the federal government to adopt a comprehensive program of medical care for all United States citizens, the negative must determine if the affirmative plan actually constitutes a comprehensive program of medical care. Relying on the reasonableness standard for definitions, the negative would in all likelihood conclude that a national health insurance program would be topical, while a polio vaccine for public elementary school students would not be topical.

Establishing Extratopicality

At times, some components of the affirmative plan fall within the scope of the resolution and other components fall outside of the resolution's boundaries. In debate, the parts of the plan that go beyond the resolution are **extratopical.** If negative debaters do not carefully consider whether each component of the plan is topical, the affirmative has a great advantage in the debate.

For example, in a plan supporting the resolution, "Resolved: that the United States should reduce substantially its military commitments to NATO member states," an affirmative team could propose to eliminate all nuclear weapons in the American arsenal. An affirmative debater could then argue that complete nuclear disarmament would lead to worldwide peace. A negative debater could easily respond that the only nuclear weapons that can be eliminated topically are those weapons committed to the defense of NATO. Any nuclear weapons committed to the defense of the United States or Southeast Asia would not fall within the boundaries of the NATO commitments. In such a scenario, the negative could argue that those elements of the plan that eliminate other nuclear weapons are extratopical because they go beyond the resolutional bounds of NATO military commitments.

Ordinarily, debaters do not consider the funding and enforcement provisions of the affirmative plan to be extratopical. Funding and enforcement are considered integral components of any course of action specified by a resolution. The exception to this general rule occurs when the affirmative attempts to gain an advantage from the type of funding or enforcement it presents. If an affirmative plan funded a proposal through a 75 percent reduction in the defense budget, the negative could argue that disarmament advantages from the funding cutbacks would be extratopical. Unless the resolution deals with reducing U.S. military commitments, the advantages of disarmament would seem to fall outside of the resolution's discussion area.

What are the consequences of extratopical plan components? Debaters can treat the impact of extratopical plan components in several different ways. First, a negative debater might argue that the affirmative team should lose the debate because the extratopical portions of the plan distort the focus of the debate away from the debate resolution. In the NATO example, negatives could point out that they have devoted their debate research and arguments to NATO commitments, not global military commitments. They could argue that the affirmative's interpretation unfairly expands the scope of the debate topic.

Negative debaters could also argue that the affirmative should not be able to claim any advantages from extratopical portions of the plan. In the NATO example, the negative might argue that the judge should not consider the affirmative advantage of world peace because that advantage flows from an extratopical portion of the plan, the elimination of all nuclear weapons. However, the negative might also argue that it would be disadvantageous to eliminate nuclear weapons because war would be inevitable without the deterrence offered by nuclear weapons. The negative can argue that the judge cannot consider advantages stemming from extratopical portions and, at the same time, that the affirmative must answer disadvantages stemming from the entire plan, because debaters are responsible for the policies they advocate.

Debaters might finally argue that the judge should completely eliminate all extratopical elements from the plan. The merits of the topical portions of the plan should become the only arguments the judge considers. In this case, neither the advantage of world peace, nor the disadvantage of nuclear deterrence are relevant to the debate. Instead the judge should consider only the topical portions of the plan to determine if reduced commitments to NATO are sufficient to justify the resolution.

Lines of Argument for Comparing Topicality Claims

As in all other debate arguments, the side that compares competing topicality arguments and resolves the conflict between the arguments in its favor will usually be more persuasive with the judge. When attempting to resolve competing claims, all debaters should focus on several key questions.

Does the affirmative plan fall within the definitions of the resolution? The affirmative debater must be able to prove that the affirmative proposal actually meets the requirements of the resolution. The negative debater, usually by offering alternative definitions, attempts to argue that the affirmative is not fulfilling the requirements of the resolution. If the negative can convince the judge that the affirmative plan does not fall within the scope of the debate topic, the negative will probably win the debate.

Does the affirmative interpretation of the resolution fall within the interpretation of the resolution offered by the negative? At times, the affirmative debater may be able to argue that the affirmative definition of the resolution is consistent with the negative's definition of the resolution. If the affirmative debater can prove that their interpretation of the resolution can even fulfill the requirements of the negative interpretation of the resolution, then the affirmative team will probably win the topicality argument.

What are the optimal standards for evaluating competing definitions of resolutional terms? It is possible that both sides will offer topicality standards for evaluating definitions in the debate. The difficulty is that some standards can and do conflict. For example, consider the resolution that all military intervention in the internal affairs of any nation or nations in the Western Hemisphere should be prohibited. This may mean grammatically that all military intervention should be prohibited. However, this grammatical interpretation may not promote the debatability of the topic. The grammatical standard arguably overlimits the debate topic because only one affirmative plan would be topical: banning all intervention into any nation in the Western Hemisphere. The possible conflict between the standards means that debaters must persuade the judge that their standards are more appropriate in any specific debate.

Are the definitions consistent with the guiding standards for definition evaluation? At the end of the debate, the judge must decide if the definitions meet the standards. A debater could conceivably win the argument that their standards should govern the debate, but lose the argument that their definition fulfills the standards. For example, a debater could argue for a grammatical standard and then read a definition of a noun in place of an adverb. Or the debater could argue for a reasonability standard and then read a definition that is unreasonable. Careful application of standards is critically important in persuading a judge in an argument over the meaning of words.

Does the affirmative plan have to fulfill all of the terms of the resolution? In addition to establishing that the affirmative is not topical, the negative should be prepared to argue that fulfilling the terms of the resolution is necessarily a voting issue. A voting issue is an argument that the judge considers so important that it can, by itself, justify a decision for one of the two teams. Many affirmative debaters have argued that they do not have to fulfill all of the terms of the resolution. In short, affirmative debaters have been known to argue that topicality is not a voting issue. These debaters assume that the goal of the debate topic is met if they debate subjects germane to the resolution. As long as the negative has adequate opportunity to prepare for such subjects, topicality remains intact. Rigid adherence to the topicality argument, they maintain, is not necessary.

There are several problems with this approach to topicality arguments. First, many debate judges find it wholly unpersuasive and may even take offense at its use. To argue positions that many judges find unacceptable violates all tenets of audience analysis and persuasion.

Second, topicality is traditionally a voting issue, which is perhaps why so many judges take offense at the suggestion that the affirmative does not have to support the resolution. Many national debate tournaments including the Cross-Examination Debate Association National Tournament, the National Debate Tournament, and tournaments sponsored by the American Debate Association require topicality to be a voting issue. The norm clearly expressed through the traditional institutions of competitive academic debate indicates that topicality is a voting issue.

Third, there are theoretical considerations that justify the argument that topicality is a voting issue. Affirmative debaters begin the debate advocating the resolution. Thus, any arguments they make should support that resolution. To argue at some point that the resolution is irrelevant is to say that the initial affirmative is irrelevant. By that token, any negative arguments against the resolution would also be irrelevant. At this point, the basis for debate becomes absurd.

Fourth, many analogies give support to the claim that topicality is a voting issue. Analogies may be a weak form of argument but, in this instance, they may provide some understanding of the reasons why topicality is a voting issue. Jurisdictional analogies are available. Courts, congressional committees, and administrative agencies frequently dismiss cases that are not within their jurisdiction. Some debaters argue that debate judges should also dismiss cases that fall outside of their "jurisdiction." The analogy of the social contract can also justify the argument that topicality is a voting issue. Many debaters argue that debaters borrow from political philosophy and adopt a social contract theory of debate participation. In democratic governments individuals enter into a de facto social contract to abide by the rules and laws of the society's elected representatives. In exchange, they receive essential services such as the administration of justice, enforcement of public peace and welfare, and the national defense. Similarly, some debaters argue that by agreeing to debate a resolution, they have entered into a social contract to abide by the words of the resolution.

Fifth, and finally, real-world implications can justify topicality as a voting issue. There are many historical examples where the meaning of words were essential to resolving important disputes. Defining terms too broadly or too narrowly can lead to negative consequences. Debaters have the same responsibility that policymakers do to define terms carefully and make topical claims. If a debater can maintain that a definition has important implications for public policy, topicality arguments become more than a mere semantic game.

Summary and Conclusions

Topicality is a fundamental argument in academic debate. To uphold the resolution a judge must be clear as to its meaning. To provide fair argumentative ground in a competitive debate, there must be some degree of predictability in interpreting the debate topic. Debaters should strive to understand and apply the topicality argument and its defenses when and where it is appropriate. Several important lines of argument aid the development, coherence, and clarity of topicality arguments.

First, debaters must understand the processes of definition. When debaters learn what topic they will be debating, it is very important that they proceed to familiarize themselves with the relevant definitions generally available in dictionaries, legal and legislative documents, and academic articles and books. The affirmative needs to know what definitions exist in order to identify what arguments are available and to be able to defend their case for the resolution as a topical one. The negative needs to know what possible ways the affirmative might defend the resolution, and they need to explore definitions available in their preparation of arguments. Definitions can indicate what a term includes and what it excludes; giving examples of terms promotes a clear understanding of the resolutional interpretation.

Second, debaters need to familiarize themselves with the standards available for evaluating the appropriateness of a definition. There are several definitions available for most words. The debater needs to neutralize the subjectivity of judges as much as possible by persuading them that debatable standards of evaluation can determine the appropriate definition for the debate. Several conventional standards are used for determining the meaning of the resolution: grammatical context, each word should have meaning, reasonability, better definition, and debatability.

Third, debaters must be able to show how the affirmative plan does or does not meet the preferred interpretation of the resolution. To prove that the affirmative is not topical, negative debaters can either show that the proposed plan does not fall within the boundaries of the topic as defined by the affirmative or that the plan does not fall within the boundaries of the topic as defined by the negative. For this latter argument to be successful, the negative must persuade the judge that their interpretation of the resolution is superior. To win the topicality argument, the affirmative must show that their plan falls within the definitional limits of the topic.

Clarity of presentation and resolving competing arguments are critical when making topicality arguments. These semantic arguments require the utmost precision, but because they are delivered under the pressure of a timed speech, they can be very difficult to resolve. If the debaters do not resolve them, the judge has no choice but to make a subjective evaluation. There is little the debater can offer in the way of objective evidence to support a topicality argument. The ability to persuade the judge hinges on fair standards and definitions, appropriately applied and compared.

Exercises

1. Assume that your opponent is defending the resolution, "Resolved: that the powers of the presidency should be significantly curtailed with a plan that removes the CIA from executive oversight." Identify the implicit definitions of the key terms in the resolution. How is your opponent defining "powers of the presidency"? How is your opponent defining "curtailed"? Are these reasonable definitions?

2. Define *freedom of speech* using a general dictionary, a specialty dictionary, legislative history, and an academic article or book. How do the definitions compare? How are they similar and how are they different? What does the comparison tell you about the biases of the definitional sources?

3. Suppose you had two definitions for the term "arm sales" in the resolution, "Resolved: that the United States should significantly curtail its arms sales to foreign countries." Government sources define the term to mean any sale of weaponry constituting more that $7 million to a foreign country. The other definition, from an academic, argues that arms sales are the commerce of all weapons and spare parts used in the operation of those weapons. Defend each definition as superior to the other. Use the standards of definition identified in this chapter to fortify your arguments.

4. Identify five affirmative plans that you suspect would be topical if the resolution is "Resolved: that the federal government should provide social services for the homeless." Can you find definitions of "social services" and "homeless" that support an interpretation of the resolution that make your plans topical?

5. Suppose the resolution you are debating against is "Resolved: that the United States should adopt a comprehensive energy policy which decreases fossil fuel consumption." The affirmative plan mandates that all automobiles must undergo a stringent emissions test. Make an argument for why the affirmative case is not topical. Do you need to define terms or can you rely on the implicit definitions of the affirmative? What standards for evaluating competing interpretations of the resolution do you offer? Why does the affirmative fail to meet your interpretation?

6

Counterplans

Chapter Outline

Key Terms

counterplan
competitiveness
mutual exclusivity
net benefits
redundancy
conditional argument
permutation

Jason: Don't you think the government could do a better job of decreasing tobacco use? Cigarettes kill hundreds of thousands of people a year and the government does very little. I think the federal government should set limits on tar and nicotine in cigarettes, ban tobacco advertising, and strengthen the warning labels on cigarette packages.

Ann: I won't disagree with you that out of the tens of millions of people who smoke, many of them die. But you can never count on the government to regulate adequately or effectively. I think if you removed government regulation and let people sue the companies for the damage they cause people's health, it would be better.

Jason: I think you can let people sue *and* regulate more. Make the tobacco companies pay and make the industry safer.

Ann: No way. The tobacco companies use government regulations to defend themselves in court now. They have convinced the courts that since they meet the current regulations and provide consumers with warnings of the harm smoking causes, they are immune from suits. No, I think you have to pick one side or the other.

Should the government regulate the tobacco industry? Or would removing all government regulation and increasing litigation be a better policy for reducing the harms of smoking? In the debate between Jason and Ann, Ann is presenting an alternative proposal for solving the harm perpetuated by current policies. Such alternatives are known in debate as **counterplans.** Counterplans can range from small steps to radical alterations of established procedures. Regardless of the specifics, all counterplans provide alternatives to the affirmative's plan for solving a significant problem.

We use counterproposals, or counterplans, every day of our lives. Someone suggests we go to a movie, a play, or visit the zoo. We say no, I'd rather go skydiving, write a play, or go big-game hunting. Instead of doing what someone proposes, we suggest an alternative.

When negatives presents a counterplan, they can effectively undermine the rationale behind the entire affirmative case, rather than focus on a single line of argument. Some counterplans eliminate any significance that the affirmative argues in support of changing policies. Other counterplans overcome the barriers toward solving the problem with the status quo as well or better than the affirmative plan. In these instances, the counterplan eliminates the necessity of having the resolution solve the problem. At times, the result of adopting a plan is that you must forego a counterplan that would be more beneficial.

Presenting a counterplan is an important strategy that negative debaters can deploy to their advantage. This chapter begins by demonstrating how to develop a counterplan, and describing the lines of argument necessary for its defense. Next, we examine the lines of argument useful for denying a counterplan's impact. We conclude by exploring the lines of argument useful for resolving conflicting claims concerning counterplans.

Writing the Counterplan

When arguing a counterplan, negative debaters must provide a straightforward account of what their proposal would do. The counterplan should usually include (1) the specific mandates or actions advocated, (2) a funding provision that specifies how the negative will cover the costs of the proposed policy, (3) an enforcement provision that explains how the counterplan will encourage compliance with its mandates, and (4) an intent plank which reserves for the negative the right to interpret the meaning of the counterplan.

In the debate between Jason and Ann, the counterplan might take the following form:

I. All government regulations regarding the production, distribution, sale, and use of tobacco will be prohibited.
II. The courts will adopt a standard of strict liability for all tobacco companies that sell or distribute tobacco.
III. Funding for the proposal will come from reductions in wasteful governmental spending and general revenues.
IV. Failure to comply with counterplan mandates will result in fines and/or imprisonment.
V. Negative speeches will answer questions about counterplan intent.

Keep in mind that this example represents only one way to construct a counterplan. Some debaters will want to be more specific in their mandates, while others will want to be more general. When writing the counterplan, negative debaters should ask themselves, how much specificity is needed to accomplish the counterplan objectives? Some counterplans will need to be very specific, particularly if many groups have a motive to circumvent the counterplan mandates.

Lines of Argument for Defending Counterplans

Negative debaters need to remember that when they present a counterplan, they no longer are assured of having presumption in a debate. Many judges traditionally assign presumption to the negative because the negative represents the policy of least change and consequently least risk. If the counterplan requires more change than the affirmative plan, presumption may rest with the affirmative. Other judges will insist that presumption is always with the negative, but may still expect the negative to prove certain lines of argument. In either case, the negative team that presents a counterplan assumes the burden of proving several lines of argument. Usually, the negative posits these lines of argument when they initially present their counterplan.

Nontopicality

The counterplan should be nontopical. If the counterplan falls within the scope of the resolution, it arguably becomes another justification for affirming the resolution.

Trying to avoid this, negative debaters attempt to characterize their policies as nonresolutional alternatives to the affirmative proposal. In the debate between Jason and Ann, the resolution might be "Resolved: that the federal government should increase regulations to protect the safety of American citizens." Ann would need to indicate why the counterplan does not fall within the boundaries of the resolution. She could argue that the counterplan is the antithesis of the resolution. Rather than increasing government regulations, the counterplan prohibits all existing laws applicable to the production, distribution, sale, and use of tobacco.

Some controversy exists concerning whether a counterplan must be nontopical for the negative to win the argument. Some judges feel that as long as the counterplan presents an alternative that clashes with the affirmative proposal, the negative has a legitimate right to defend a topical counterplan. This view stems from the perception of debates as a comparison of two competing policies. As long as the two policies provide opposition to one another, the negative meets its obligation to clash in the debate. Other judges feel that the counterplan must be nontopical to provide a test of the truth of the resolution. Only by having a topical and a nontopical option can these judges decide whether to affirm the resolution. Given that the acceptance of topical counterplans is not universal, negative debaters should offer reasons why their counterplans are nontopical and rely on topical alternatives only if unusual circumstances require it.

Competitiveness

The counterplan must be competitive with the affirmative proposal. **Competitiveness** holds that the counterplan could not, should not, or would not be adopted simultaneously with the affirmative plan. This line of argument is critical for defending a counterplan because it is the rationale for why the counterplan forces a choice to be made with the affirmative plan. Ann must be able to explain why a policy of making it easier for citizens to sue could not, should not, or would not be implemented with a policy of increased regulations on tobacco companies. Failure to convince the judge that the two policies are competitive means that Ann's counterplan does not provide a reason to reject Jason's proposal. The judge could accept both alternatives as worthwhile choices. Ann has several options for arguing that her counterplan competes with the affirmative plan.

When we are faced with a variety of options about what to do with our lives, we find that some of them are competitive and some are not. For example, if you and a friend want to go to a movie, and you want to see a lurid docudrama and your friend wants to see a sophisticated foreign film, you would have to choose between the two. We would say that the options compete with one another.

Mutual Exclusivity

The first type of competitiveness in debate is called **mutual exclusivity.** A counterplan and plan are mutually exclusive if they could not coexist. The existence of one policy must absolutely prevent the existence of the other. Ann could argue that her counterplan is mutually exclusive with Jason's policy of increased regulation. She could explain that the courts do not allow individuals to sue companies when those companies are abiding by the standards established through the federal government. Only when *no* laws or regulations are present is the court free to hear cases of individual harm. The two plans, in effect, could not exist together because the existence of the regulations prohibits the use of common law court remedies.

Our movie choices could be mutually exclusive if we could not possibly see both movies. If the mushy movie and the sophisticated film were both showing at the same time, for the last time, and we had no other opportunity to see both movies, then we would have to choose. The movies would be competitive.

Net Benefits

The second type of competitiveness is based on **net benefits.** To argue net benefits is to suggest that adopting the counterplan or the plan will be more advantageous than adopting both plans concurrently. In other words, the plan and the counterplan should not exist together. The plan and the counterplan together would be worse than the adoption of the counterplan alone.

To decide whether a counterplan is net-beneficial, the debaters assess the costs and benefits of adopting the counterplan alone. Then, they determine the costs and benefits if the plan and the counterplan came into existence together. If the counterplan alone is more beneficial, the negative has proven that the counterplan is competitive. If the counterplan and the plan in tandem are superior, the affirmative has shown that the counterplan is not competitive.

In the movie example, suppose it would be possible for you and your friend to see some of both movies because one starts an hour before the other. You would probably not want to only see part of both movies and would, instead, decide to see all of one. The plan to see one movie thus produces a greater net benefit than the plan to try to see both.

> Ann: Tobacco companies would never let a product that has been proven to cause cancer and heart disease on the market if they were afraid they would get sued. They would be too afraid that the juries would take their profits and hand them over to the people that are suffering. It is simple justice that those with preventable cancer and heart disease get compensated by the companies that are just in it for the money.

Here, Ann is making the argument that her counterplan is competitive by the net benefits standard. If the counterplan and the plan exist together, the advantage is minimal. The courts will not consider claims against the tobacco companies as long as those companies comply with current government regulations. The result is no justice for those who are injured by smoking. The benefits of the counterplan alone, however, are substantial. The counterplan has the effect of increasing the safety of American citizens, because the tobacco companies would fear the lawsuits. Additionally, the counterplan would lead to a more just system, where those people who suffer because of a company's monetary gain get compensated.

In short, the counterplan and plan taken together may increase safety, but the counterplan alone would both increase safety and improve justice. Ann would conclude that her counterplan is competitive by the net benefits standard.

Redundancy

The final type of competitiveness, redundancy, occurs when the plan and the counterplan *would* not exist together. If you claim **redundancy,** you argue that the counterplan proves that the action called for in the resolution is not necessary to solve the problem because a nonresolutional alternative can solve it equally well. If an effective nontopical solution exists, a judge would not have to affirm the resolution. Ann could argue that the existence of a strict liability standard would provide an effective remedy for all American citizens suffering from the harms of cigarette smoke. Given that this effective alternative exists, there would be no reason to adopt the resolution.

The redundancy standard of competitiveness can be a difficult one to sustain. If some advantage accrues from having duplicative agencies or policies for dealing with a problem, then the counterplan is not completely redundant. The affirmative could argue that their plan would be justified if it prevented only an individual or two from getting cancer. Thus, negative debaters will usually want to rely on the redundancy standard in only rare cases, and will usually want to couple the standard with arguments for mutual exclusivity or net benefits.

In short, the negative has the option of arguing that the counterplan and plan are mutually exclusive, that the counterplan yields a greater net benefit alone than when combined with the plan, that the counterplan is redundant with the affirmative proposal. The negative could choose to argue all three, but given the lack of persuasive force for the claim of redundancy, debaters would probably want to rely on the mutual exclusivity and the net benefits standard.

Solvency

Many times the counterplan attempts to reduce or eliminate the affirmative's harm. Just like the affirmative's defense of the plan must involve a consideration of solvency, so must the counterplan solve a significant problem to produce any advantage. The negative team offering a counterplan usually shows that the proposal provides an alternative means for reducing the harm identified by the affirmative. By addressing the same problem, the counterplan and the plan become two competing options that can be weighed against one another. Ann can argue that her counterplan works to solve the problems cited by Jason. The significance of current policies is that thousands of individuals are dying from tobacco-related diseases. If tobacco companies fear that successful suits would be brought against them, they will take efforts on their own to ensure the safety of their products. Otherwise, their profit will not be secure.

Negative debaters do not have to show that their counterplan solves more of the harm than the affirmative. The counterplan can clash with the affirmative by (1) solving the harm cited by the affirmative or (2) having advantages if adopted alone would outweigh the advantages of both the counterplan and the plan together. An example of this latter approach occurs when the counterplan takes the opposite approach of the affirmative plan. Instead of increasing regulations against tobacco companies, the counterplan removes all existing restrictions. To provide a rationale for such an action, the negative might argue that the counterplan would solve the trade deficit that the United States has with certain foreign countries. The negative could indicate that regulations are the cause of the U.S. trade deficit; by removing these bureaucratic obstacles, the counterplan would increase the flow of tobacco products to foreign countries. If tobacco products make up a substantial portion of the exports of the United States, the elimination of regulations could turn the entire trade deficit into a trade surplus. In this fashion, the negative can show that it not only solves the affirmative harm but achieves other benefits as well through the counterplan. Note that these additional benefits need not be limited to the affirmative need area. Once the affirmative need area is addressed, additional benefits might accrue in any category. We develop this line of argument more extensively in the next section.

Imagine what would happen if the counterplan did not have to address the same harm as the affirmative or have advantages that outweigh the advantages of adopting both plans together. The assistance of one plan would not force the rejection of the other. While Jason discusses the problem of tobacco-related illnesses, Ann would be defending a counterplan that decreased the problem of air pollution. Unless a reason exists why a judge would not want to reduce tobacco-related illnesses and air pollution, a judge could vote for Jason's plan and Ann's counterplan as well. At that point, however, the plan and the counterplan should exist together. Ann would not have proven that Jason's plan should not be adopted. The potential for such absurd debates requires that the burden be placed on the negative to show that the counterplans will reduce the harm claimed by the affirmative or have advantages that outweigh the advantages of adopting both the plan and the counterplan.

Added Advantages

The counterplan can have added advantages. Beyond showing how the counterplan reduces harms cited by the affirmative, many negative debaters will offer additional benefits to adopting their counterplans. While not a necessary point, you may see strategic advantages to making this type of argument. Taking this step allows you to magnify the rationale for adoption of the counterplan, while expanding the costs of ignoring your policy.

> Ann: If the federal government would just leave things alone, we would be a lot better off. Every time they increase regulations on business, they distort the free market system that forms the basis of our country's economy. Having business bear the cost of the damage they do will reinforce the free market system.

At this point in our debate, Ann has offered two additional advantages for adopting her counterplan. Earlier, under the competitiveness standard of net benefits, she argued that the counterplan would bring justice for the victims—something increased federal regulations would not do. Here, she adds that by eliminating restrictions on tobacco producers, distributors, promoters, and users, the counterplan would enhance the free market economic system.

Conditionality

In some instances, negative debaters may not be confident that they can successfully argue that their counterplans are nontopical, competitive, solvent, and advantageous. To guard against the possibility that the counterplan may not be successful, some teams argue their counterplans as conditional arguments. **Conditional arguments** are arguments that depend on a set of circumstances for their consideration in debates. Conditional counterplans do not commit the negative team to defending the alternative proposal. The negative specifies certain conditions that must be present before they will commit to the argument.

When the conditions are in place, then and only then does the alternative policy become part of the judge's evaluation of the debate. These conditions can vary. Sometimes they are dependent on the negative team winning or losing another issue in the debate. For example, Ann might argue that her counterplan is conditional on her successfully refuting any disadvantages that the affirmative might argue against the counterplan. At other times, the counterplan is conditional on the negative team's ability to successfully defend the four burdens of the counterplan.

Once the negative introduces the counterplan, defines whether or not it will be conditional, and proves that it is nontopical, competitive, solvent, and advantageous, they have met their burden of proof. As a result, the affirmative must identify the weaknesses of the counterplan, indicating why the argument does not constitute a reason to vote against the resolution.

Lines of Argument for Attacking Counterplans

When responding to a counterplan, the affirmative has six options. These include arguing that the counterplan is topical, that it is not competitive, that it will not solve the problem, that it will be disadvantageous, that it violates the convention of fiat, and that it should not be accepted as a conditional argument. This section will explore these approaches, indicating how each can be defended.

Topicality

In many debates the affirmative team will attempt to persuade the judge that the counterplan is topical. By doing this, the affirmative maintains that the negative has simply offered another reason for affirming the resolution. If the counterplan falls within the boundaries of the resolution and it is advantageous, the affirmative could arguably ignore their own plan and support the resolution with the counterplan. Either plan, the one offered by the affirmative or the one offered by the negative, would justify the resolution.

> Jason: If we let people sue tobacco corporations for the harms to their health, that is still regulating business. Whether we go through the legislature or the courts, we should still require regulations to improve the safety of American citizens.

Recall that the resolution presented earlier for the debate between Jason and Ann is "Resolved: that the federal government should increase regulations to protect the safety of American citizens." Defining *regulate* as "to direct or govern by rule," Jason argues that the resolution encompasses Ann's counterplan to impose strict liability on tobacco companies. Jason maintains that the federal government has three components: the executive, the legislature, and the judiciary. Thus, direction from the judiciary is just as much an increased regulation for safety as would be his plan calling for additional laws from the legislature. By making such an argument, Jason argues that either his plan or Ann's counterplan justify affirming the resolution.

Noncompetitiveness

In the lines of argument that affirm counterplans, we indicated that negative debaters must prove that the counterplan could not, should not, or would not exist with the affirmative plan. Otherwise, the two proposals would not force a choice on the judge. In responding to the counterplan, the affirmative attempts to show how the counterplan is not competitive. Indeed, it could, should, and would exist together with the affirmative plan. Affirmative debaters must prove that all of the potential competitiveness arguments presented by the negative are untrue. If the negative can sustain one reason why the counterplan and the plan could not, should not, or would not exist, they will win the competitiveness argument. Any of these lines of argument would justify making a choice between the two alternatives.

Could Exist Together

When seeking ways to argue that the two proposals could exist together, the affirmative needs to examine carefully the impediments to mutual adoption. Many times, the affirmative can insist that the reasons for why the two proposals could not exist together are artificial. Perhaps the wording of the counterplan makes it appear that the two could not exist together, but in actuality the opposite may be true. Frequently, claims of mutual exclusivity are artificial when negative counterplans (1) ban the provisions of the affirmative and (2) proceed to add further mandates. The ban on the affirmative provisions does compete with the affirmative plan, but the additional mandates regularly can coexist with the plan. Thus, any advantages stemming from additional mandates could also be gained from adopting that part of the counterplan with the affirmative proposal.

Let's return to our debate between Jason and Ann to illustrate the point. Ann's counterplan initially prohibits the existence of any federal regulations on

COUNTERPLAN NONTOPICALITY ARGUMENT

In the final round of the 1982 National Debate Tournament, the University of Redlands (Jeff Wagner and William Isaacson) affirmed the resolution, "Resolved: that the federal government should significantly curtail the power of labor unions." The University of Louisville (Dan Sutherland and Dave Sutherland) negated the resolution. Redlands affirmed the resolution by arguing that labor unions should be required to represent minority members. In response, Louisville argued that labor unions should not be required to help minority members; in fact, they should not exist at all. Rather than curtail union power, the government should eliminate labor unions completely.

The Louisville team explains why the counterplan is not topical in the following speech. Mr. Isaacson, for Redlands, responds that the counterplan is topical and explains why in the accompanying speech.

Negative

[The counterplan] is not topical, and we can show this by their own definitions. The counterplan abolishes unions, which is clearly distinct from curtailing them. Abolish does not mean to curtail.

Explicitly definitions prove this. As Words and Phrases says: "Curtail means to cut off the end or any part of; hence to shorten, abridge; diminish; lessen; reduce; and has no such meaning as abolish." Now, Black's Law Dictionary, which he says has a good definition for labor union has the same phrase . . . "has no such meaning as abolish." Let me read the consensus of legal and dictionary definitions. Corpus Juris Secundum, a legal source: "It has been held that it [curtail] has no such meaning as 'abolish,' and that the words 'abolish' and 'suspend' are not given in the dictionaries as meanings of the word 'curtail.'" In other words, all legal opinion and all dictionary opinion agree the counterplan is not topical.

Affirmative

The counterplan is clearly topical. (a) The counterplan curtails a union power, legal authority. (b) Unions will continue to exist, simply void of legal recognition and curtailed of some powerful functions. Indeed, they could do all of the things that unions do right now; they are just not under the scope of the NLRA [National Labor Relations Act]. (c) The negative position to abolish, not to curtail, assumes the counterplan abolishes union power. Black's Law Dictionary: "Abolish: to do away with wholly; to annul . . . put an end to." Note: Neither Black's definition of labor union . . . nor any other definition suggests that union power is exclusively limited to legal recognition or sanction. (d) The counterplan does not abolish labor unions nor their power. History is replete with union actions which were illegal prior to the labor legislation of the 1920s and 1930s. These organizations had immense power and used it. (e) The negative burden is to prove they abolish all segments of union power, which requires making all former functions of unions illegal for any group of employees.

In this excerpt the Louisville team explains why the counterplan is mutually exclusive with the affirmative plan by arguing that both plans cannot operate simultaneously. Redlands responds in the accompanying speech.

Negative

(A) [The plan and counterplan] mutually exclude each other. The affirmative plan places restrictions on labor unions. The counterplan bans, or eliminates from existence, labor unions. Obviously you cannot pass legislation on something which yet doesn't exist. Now, maybe this is better termed "operational competitiveness." The two plans could not both operate. Let me give you examples from the affirmative plan. They say they will amend the NLRA which . . . it doesn't exist anymore under the counterplan. They say they'll impose duty of fair representation which doesn't exist anymore. They say they'll talk about the NLRB [National Labor Relations Board] and the general counsel will codify this and then make unions file information about this. That's all in the first plank [of the affirmative plan]. [The affirmative plan] could not operate at all [under the counterplan].

Affirmative

Competitiveness? (A) Point: mutual exclusivity. (1) These standards are artificial. You can bar unions except for purposes of bargaining for discrimination and gain the advantages of both systems. (2) The standard is artificial. You can ban all unions except one, and then get the advantages of both systems. (3) Mutual exclusivity must be linked to advantages of the counterplan. [The advantages of the counterplan do not stem from competitive counterplan planks.]

tobacco companies. Certainly, there is little doubt that this portion of the counterplan could not exist simultaneously with Jason's plan. The second plank of the counterplan establishes a standard of strict liability for tobacco companies. Could this portion of the counterplan coexist with the affirmative plan? Could we adopt both the strict liability standard and increased regulations on tobacco companies simultaneously? Perhaps the standard of strict liability could be imposed in instances where the federal government has not moved in to regulate the industry.

Should Exist Together

The affirmative can show that the counterplan and the plan should exist together by showing that the advantages of having both policies in effect are greater than those of having the counterplan alone. To indicate that mutual adoption would be more advantageous, the affirmative can make one or more of the following arguments: that mutual adoption would lead to more solvency of the significant problem, that mutual adoption would lead to fewer disadvantages, or that the affirmative plan alone would be more advantageous.

First, the affirmative can maintain that the plan and the counterplan together would solve the problem better. Here, the affirmative debaters maintain that the interaction between the two proposals results in positive reductions of the significant problem. Jason could argue that Ann's strict liability standard would fill in the gaps of his regulations. Take the problem of secondhand smoke. Jason's limits on tar and nicotine, his ban on advertising, and his strengthened warning labels would do little for citizens suffering from the smoking of others. Ann's counterplan could easily fill this void. Jason's proposal would solve the problem in the areas of regulation, and the counterplan would address additional harms outside the reach of the governmental regulations. The plan coupled with the counterplan would solve the largest amount of the problem.

Jason could also point out that Ann's strict liability standard would not serve as an effective remedy for all American citizens. Many poor people are suffering from the harms of cigarette smoke. They cannot afford to sue the tobacco industry. The affirmative plan, by contrast, provides a remedy for all American citizens, rich and poor. In short, the affirmative plan addresses all interests not effectively covered by the counterplan.

Second, the affirmative can argue that the counterplan and the plan together would result in fewer disadvantages. Both the plan and the counterplan are likely to produce negative results, but the adoption of both together may interact to reduce these effects. The affirmative denies that there is a net benefit to adopting the counterplan alone by showing how mutual adoption reduces any negative effects overall. Jason could easily make such an argument in his debate with Ann. He might be forced to address the disadvantage that the regulations would not provide a remedy for citizens whose particular cases do not meet the specific requirements of the legislation. He could argue that if we adopted the plan and the counterplan together, justice for all Americans would be ensured. His regulations would prevent a large bulk of the population from being harmed by tobacco products, but strict liability would cover any loopholes in the legislation.

The final way to argue that the counterplan does not produce a net benefit is to indicate that the affirmative plan alone is more advantageous. If the counterplan accrues multiple disadvantages and the affirmative plan does not, little reason would exist to endorse the counterplan. Jason might conclude that the counterplan of strict liability would be disastrous, causing devastating consequences for the business community. The impact on the trade balances with other countries, as well as the impact on employment here at home, might justify adopting the affirmative plan alone.

Would Exist Together

Not all debaters agree that redundancy is a legitimate form of counterplan competitiveness. As a result, affirmative debaters can sometimes succeed in maintaining that this argument does not justify rejection of the affirmative plan. Affirmative debaters can argue that redundancy is an illegitimate form of competitiveness because it does not indicate why the counterplan should be selected over the affirmative plan. If both plans do the same thing, why not choose the affirmative? The affirmative would still have to offer good reasons for adopting the resolution.

Even if it cannot dismiss the issue altogether, the affirmative can argue that no plan and counterplan are ever completely redundant. Our government is filled with examples of duplicative laws that address precisely the same problem. Air pollution laws at the federal level are frequently codified into state laws simultaneously. Federal laws against discrimination are reinforced by state laws that prohibit specific types of discrimination. Both sets of laws are arguably redundant, but in practice several layers of law are needed to completely protect society's interests. If even a small amount of additional solvency can be accomplished through additional policies, the benefit may warrant adoption of both proposals.

Permutations

In order to determine whether a plan and counterplan could, should, or would exist together, debaters need to assess the compatibility of two proposals. In debate, the creative process of testing the compatibility of two policies through plan or counterplan alterations is called **permutations.** The affirmative team tests the compatibility by seeing if either the affirmative or negative proposal could offer a permutation (or alteration) to allow the two proposals to exist together. Even in something as simple as two friends deciding where to eat, permutations may be helpful. Assume for a minute that one friend wants rich food; the other is on a diet. Harry says, "Let's go get pizza." Larry says, "I'm on a diet; I'd rather have salad." Harry and Larry have to compromise. They can alter their original proposals to select a restaurant that will let Harry have his pizza and Larry have his salad.

If affirmative debaters could not rely on permutations to test the competitiveness of the counterplan, the negative could argue that any proposal would be competitive with the affirmative. Negatives would merely ban the affirmative proposal and institute their own policy. Harry, for example, would exclude from consideration any restaurant that did not have salad but did have pizza. Such a posture would be silly, preventing the two friends from eating together for no good reason. The process of permutation, then, acts as a test of the true competitiveness of a negative alternative. However, it does not commit either team to advocacy of an altered proposal. Just as Harry and Larry do not have to go to a restaurant that offers pizza and salads, so too can judges reject permutations if the test fails.

Several permutations are recurrent in debates because they demonstrate common errors assumed about competitiveness. These include time frame, exceptions, and agent compatibility. In each case, these standard permutations can unmask false competitiveness claimed by negative teams.

Time Frame. In this permutation, the affirmative assumes the adoption of the one policy first and the second policy at a later time. This permutation addresses counterplans that are justified according to the system's lack of readiness to implement one of the proposals. In our debate, Jason could rely on a time-frame permutation. He could advocate that Ann's counterplan be placed into existence to accommodate claims of past wrongs. When regulations were not in place, citizens should have the right to sue for damages. Jason's own plan would address future harms by requiring tobacco companies to inform citizens of the consequences of using their products.

Exceptions. Here, the affirmative accepts a counterplan that bans much of the affirmative proposal, but the affirmative retains a modified and specific plan mandate. This allows the affirmative to claim the advantages from the counterplan, while still receiving the benefits of their proposal. Jason could accept the portion of Ann's counterplan that bans government regulations and implements strict liability in all instances not covered by the affirmative plan. Jason could retain the ban on cigarette advertising, the strengthened warning labels, and the stricter standards for tar and nicotine. Those citizens who develop diseases because of secondhand smoke, those who suffer from diseases not specified on the warning labels of cigarette packs, and those who lose their homes to fire caused by cigarettes that lack self-extinguishing features could all still recover damages.

Agent Compatibility. With this permutation, the affirmative attempts to reconcile conflicting use of agents to execute the same proposal. Many resolutions will specify an agent, such as the federal government, to carry out the new proposal. Negative teams will offer counterplans at the state and local level, arguing that the plans are competitive because the federal and state governments cannot both implement the same plan. Generally, the negative then claims advantages from having state and local oversight of community problems. They argue that the government closer to the people tends to be more responsive to the people's needs. Affirmative debaters can use permutation on this counterplan by having the federal government provide monetary incentives to the states to carry out the program or by having the federal government provide a general outline of the proposal to be developed more specifically at the state level. The affirmative can thus remain within the bounds of the resolution by letting the federal government have ultimate authority but capture the negative's advantages by allowing the states to carry out the day-to-day implementation of the proposal.

Permutation provides the affirmative with a means for testing whether the a counterplan is truly competitive. Debaters should think about small alterations that would make the plan and counterplan compatible. If a small change is suggested, negative debaters need to consider why that permutation means the plans could not, should not, or would not exist together.

Solvency

If the counterplan does fall outside the resolution and competes with the affirmative proposal, the affirmative can still undermine its impact in the debate by showing that it fails to solve the problem. Assuming that the affirmative can show that their own plan can solve a significant problem, the pressure shifts to the negative to show that their proposal can also solve the problem.

> Jason: Tobacco companies would never be afraid of suits brought by the little people. They have so much money that they can afford to hire attorneys who will win the cases even if the companies have been in the wrong. Their lawyers will blame other factors for our lung cancer or our heart disease. You can't change a tobacco company that easily.

Here, Jason argues that the strict liability provision of Ann's counterplan will not deter tobacco companies from producing and distributing unsafe products. Their financial backing alone makes them invulnerable to most of the suits that average citizens could muster. Even against wealthy complainants, the tobacco companies can always point out multiple factors that contribute to the diseases. If attorneys cannot prove responsibility, the effects of the counterplan would do little to change the tobacco company's behavior.

Affirmative debaters can take advantage of all of the usual lines of argument for denying solvency when arguing against a counterplan. They can argue that attitudinal barriers will prevent the counterplan's solvency, that structural barriers will undermine positive effects, and that circumvention will completely eliminate any hope of success. (For a fuller treatment of the lines of argument for arguing against solvency, see Chapter Four of this text.)

All debaters should recognize that the solvency of the counterplan has a direct bearing on the net benefits of adopting the counterplan. If the affirmative can reduce or eliminate the solvency of the counterplan altogether, then the benefits claimed by the negative may not continue to exist. Affirmative debaters should always evaluate the net benefits of the counterplan in light of the solvency claims of the counterplan.

Presumption

Particularly in cases where debates are very close, affirmative debaters will attempt to argue that presumption should rest against the counterplan. In Chapter One, we explained that presumption is usually against the affirmative plan. One reason for this convention is that risks tends to accompany change. With a plan and a counterplan, however, both teams are advocating a change in the course of action. The question becomes, which policy will bring the most change? Is the plan to increase regulations more of a change than the plan to abolish all restrictions and impose a system of strict liability? Probably not. Jason could argue that the unknown risk of adopting the counterplan means that we should play it safe and adopt the affirmative plan.

Disadvantages

The counterplan is also vulnerable to attacks that it will cause disadvantages. The negative may be correct in claiming that the counterplan has some positive effects, but the change in policy may also produce negative consequences. Just as with disadvantages offered by the negative against the affirmative plan, affirmative debaters interested in discussing the disadvantages of a counterplan must prove (1) that a link exists; that is, the counterplan causes the disadvantage to occur, (2) the disadvantage is unique; that is only the counterplan will lead to the negative consequences, and (3) the disadvantage has a significant impact, that is the negative consequences are important enough to consider in the context of the debate. (For a fuller treatment of the lines of argument necessary to prove a disadvantage, see Chapter Two of this text.)

> Jason: Fear of suits would force the tobacco companies to shift to other, safer, products. Thousands of tobacco farmers would be hurt. They would go bankrupt, leading to large numbers of foreclosures.

With this argument, Jason offers a disadvantage. He shows a link to the disadvantage by indicating that the fear of lawsuits would force the tobacco companies to shift to other products. He could have argued that this disadvantage is unique by proving that tobacco companies have no intention of decreasing the products they buy from farmers under a regulated market. Finally, he shows the impact of the disadvantage by pointing out that the shift away from tobacco would lead to bankruptcies and foreclosures for individual farmers.

All affirmative debaters should be alert to the interrelationship between counterplan disadvantages and net benefits. The counterplan may not be net-beneficial if it results in multiple disadvantages. If the affirmative feels that the negative consequences of a counterplan are substantial, they may want to reexamine their initial interpretation of its competitiveness.

Fiat

In Chapter One, we introduced the notion of fiat, the assumption that the affirmative plan would come into existence. This convention raises the question, can the negative assume their counterplan is entitled to fiat? There is no consensus among debaters about the answer to this question. The affirmative may be able to capitalize on this ambiguity by arguing that the negative does not have the right to fiat, rendering the argument of minimal importance in the debate.

Affirmative debaters initiating the argument that the negative does not have the right to fiat usually ground their position in the terms of the resolution. These debaters argue that power of fiat stems from the word "should" in the resolution, as in "The federal government *should* increase regulations to protect the safety of American citizens." Because there is no comparable resolution for the negative position, they claim the negative cannot assume the proposal would come into existence.

Many debaters and judges disagree with this line of thinking. These individuals want to see competing proposals debated for the purpose of determining the best approach to solving a problem. Nevertheless, they would still argue that there should be some restrictions on the negative's claim to fiat. Can the negative assume enactment of the counterproposal through another agent, such as state or local governments? Or is the negative limited to the agent identified in the resolution? Must the negative assume only policies would be in effect or can they assume the existence of attitudinal changes that would improve compliance with the counterplan? Questions such as these show the range of possible limits that debaters and judges may place on fiat. The affirmative normally chooses to defend a narrow interpretation of fiat to prevent the negative from having a greater argumentative advantage.

Conditionality

In the lines of argument for defending counterplans, we explained that on occasion the negative offers their counterplans as conditional arguments. The final option for attacking counterplans is to point out that conditional arguments are not legitimate. The affirmative usually wants to commit the negative to the counterplan. Otherwise, they may discover that they have spent a great deal of time establishing that the counterplan is topical, not competitive, not solvent, disadvantageous, and an abuse of fiat only to have the argument conceded by the negative. This situation can be extremely frustrating for affirmative debaters.

Many times, the basic reason why conditionality is argued to be illegitimate is fairness. The affirmative argues that they must remain committed to their proposal, so the negative team should have to assume this burden as well. The affirmative does not have the option to concede their plan; negative attacks on the plan are relevant throughout the debate. If conditionality is an acceptable form of argument, the negative can concede arguments that they are losing.

If not attacked as unfair, conditionality is usually criticized because the practice is harmful to the educational value of debate. If the negative can concede a major argument in the debate that the affirmative has spent a great deal of time arguing, the negative avoids clash. Confrontation is necessary in debate because it teaches participants how to be persuasive when their viewpoints are challenged. If the negative can avoid rather than face confrontation, both the affirmative and the negative are deprived of the chance to learn the essential processes of debate.

In an attempt to level the field, many affirmative debaters will argue that negative conditional arguments justify the use of conditional arguments by the affirmative. In practice, this may mean that the affirmative dismisses some of their plan provisions. If one of their planks links to a disadvantage, the affirmative can indicate that it should be considered conditionally. If the affirmative defeats the disadvantage, the plan plank should remain in the consideration of the affirmative plan. If not, the plan plank should be dismissed from the judge's evaluation altogether.

Lines of Argument for Resolving Counterplan Claims

The lines of argument useful for resolving competing claims about the counterplan focus on the topics discussed previously in this chapter: topicality, competitiveness, solvency, presumption, desirability, fiat, and conditionality. Assessing how the arguments used by both the affirmative and negative interrelate helps debaters determine the persuasive impact of a counterplan.

Topicality

The first question that both the affirmative and negatives must answer is whether the counterplan is topical. *Is the negative's defense of the counterplan as a non-resolutional alternative more persuasive than the affirmative's insistence that the topic encompasses the counterplan?* In our debate between Ann and Jason, Ann would probably win the argument that the counterplan is not topical. Even if she concedes that Jason is correct in defining *regulate* as "direct or govern," the resolution would still exclude the counterplan. Given that the counterplan abolishes many regulations outright, it probably decreases regulation overall.

If a counterplan is proven to be topical, both affirmative and negative debaters should ask whether a topical counterplan justifies a win for the affirmative team. In the lines of argument for attacking counterplans, we indicated that the affirmative is likely to maintain that any approach falling inside the parameters of the resolution justifies an affirmative decision. However, the negative can defend that this conclusion is premature. If the counterplan is competitive with the affirmative plan (thereby showing the counterplan could, should, or would not exist with the plan), critics of the debate have a clear choice. They can either decide that the affirmative plan is a superior alternative or that the negative counterplan is better. The negative would therefore suggest that the affirmative's reasoning is an artificial reason that ignores the clash in the debate. Whatever the reasoning employed by the debaters, the impact of showing that a counterplan is topical will likely be one of the central issues of resolving the argument.

Competitiveness

If the counterplan is nontopical or if the negative wins that their topical counterplan is legitimate, the debaters should then focus on *is the counterplan competitive with the affirmative proposal?* In our debate the mutual exclusivity of increasing regulations and a complete ban on government regulations is persuasive. The competitiveness of the strict liability component of the counterplan is less clear. Some benefit would seem to derive from using governmental regulations to help those citizens too poor to sue the government. Strict liability imposed with the affirmative plan would also help cover individuals suffering harms prior to the introduction of the regulations and individuals suffering harms not covered by the regulations. In short, the affirmative is on strong ground in arguing that strict liability should be coupled with the affirmative plan. The negative would certainly respond that the government's regulations prohibit citizens from being able to sue in the area of the regulations. Thus, to maximize the claims against the tobacco company, all regulations should be removed.

Earlier, we discussed how the affirmative might rely on permutations to test the compatibility of their plan with any counterplans. Debaters should realize that they may need to debate whether or not the use of permutations is a persuasive form of argumentation. In the lines of argument for attacking counterplans, we identified possible reasons the affirmative could give to defend the view that permutations are legitimate. The negative in response may wish to consider several arguments.

When attempting to respond to permutation arguments, the negative attempts to commit the affirmative to any alterations it might suggest. Unless the affirmative commits to defending the altered plan, the negative argues that the affirmative plan becomes a moving target. Moving targets, the negative suggests, are unfair because they prevent the negative from knowing what plan to attack in the debate; the plan changes as the debate progresses. The affirmative places an unfair burden on the negative by changing what their plan will be with the introduction of each new negative argument. If the negative can convince the judge that the affirmative should be responsible for any permutations they suggest, a number of lines of argument become possible. The negative may be able to argue that the permutation represented by the new plan is not topical, that it is disadvantageous, or that it renders the affirmative unable to solve the problem. If, however, the affirmative can argue that the new plan is merely designed to test the competition between the plan and the counterplan, any of these arguments—nontopicality, disadvantages, or solvency—merely becomes a reason to nullify the test, not to reject the affirmative completely. If the judge were merely testing to see if the counterplan and plan could coexist, these negative arguments would allow the judge to dispense with the permutation. At that point, the judge could look at other issues in the debate to see if the counterplan or the plan is superior.

If the negative cannot encourage the affirmative to commit to the permutation, it must undermine the notion that a permutation is a fair test. Some debaters argue that the number of possible permutations is infinite. As a result, it would be unfair for the judge to ask the negative team to prepare for each and every one of them. Other debaters attempt to place burdens of proof on the affirmative's permutations. Since each permutation represents essentially a new plan, the affirmative should have to show that the altered plan can solve the problem, and that inherent barriers will prevent its adoption.

Despite the myriad of approaches available when discussing permutations, debaters need to remember that the purpose of this line of argument is to determine the compatibility of the affirmative and negative proposals. If the policies could not, should not, or would not exist together, the negative has sustained its burden to show that the counterplan is competitive.

Solvency

In attempting to assess the benefits of adopting a counterplan, the debaters should determine the relative solvency of the various proposals. *Will the counterplan produce more, less, or equal solvency compared with the affirmative plan?* Will the counterplan and the plan together improve or diminish the potential benefits? In the debate between Jason and Ann, the choice is straightforward. Does the deterrence value of the court's use of strict liability result in fewer health harms for cigarette smokers? If so, how does the amount compare with the solvency claimed by the affirmative plan? Will using the policy of strict liability with the specific regulations of the affirmative maximize the potential benefits? Both affirmative and negative debaters should explore which alternative or set of alternatives maximizes solvency in the problem area. Debaters should remember that the solvency arguments concerning the counterplan have a direct effect on the net benefits of adopting the counterplan.

Desirability

Here, the debaters engage in a cost-benefit analysis of the counterplan, the plan, and the counterplan and plan together. *Does the counterplan on balance produce positive or negative effects?* To assess the disadvantages of the counterplan, debaters will want to refer to the lines of argument useful in resolving disadvantages and advantages (see Chapter Two). Overall, if the counterplan does have a positive effect, does that effect outweigh the benefits of the affirmative plan? If the counterplan is more advantageous, the negative will ordinarily win the debate; if it is less advantageous, the affirmative is more likely to be persuasive.

If the counterplan appears more advantageous, however, both teams must ask whether the plan and the counterplan together would be more advantageous. On balance, the strict liability counterplan could arguably have more advantages than the affirmative plan of increasing regulations. Nevertheless, the affirmative would not lose the debate unless the counterplan and plan together were also shown to be inferior to the counterplan alone. Strict liability could cover those harmed previously and those who lack coverage after the regulations go into effect. The regulations could cover the rest of the citizenry that is harmed by cigarette smoking. The proposals taken together might offer the strongest possible approach to the problem. If mutual adoption of the plan and counterplan produce the strongest positive effects, the negative will in all likelihood lose the debate.

In many debates, deciding which alternative is superior can be difficult. Multiple advantages for the plan and the counterplan, coupled with multiple disadvantages for each, can make the debate difficult to evaluate. Consequently, both affirmative and negative debaters should attempt to convince the judge that presumption rests with their alternative. If the debaters agree that presumption rests with the policy of least change, the question becomes, which policy is a smaller step? If they do not agree, then the debate will focus on the role of presumption in the debate.

Presumption

Like their affirmative counterparts, negative debaters will want to ensure that presumption rests with their course of action in case the debate is close. Presumption can rest with a counterplan for two reasons. First, the counterplan may be less of a change than the affirmative plan. With less change comes less risk of the unknown. Ann could point out that the risks to completely abolishing advertising of tobacco products represents a sharp departure from existing laws. The counterplan, by contrast, simply expands the common law standards to be used in many instances of deregulation. The second method of arguing that the counterplan has presumption is to maintain that presumption always exists against the resolution. Many debaters and judges believe that the process of debate is a test of the truth of the resolution. Before we can conclude that something is true, we must dismiss all alternative explanations. Likewise, debaters can argue that the counterplan simply offers another test of the resolution and thus should retain presumption during the debate.

Fiat

Does the negative have the right to assume enactment of the counterplan? The answer often determines whether the counterplan will have an impact in the debate. Affirmatives might argue that the negative is not entitled to fiat because the word "should" appears only in the resolution defended by the affirmative, not in the counterplan. In response, the negative might want to indicate that such a stance would make debate unrealistic. In the world outside of debate, individuals do not evaluate policies in a vacuum. If they recognize a problem, they seek the best alternative for how to solve that problem. If negative debaters are denied the right to assume their counterplans would exist, neither the affirmative or negative has the option to pursue realistic debates about policy.

Since most debaters and judges allow the negative some latitude with respect to fiat, debaters should be prepared to argue what the proper scope of that power should be. Should the negative be able to defend alternative actors for implementing the affirmative's proposal? Should they be able to assume supportive attitudes so that circumvention and disadvantages will not occur? Debaters should strive to defend counterplans that fall within a reasonable range of acceptable fiat. Using a different agent might be reasonable given that both sides should explore who would best implement the plan. To assume certain attitudes, by contrast, might go too far because the negative would be excluding the possibility of circumvention or disadvantages against the counterplan.

Conditionality

The final issue in resolving competing claims of counterplans is conditionality. Initially, debaters should discuss *is conditional argumentation legitimate?* While the affirmative will want to rely on the previously discussed arguments that conditionality will hurt both fairness and education, the negative also has options. Some negative debaters argue that conditional arguments form the best test of the resolution. Multiple attacks on the resolution force the affirmative to explore as much of the resolution as possible, instead of limiting the debate to a few isolated arguments. Other debaters argue that conditionality is a legitimate form of argument because all arguments are conditional. Debaters can concede any other argument in the debate. Why not a counterplan? Finally, the use of conditionality prevents debaters from advocating a false choice. Policies are not compared only against one alternative. Frequently, multiple options are available that require debaters to assess the relative merits of each.

If the negative wins the point that conditional argumentation is legitimate, the final question becomes *have the conditions outlined by the negative been met?* Does the negative lose the disadvantage that serves as the condition for the counterplan's adoption? Both affirmative and negative debaters should be alert to what arguments are affected by the set of conditions that must be present for them to impact in the debate.

Summary and Conclusions

Counterplans are alternative courses of action advocated by the negative to solve the significant problem identified in the affirmative plan. They interact with each of the four general lines of policy argument. Counterplans usually include specific mandates, funding provisions, enforcement procedures, and an intent plank which reserves for the negative the right to interpret the meaning of the counterplan.

When defending a counterplan, the negative needs to initiate four arguments. These include that the counterplan is not topical, that the counterplan is competitive with the affirmative plan (that is the counterplan could not, should not, or would not exist with the affirmative plan), that the counterplan solves at least a portion of the significant problem cited by the affirmative, and that the counterplan has additional advantages. Counterplans may be presented as conditional arguments, requiring specific conditions to be in place before the argument should be considered in the debate.

When attacking a counterplan, the affirmative can maintain that the counterplan is topical, that the counterplan is not competitive, that the counterplan does not solve the harm identified by the affirmative, that presumption rests against the counterplan, that the counterplan would be disadvantageous, that the counterplan would overextend the definition of fiat, or that conditional counterplans are illegitimate.

To test whether a counterplan is competitive, affirmative debaters can use permutations. Permutations are alterations that test the compatibility of two proposals. Common permutations include adopting one policy first and the second policy at a later time, adopting the bulk of the counterplan but leaving an exception for a portion of the plan, and using multiple agents to implement the counterplan and plan together.

When resolving conflicting claims of topicality, all debaters should decide if the counterplan is topical, and if it is, does a topical counterplan justify affirming the resolution? Resolving compatibility questions involves a determination of whether the counterplan could, should, or would exist together and whether permutations can be employed to determine the compatibility. Debaters should determine which proposal has more solvency and benefit: the counterplan, the plan, or the counterplan and plan together. In the final analysis, presumption may play a role in determining which policy is the superior alternative. The debaters should attempt to resolve whether the use of fiat is overbroad and unwarranted. Finally, they should consider the appropriateness of conditional arguments and whether the debaters have fulfilled the conditions posited for consideration of the counterplan.

Exercises

1. Assume that you are debating against an affirmative plan that would require all welfare recipients to work for their government check. The affirmative claims this plan will make the poor more productive. Write a counterplan that would address this same problem area. Be sure to include mandates, funding, enforcement, and an intent plank.

2. Assume that the resolution in the previous example had been "Resolved: that the federal government should increase the employment opportunities for the poor." Can you argue that your counterplan is nontopical? Is it competitive? By what standard(s)—mutual exclusivity, net benefits, or redundancy? What added advantages can you claim beyond those offered by the affirmative?

3. In the 1992 presidential campaign, Democratic candidate Jerry Brown advocated a 13 percent flat tax rate, i.e. everyone in America would pay 13 percent of his or her income to the federal government. His Democratic opponent Bill Clinton argued that we should keep the current tax system but give a tax cut to the middle class paid for by the rich. Can you use a permutation of Clinton's plan to show that it is not competitive with Brown's proposal?

4. Pair yourself with another student and conduct a mini-debate on a single counterplan. For three minutes, let the affirmative outline a

plan and a potential advantage that stems from the plan. In the next three minutes, have the negative outline a counterplan arguing why it is competitive, how it has solvency, and how it produces added advantages. Allow each debater one rebuttal of three minutes. Each debater should attempt to resolve the major issues of the counterplan according to the section of this chapter entitled, "Lines of Argument for Resolving Conflicting Counterplan Claims."

7

Interaction Among Lines of Argument

Chapter Outline

Interactions That Minimize Your Opponent's Arguments
    Trivializing Opposing Arguments
    Making Opposing Arguments Irrelevant
    Exposing Contradictory Arguments
Interactions That Maximize Your Arguments
    Identifying Complementary Arguments
    Initiating Independent Arguments
    Repeating Critical Arguments
Summary and Conclusions

Key Terms

cross-application
trivializing arguments
probability
time frame
threshold
brink
linear argument
irrelevant argument
contradictory argument
doubleturn
complementary argument
independent argument
repetition

In Chapters One through Five we introduced the general lines of argument in policy debate: significance, inherency, solvency, and topicality. All arguments in debate revolve around these four arguments which determine whether the judge will affirm or negate the resolution. Winning each argument is necessary for the affirmative to prevail in the debate. However, you should not view each of these arguments strictly in isolation. Each argument can, and should, be combined to establish a consistent defense of the resolution. The negative can win the debate by defeating any one of these four lines of argument. However, it is rare that the negative overwhelmingly defeats one of the lines of argument. Frequently, they must win several arguments in order to win the debate. The negative significantly enhances its chances of winning the debate if they attack the affirmative policy from a coordinated perspective rather than attacking individual lines of argument separately.

Debate arguments can interact in six general ways. Arguments may have a trivial relationship to each other; they may be irrelevant to each other; they may contradict each other; they may complement and support each other; they may independently support the overall position; or they may repeat each other. The first three forms of interaction (trivial, unrelated, and contradictory) tend to minimize your opponent's arguments. The latter three forms of interaction (complementary, independent, and repetitious) tend to reinforce your own position.

Understanding how arguments interact is critical for developing your debate strategy. If you merely deny every argument your opponent offers, you will make several mistakes in the debate. You will waste time answering arguments unnecessarily, fall into the strategic ploys of your opponent, and undermine your own arguments. Debaters who are acutely aware of argumentative interaction are more likely to be strategically successful. For example, when debaters use an answer to one response as an answer to another, they engage in the **cross-application** of arguments. Cross-application can make speeches more efficient, argument selection more effective, and debates more interesting.

This chapter identifies how general lines of argument tend to interact. After describing these relationships, we discuss their strategic implications for argument construction and resolution. The first section discusses arguments that minimize your opponent's position. The second section discusses arguments that maximize your own position.

Interactions That Minimize Your Opponent's Arguments

For many judges, debate is the process of cost-benefit analysis. What are the costs and benefits of the affirmative proposal compared to those of any negative alternatives? You must be able to reduce the impact of the arguments your opponent presents. By taking this step, you maximize the changes that the impact of your own arguments will be more substantial. To minimize your opponent's arguments, you can argue that they are trivial, that they are unrelated, or that they contradict each other.

Trivializing Opposing Arguments

In a debate where the topic is relatively balanced, where there is a fair division of ground, and where the debaters have relatively similar levels of argumentation and presentation skills, the debate may hinge on your ability to trivialize the importance of your opponent's arguments while maximizing the importance of your own arguments. **Trivializing arguments** is the process of reducing the impact of a specific argument in the context of the entire debate. The ability to distinguish trivial from substantial relationships is a critical thinking skill necessary for thoughtful argumentation.

Most of us place a high value on life. If you could save one life without negative consequence, you would probably do so. If, however, saving one life required you to forfeit the freedom of 200 million people, you would probably not save that life. The scope of freedom lost (200 million people) is so much greater than the scope of one life lost that most of us would sacrifice that life to preserve freedom for so many, even if we thought that life is more important than freedom. A debater opposing the argument that life is more important than freedom in this case would attempt to trivialize the magnitude of the loss of life in comparison to the scope of the lost freedom.

Assessing the impact of two competing positions is one of the most difficult aspects of judging a close debate. In many debates both sides will win some arguments, and the judge must compare the impact of the opposing arguments. Debaters should help judges resolve these difficult decisions. The six most frequently used arguments for resolving the impact of competing claims are probability, magnitude and scope, time frame, linearity and threshold, specificity, and degree of irreparability. These arguments are usually essential for a judge to evaluate the strengths and weaknesses of affirming or negating the proposition.

Probability

When attempting to resolve impact conflicts, a primary question you should ask is, what is the probability of each argument? The **probability** of an argument is the likelihood that one thing will lead to another. The impact of an argument can be extremely significant, but the probability of that impact may be sufficiently low that the risk may be worth taking. Human beings take chances with their lives regularly because they enjoy activities that provide big thrills; they sky-dive, race stock cars, go hang gliding. People can minimize the probability of danger through the use of safety equipment, training, intelligence, and physical prowess. They minimize the probability of losing their lives for the certain thrill of engaging in the activity. Arguments that are more probable are frequently more persuasive than arguments that have more impact but are highly improbable.

Magnitude and Scope

A second question you should ask is, how substantial is the impact? The more consequential argument is frequently the more persuasive argument. Physical activity, like that found in amateur sports, can result in injury to many people who participate. However, most amateur sports, such as basketball, softball, hiking, and jogging, result in only minor injuries which most participants are willing to risk because their impact is so small. Compared to the positive impact of participation, whether that is fun or overall physical conditioning, most of us are willing to risk a sprained ankle or shoulder.

Time Frame

A third question you should ask is, what is the time frame of the argument? The **time frame** of an argument refers to when the argument is likely to occur. Frequently people make important decisions on the basis of immediacy rather than impact or probability. Many individuals smoke cigarettes, drink alcohol excessively, or eat fatty foods because such consumption provides immediate gratification. Some of these people reason that the development of medical technologies will outpace the problem, providing options for treatment in the long term that are not available today. The probability that these activities will shorten their lives by several years does not deter the behavior. The risks are just too far in the future. Stressing the short time frame can be persuasive if the immediate benefits gained or harms averted are significant.

Interaction of Competing Trivialization Claims. Frequently a tension exists between the probability of impacts, the magnitude and scope of impacts, and the time frame in which the impacts occur. The debate resolution, "Resolved: that the federal government should adopt an energy policy that substantially reduces the nonmilitary consumption of fossil fuels in the United States," could give rise to many conflicting scenarios involving probability, impact, and time frame. Milo might offer a proposal to decrease fossil fuel consumption by arguing that the continued use of fossil fuels ensures the continued release of carbon dioxide into the atmosphere. More carbon dioxide will accelerate global warming, causing a loss in agricultural production, coastal flooding, and increased international conflict as the world attempts to adapt to a changing climate.

Milo's opponent Kate could argue that any attempt to decrease fossil fuel consumption at this time would trigger immediate economic dislocation and hardship, perhaps leading to international conflict. Both debaters must compare the probability of the impacts they present. If, at the end of the debate, the judge decides that the affirmative impact is more probable but that the equally devastating negative impact is likely to occur sooner, how does the judge decide which argument is more compelling? Should the judge vote to avoid the more certain harm, or to avoid the near-term harm? Resolving these conflicts is the debater's responsibility. You need to provide arguments to guide the evaluation of the debate in favor of your position.

It is often difficult to discern which of these three arguments is more important—probability, magnitude and scope, or time frame. Many of us who are willing to play amateur sports are willing to risk small injuries for the enjoyment of the sport. However, those same individuals would not risk skydiving and hang gliding because the potential negative impact of these sports—broken legs, spinal injury, death—though less likely than a twisted ankle in other sports, is too great to justify the risk. Many individuals who are willing to smoke and drink are not willing to sky-dive or play basketball. Different individuals have different perspectives on risky activities which lead some to focus on the probability of negative consequences, others on the immediacy of the consequences, and still others on the magnitude of the consequences.

Despite the difficulty of doing so, debaters must frequently convince a judge that one of these issues should be the deciding factor in evaluating the debate. Is a short time frame more important than a certain impact? Is the magnitude of an impact more important than a certain impact? To illustrate how debaters make these types of comparisons, let's examine a few options for the debate between Milo and Kate.

Time Frame Outweighs Probability. Kate wants her short-term economic dislocation from reduced use of fossil fuels to outweigh Milo's certain claim that global warming will result if we do not act now. She can argue directly that the time frame of an argument is more important because we should always seek to avoid the nearest disaster. If we stop a short-term war caused by economic dislocation, we'll have time to address the problem of global warming. If we don't, we won't care about the problem.

Besides demonstrating that the time frame is more important, Kate might want to undermine the probability of Milo's scenario. After all, a lot of things cause global warming besides the United States consuming fossil fuels. Car pollution and fossil fuel consumption by other countries are just two examples. If several factors contribute to the existence of a problem, then the probability that a plan aimed at any one of them will solve it is lower. Milo's plan to reduce fossil fuel consumption in the United States, then, will not have the certain impact that he initially claimed.

Finally, Kate might want to concede that Milo's scenario is certain but point out how it poses no real problem. The probability of a scenario is meaningless if there is no impact to the scenario. Global warming might occur, but several mitigating factors will prevent it from becoming the worldwide threat that Milo claims. Oceans absorb a lot of the heat from the air, clouds formed by pollution reflect solar radiation preventing some heat from entering the atmosphere, and the earth's natural cooling cycle may offset the effects of the rise in temperature.

With each of these arguments, Kate bolsters her claim that the time frame of her war scenario should be a more important factor than the probability of Milo's war. To show that the probability outweighs the time frame, Milo should simply ask himself the same questions in reverse. Why should probability be the most important issue? Is the time frame of Kate's scenario really short? And is there a significant impact to Kate's scenario if it does occur?

Impact Outweighs Time Frame. Here, Milo wants the impact of his global warming argument to outweigh the short time frame of Kate's economic dislocation argument. Again, Milo's first option is to directly make the claim that the impact of an argument outweighs the time frame. Since both debaters cite war as an ultimate impact, Milo must begin by showing that global warming would have a larger effect than economic dislocation. He might argue that wars from economic dislocation would be regional and low-level because the greatest economic impact would occur in impoverished nations. These nations are too poor to buy sophisticated weaponry. Then Milo should explain why global warming is a more important impact than Kate's war. He could indicate that we should risk some short-term regional wars to avoid the worldwide risk of atomic warfare caused by global warming.

Milo's second approach could be that Kate's short-term war is not probable. If the consequence is unlikely, it does not matter when it might occur. Milo could point out that war seldom occurs during economic depressions. Countries are too busy and too poor to engage in conflict. Milo could draw a sharp contrast between this unlikely war and the strong probability of his own war scenario. He could point out that war would very likely occur when land begins to be covered by the sea and countries losing productive agricultural land must turn elsewhere for food.

With these two arguments, Milo can bolster his claim that the impact should outweigh the time frame in comparing the two arguments. In response, Kate would examine why time frame should outweigh impact, whether Milo's impact really is as large as he says it is, and what the actual probability is that Milo's war will occur.

In debate, you have the opportunity to persuade the judge which arguments—probability, time frame, or impact—should guide his or her decision. These general lines of argument need to be developed into specific lines of argument. To persuade the judge you need to compare the probability, time frame, and impact of two competing policies. Develop some specific lines of argument for the types of impacts you are comparing. Your ultimate goal is to maximize the strengths of your argument while trivializing the strengths of your opponent's argument.

Threshold and Linearity

A fourth strategy for comparing impacts is the examination of threshold and linearity. The impacts of events occur in different ways. Sometimes a chain of events is put into place leading to a point at which the events become inevitable. The point at which the impact of an argument becomes inevitable is called the **threshold** or **brink** of the argument. For example, debaters might argue that international relations may deteriorate to the point where war becomes inevitable. This is a classic example of a threshold or brink. Whatever causes a war must, at some time, reach a threshold point where the war becomes unavoidable. When there are substantial international tensions, the media uses phrases such as "threshold of war," "brink of war," and "brinkmanship" to describe these situations. If Kate could argue that we are on the brink of economic collapse now, she could enhance the persuasiveness of her claim that now is a bad time to alter energy policies. She could argue that we need time to withdraw from the brink of economic collapse before we begin to develop new energy policies.

Other effects, by contrast, unfold gradually as the cause of the problem increases. Rather than establish a threshold where an impact becomes inevitable, a **linear argument** establishes that for every incremental increase in cause, there is an inevitable incremental increase in effect. Some experts say that there is a linear relationship between the consumption of cigarettes and the incidence of lung cancer. If more people smoke, more cases of lung cancer will occur. This is a classic example of linearity. In our debate, Milo might argue that there is a linear relationship between the amount of carbon dioxide released into the atmosphere and the amount of global warming. Given the dangers of global warming, he might reason, we should attempt to minimize the amount of warming whenever possible. By voting affirmative to decrease fossil fuel consumption, Milo argues that the effects of global warming can be reduced in a linear fashion.

Arguments based on threshold relationships can be persuasive because the debater can discuss the closeness of the threshold, emphasize how much closer a cause can push us toward the threshold, and note the irreversibility of crossing the threshold. Such arguments can sound very urgent and be very compelling. Arguments based on linear relationships can be persuasive because the debater can emphasize that any increment in cause is certain to create an equal increment in harmful effect. Such arguments can remind a judge that even a small change in action will have some consequence.

When debaters offer competing threshold arguments, judges can resolve the debate by approximating which policy is more likely to cross the threshold. When debaters offer opposing linear arguments, judges can resolve the debate by approximating which policy is more likely to generate a greater cause and effect. However, when one side stresses a threshold relationship and the other a linear relationship, it is sometimes difficult to compare the arguments. The circumstances that would trigger the impact of both arguments are so dissimilar that it may be difficult to develop a clear rationale for choosing one policy over another.

Exploiting some general weaknesses of both threshold and linearity arguments will enable debaters to trivialize the impact of their opponent's position. Generally, if an impact is on the threshold of occurring, there are many potential causes that will result in that impact. Milo could agree with Kate that we are on the threshold of massive economic turmoil. However, many factors have brought us to this point, such as lagging productivity, increased trade friction between nations, and massive expenses on military armaments. Milo could argue that the factors that have brought us to the brink of economic depression are far more likely to push us over the brink than the affirmative proposal to change energy consumption patterns. The arguments that prove we are on the brink, prove that crossing the threshold is not a unique result of the affirmative plan (See Chapter Two on significance for an exploration of uniqueness arguments.)

Generally, if there is a linear relationship between cause and effect, there is some doubt as to how much unique increase in effect can occur from one cause. Kate could agree that global warming might increase in a linear relationship with an increase in the consumption of fossil fuels. However, since Milo's proposal merely decreases United States consumption of fossil fuels, other nation's massive consumption rates would overwhelm any minimal positive effect.

You should familiarize yourself with the interaction between linear and threshold issues so that you can become an effective debater. Sometimes linearity and threshold questions may be difficult to resolve, but debaters who can resolve these conflicts will maximize their chances of winning the debate.

Specificity of Impact

Another area of conflicting impacts has to do with generalized and specific impacts. Arguments can fall along a continuum between being very specific to very general. The specificity of the impact is based on the degree of detail provided in the argumentative scenario. At times, your opponent may describe a very specific scenario to explain the implication of their argument. At other times, your opponent may state the impact of a policy in very general terms and not specify a scenario in which the impact will occur. Milo, for example, might identify some specific regions of the world that would experience conflict in the event of global warming. He could point to specific, heavily populated coastal regions that would become destabilized as people attempted to migrate away from floods to safer areas. He could also identify specific agricultural regions that might lose productivity where people would begin to fight over the availability of food. Kate could, by contrast, argue that the economic downturn she predicts would affect the global economic system. It would be difficult to specify the warring countries, but many countries could potentially engage in conflict.

Milo's position might be stronger because he can identify a specific region of war. However, Kate could argue very specifically that conflict can be averted in those areas because they can be identified in advance. Governments can plan for and solve refugee problems from coastal regions in advance. They can stockpile emergency food supplies to cope with future shortages in regions likely to lose agricultural productivity.

Kate's position on the other hand, might be stronger because it is unpredictable, but Milo could argue that the lack of specificity renders the impact of her scenario much less certain. Generalizing from a theory that economic downturns cause war is not nearly as persuasive as the certainty that some regions will engage in war. A judge cannot evaluate a general threat if it is unknown who the potential combatants are. Many individual circumstances might act to reduce the general threat of war.

You should constantly be alert for arguments that distinguish between circumstances that might lead to a specific impact and those that might lead to a more generalized impact. You should be able to use the differences between specific and generalized impacts to trivialize your opponent's impact while magnifying your own impact.

Degree of Reparability

A final line of argument for comparing the impact of two arguments is to consider whether or not society can recover from the effects. Some harms are difficult to endure but are nonetheless tolerable if recovery is possible. It would certainly be better for most of us if the economy never again suffered from a recession. However, if we have to endure another recession we will probably survive it. Other impacts are not reparable. Certainly the damage suffered from a nuclear war would be difficult to overcome. Many environmentalists are concerned that a number of serious environmental problems are already beyond repair, such as depletion of the ozone layer or species extinction.

In our fossil fuel debate, we witness a classic attempt to determine which impact has more irreparable consequences. Milo argues that global environmental damage is irreparable and that the damage from war will be too devastating for society to overcome the consequences. However, Kate argues that the global war caused by economic collapse would produce greater levels of destruction for the earth and its inhabitants. Therefore, her impacts are similarly irreparable.

As a debater you need to develop the skill to distinguish trivial from substantial relationships when advocating one of two competing policies. In this section, we have outlined some of the possible strategies that can be used to exploit the interaction between arguments. These possibilities are not limited to the strategies discussed here, but they provide a starting point for comparing competing impacts.

Making Opposing Arguments Irrelevant

Some interactions between arguments make one or more of the arguments irrelevant. An **irrelevant argument** is one that does not relate to the final outcome of the debate. Sometimes, your opponent's arguments may render some of your own arguments irrelevant. You should be alert to notice if an opponent makes their own arguments irrelevant.

First, topicality arguments may make some arguments irrelevant. In the debate between Milo and Kate, say that Milo had included a provision in his plan that required trees to be planted to help absorb carbon dioxide from the atmosphere. Milo could reason that this provision, coupled with requiring decreased consumption of fossil fuels, would help solve global warming. Kate, could make two arguments against this provision. First, she could argue that requiring the planting of trees is an extratopical provision of the plan (see Chapter Five), and therefore the judge should ignore the provision altogether. Then, she could argue that if Milo does plant trees, he will have to consume a vast amount of water resources for planting and fertilizing. Given recent water shortages, Milo would be stealing water from food production, creating food shortages, and ultimately causing starvation. If Milo could not convince the judge that the water disadvantage is untrue, he could concede Kate's argument that the provision of the plan causing the disadvantage is extratopical. As a result, the judge would dismiss the plan provision from consideration in the debate, thereby eliminating the link to the water disadvantage.

Second, solvency may render some arguments irrelevant (see Chapter Four for solvency arguments). Negative debaters may argue that the affirmative plan does not solve the significant problem and, at the same time, argue a disadvantage linked to the affirmative claim of solvency. If the plan does nothing to reduce the problem, disadvantages linked to the effect of the plan become irrelevant. In our debate between Milo and Kate, Kate might argue that decreasing the consumption of fossil fuel would drive prices so low that it would bankrupt many Middle Eastern countries that depend on oil sales. Without oil profits, these countries could not sustain economic growth and would begin warring with another to monopolize whatever oil market remains. If, in the same debate, Kate argues that Milo's plan could not solve the problem of global warming because other countries will consume as much fossil fuel as the United States, she makes a terrible mistake. Why? Because Milo could agree that other countries would consume the same level of fossil fuel. With consumption levels unchanged, Milo could argue, there would be no decrease in oil prices. Other nations would keep the demand for Middle East oil prices sufficiently high to keep these countries from going to war. Kate's attempt to prove that Milo cannot solve global warming means that Kate's disadvantage to Milo's plan is irrelevant; the Middle East will still have plenty of oil consuming customers.

A third way that two arguments can interact to render one irrelevant involves the general line of argument of inherency. Inherency arguments and uniqueness claims for disadvantages frequently render one another irrelevant. In the debate between Milo and Kate, Kate might argue a disadvantage that lowering oil consumption will wreak havoc on the world economy by shifting economic patterns. Milo, in response, might argue that this disadvantage is not unique to his proposal. He could reason that current conservation measures are going to alter consumption patterns and cause a global economic collapse even if his plan is not passed. Why is this a problem? If Milo is correct that present conservation policies will decrease economic growth, his plan becomes unnecessary and not inherent. Fossil fuel consumption will certainly decline because of conservation and slowed economic growth. By removing the cause of the problem, global warming would be unlikely to continue into the future. Kate, then, could concede Milo's argument that current conservation policies will decrease fossil fuel consumption, proving that the problem will not continue.

The fourth type of interaction that can render arguments irrelevant involves the general line of significance. In response to disadvantages, debaters using multiple strategies may use some arguments that make others irrelevant. Frequently, affirmative debaters argue that no link exists to a disadvantage and that they can turn the disadvantage, claiming that it is an additional reason to affirm the resolution. In our debate, Kate might initiate the disadvantage that altering energy consumption would disrupt global economic systems and cause an economic depression. Milo, attempting to answer the disadvantage, could argue that no link exists to the disadvantage. Energy prices would not trigger economic dislocation because nuclear power developments would offset the decline in fossil fuel consumption.

In the same debate, Milo could also impact-turn the disadvantage. He could argue that an economic depression would be good because current levels of economic growth are destroying the world's environment. The problem Milo faces in making both of these arguments is that if there will not be an economic depression his arguing the benefits of such a downturn is irrelevant. Kate, at this point, could concede Milo's link argument to dispense with his impact turn. Kate could then devote the rest of her speaking time to more fruitful arguments.

There are other ways in which arguments may interact to render certain arguments in the debate irrelevant. You should be alert to this possibility when planning and constructing your answers to potential arguments. When debating, you may find it beneficial to identify arguments that could render any of your other arguments irrelevant so that you can devote your time to the arguments that will improve your chances of winning the debate.

Exposing Contradictory Arguments

At times, debaters can make the egregious error of contradicting their own arguments. A **contradictory argument** is one that disproves the assumptions or claims made previously by the same side in the debate. You should be careful to avoid contradicting your own arguments, and you should always be alert for contradiction in your opponent's arguments. Contradictions can occur within a single line of reasoning or across very distinct arguments. In this section we discuss some contradictions that frequently occur across arguments.

In Chapter Two we noted that disadvantages can link to either the plan or to the effects of the plan claimed by the affirmative. Negative debaters frequently make the mistake of arguing that there is no significant problem and that a disadvantage links to the effects of the plan. Why is this a mistake? Our debate between Milo and Kate illustrates the problem.

Kate could argue a disadvantage that global warming is necessary at this time to offset the natural cooling of the earth. Some evidence does exist that the earth's temperatures are actually cooling and another ice age may be in the process of developing. Kate could argue that the ice age would destroy much of life on earth, as previous ice ages have done. Kate would then make a very big mistake if she tried to disprove Milo's argument that present policies cause global warming. If she made the argument that fossil fuel consumption did not contribute to increased global temperatures, Milo could concede this argument to dismiss Kate's ice age disadvantage. If fossil fuels do not increase temperatures, then the judge could hardly expect rising temperatures to offset the coming ice age. Kate's arguments to deny Milo's significance, then, disproves the significance of Kate's own disadvantage.

The negative can also contradict themselves when arguing inherency arguments and disadvantages. Frequently a natural tension exists between the uniqueness of a disadvantage and the arguments that the affirmative case is not inherent. In our debate, Kate could make this mistake if she argued that conservation measures will decrease the consumption of fossil fuels whether the resolution is adopted or not. If Kate also argued her disadvantage that decreased consumption of fossil fuels will decrease oil prices and trigger a Mideast war, Milo could conceivably grant Kate's inherency argument—conservation will decrease consumption—and argue that Kate's disadvantage on Mideast war would not be unique to his plan. Decreased consumption would occur regardless, making the Middle East war inevitable. Kate's inherency argument therefore proves that a Mideast war would occur with or without the polices recommended in the resolution.

While a variety of arguments can contradict in a debate, the most dangerous form of contradiction is usually referred to as a **doubleturn.** Frequently, in their haste to claim every argument in the debate as a potential advantage, affirmative debaters argue both kinds of turnaround arguments at the same time. The first kind of turnaround, you recall from Chapter Two, is a link turn which says that the affirmative actually prevents a disadvantage from occurring. The second turnaround is an impact turn which says that the impact of the disadvantage is actually a good thing rather than a bad thing.

In our debate, Milo could make this mistake on Kate's economic depression disadvantage. Milo could argue that by instituting a policy to decrease fossil fuel consumption now, we can avert a severe economic depression when climate change destroys agricultural production. Agricultural productivity is critical to driving the world economy, Milo could argue. If climate change decreased agricultural production, Milo could reason, it would lead to economic chaos comparable to the Great Depression of the 1930s. In this way, Milo could link-turn the depression argument. Against the same disadvantage, Milo could make the argument that economic depression would be a good thing because it would save the world ecosystem from the ravages of economic growth. If Milo foolishly offered both arguments in the same debate, Kate could concede that Milo prevents a depression and that a depression would be good for the environment. At that point, Kate would argue, Milo has "double-turned the disadvantage." Milo prevents a good impact from occurring and therefore his plan should be rejected. This argument is ideal for Kate because Milo's arguments alone are sufficient to win the debate for Kate.

There are several ways in which debaters can contradict themselves. We have outlined a few of the most recurrent contradictions and explained how debaters can capitalize on them. You should always be alert for possible contradictions. When developing and selecting arguments to run in a debate, be sure that they are consistent. When actually debating, watch for these kind of mistakes by your opponent. Even the best and most experienced debaters make these kind of errors. Taking advantage of such mistakes can make you a very successful debater.

Interactions That Maximize Your Arguments

Having minimized your opponent's claims, the next step is to ensure that you are maximizing your own. By capitalizing completely on your winning arguments, you improve the judge's cost-benefit assessment of your proposal. Employing the strategies of using complementary arguments, relying on independent claims, and repeating critical points, you maximize your chances of winning the debate.

Identifying Complementary Arguments

At times, your opponent can make arguments that prove your arguments are true. **Complementary arguments** are those that support the reasoning of another claim within the debate. Again, a number of opportunities exist for you to prove that one of the lines of argument made by your opponent actually proves one of your lines of argument. We cite several examples here, but you may discover other lines of argument that complement your arguments in any given debate.

A tension exists between the inability of the present system to solve a problem and the ability of the resolution to overcome the inherent problems in the present system. If opposing attitudes exist to solving the problem currently, those same forces may remain to undermine the solvency of the affirmative proposal. Both sides can take advantage of this tension if they are alert and careful. Sometimes affirmative debaters isolate inherency arguments that their own solvency arguments cannot overcome. In our debate, Milo could argue that the present system will not enforce laws against polluters. Administrative agencies have the capacity to grant exceptions. Enforcers take bribes. The executive branch tends to support business interests which lobby government officials for exceptions. Combined with the philosophical predisposition toward a market economy free of governmental regulation, the ability to enforce existing laws makes pollution reduction nearly impossible. Kate, recognizing the strength of Milo's inherency arguments, could elect to concede Milo's arguments that administrative agencies skirt the letter of the law. Instead, Kate could use these very arguments to advance a position that the same agencies will continue to avoid enforcing the mandates of Milo's plan. Thus, the negative can use the inherency arguments of the affirmative to complement their own position that a powerful constituency will thwart efforts to decrease fossil fuel consumption.

The same argument might work to the affirmative team's advantage under different circumstances. The affirmative team might argue that the negative inherency arguments prove that the affirmative plan can solve the harm. Kate could argue that the present system is committed to conservation of energy, that conservation is working, and that the affirmative plan is not necessary. At that point, Milo could agree that current conservation policies are effective, undermining any need for enforcement. If the success of current policies is true, Milo could reason, the affirmative plan would also be effective. We merely need to commit ourselves to conserving even more fossil fuel. The willingness of the present system to enforce conservation efforts proves that the new conservation efforts will receive little resistance and little circumvention. In this way, Milo can use Kate's inherency arguments to prove that conservation policies will work.

There are many ways for your opponent's arguments to actually prove that your own arguments are true. You must be alert to the possibility and carefully explain how these arguments prove your argument without conceding the ultimate impact of the argument to opponent. With this awareness and attention to explanation, you should be able to take advantage of these forms of argument.

Initiating Independent Arguments

An **independent argument** is a claim that relies on no other claims in the debate to serve as a reason to affirm or negative the resolution. In our example, Milo could justify his proposal to decrease fossil fuel consumption by offering two independent problems resulting from current practices He could argue, as before, that fossil fuel consumption causes global warming, so we need to decrease such consumption. Milo could also argue that fossil fuel consumption causes air pollution which shortens the lives of tens of thousands of human beings in the United States each year. If either argument proves that a significant benefit accrues from the proposal, then the affirmative maximizes its chances of winning the debate. Looking back at our previous examples, the benefit of independent significance arguments should be clear. At several points in our discussion, we suggested that Milo could concede Kate's argument that other countries would consume as much fossil fuel as the United States. However, Milo would still win the debate if he could prove that some advantage would exist even if the United States were the only country to decrease consumption. If United States consumption causes people to die from air pollution here, then it would be sensible to at least decrease the deaths from air pollution. Milo could argue that it might be impossible to stop global warming, but it is still possible to prevent some deaths from air pollution nationally.

Other varieties of independent arguments are available to support resolutions. Affirmative teams can argue that there are independent reasons why their case is inherent. They can argue that there are independent reasons why their proposal can solve the problem. They can also argue that independent arguments prove their plan is topical. The advantage of independent significance, inherency, solvency, and topicality claims is that it is easier for the affirmative debater to concede some negative arguments without forfeiting any of the general lines of argument.

Negative debaters may also offer independent lines of argument. They may choose, for example to offer two independent disadvantages to the affirmative plan. This would be a necessary first step for Kate if she wanted to concede some arguments to Milo and still have a disadvantage to weigh against Milo's significance at the end of the debate. Even within disadvantages it is possible to have independent links to one disadvantage or independent impacts to one disadvantage. In this way, if the affirmative is able to defeat one disadvantage, or one part of a disadvantage, there may be ways for the negative to still win some of the disadvantages.

Constructing independent advantages and disadvantages is strategically sound because debaters then have more than one argument to pursue to win the debate. You must be sure of the independence of your claims, however, or the previously discussed interrelationships may emerge in the course of the debate.

Repeating Critical Arguments

Communication studies show that **repetition,** or the repeating of arguments for emphasis, can be a very persuasive strategy for the public speaker. Repetition can also be effective in debates. Particularly, it is useful for stressing when an opponent has conceded an important argument to remind the judge of the concession. It can also be helpful to reiterate arguments that you believe a judge might not understand. Finally, it is sometimes useful to repeat evidence, or the particular phrasing of a quotation, to remind the judge of the impact of a particular evidenced argument on other arguments in the debate.

However, debaters should be aware of two important problems with repetition. First, debaters usually compete in timed speeches, and it may be an inefficient use of time to repeat arguments that are clear to everyone in the debate. You rarely have time for repetition. Second, debaters should be aware that repeating an argument several times in the debate also provides an opponent with several opportunities to answer the argument. Thus, if you repeat too much, you provide your opponent with a tactical advantage. Debaters should reserve the use of repetition for those circumstances where a memorable quotation or particular phrase aids the persuasive process. Excessive repetition merely wastes your valuable speaking time and provides tactical opportunities to your opponent.

Summary and Conclusions

Debaters need to be acutely aware of the interaction between arguments both before they debate and during debates. Being aware before the debate allows you to maximize your own potential for offering defensible and consistent positions. Being alert for interactions during debates allows you to take advantage of mistakes made by your opponents. It is not easy to process all of the arguments in a debate without making an error. The best debaters in the nation frequently contradict themselves or fail to notice their opponents' contradictions. An intelligent debater can take advantage of these mistakes if they are alert for interactions among arguments.

We described six types of interactions among arguments. The first three tend to minimize the impact of your opponent's arguments. These are interactions that render some arguments trivial, irrelevant, or contradictory. The next three ways in which arguments interact maximize your own position. These interactions include identifying complementary arguments, relying on independent claims, and repeating critical arguments.

By understanding these interactions, you should be able to approach debates with a sense of strategy. You should develop consistent coherent positions for debating your side of the resolution. The more coordinated your own position is, the greater the chances are that you will persuade the judge to support your position.

Exercises

1. Lab tests reveal that animals exposed to saccharin have higher cancer rates than those not exposed. Nevertheless, people who rely on sugar substitutes reduce their intake of sugar, decreasing the chances that they will suffer from heart attacks due to obesity. Do a cost-benefit assessment of choosing to rely on saccharin. Should you use the sugar substitute? Use probability, time frame, and impact assessments to reach your final conclusion.

2. Some commentators argue that boxing should be banned because it can lead to severe head injuries for the participants. Imagine that you are advocating the continuation of boxing as a national sport. Can you trivialize the previous objection? Use probability, time frame, and impact arguments to reduce the relevance of the objection to the debate.

3. Examine the editorial page of your local newspaper. Find examples of problems that commentators say we are on the brink or threshold of experiencing. Then look for examples of problems that are described as having linear risks. Is either type of argument more persuasive? Why?

4. Suppose you are advocating a ban on the use of assault weapons by nonmilitary personnel. Your opponent defends a nationwide one-week waiting period for the purchase of all weapons and then argues that your plan would violate the citizenry's right to bear arms. Can you trivialize your opponent's arguments? Can you make them irrelevant? Do they contradict? Without researching the arguments, how can you minimize the impact of your opponent's arguments?

5. Suppose you are advocating a plan that would require all attorneys to defend clients too poor to afford legal representation for one third of their billable hours. Your opponent argues that most attorneys have little interest in helping indigent defendants and supports a simple expansion in the recruitment of public defenders. Can you trivialize your opponent's arguments? Can you make them irrelevant? Do they contradict? Without researching the arguments, how can you minimize the impact of your opponent's arguments.

6. Identify three independent reasons for increasing resources for the drug war. Is their any overlap among your claims? Could the opposition think of any way to link your reasons together? How would you respond to keep the arguments independent?

8

Roles of the Speaker

Chapter Outline

First Affirmative Constructive
   Traditional Need
   Comparative Advantage
   Goals Criteria
   The Plan
   Language and Transitions
First Negative Constructive
   Introduce the Negative Position
   Refute First Affirmative Arguments
   Construct Abbreviated Plan Attacks and
      Topicality Arguments
Second Affirmative Constructive
   Rebuild the Affirmative Case
   Answer the First Negative Arguments
   Construct Additional Advantages
   Preempt Second Negative Attacks
Second Negative Constructive
   Extend the Negative Position
   Construct New Plan Attacks or Case Attacks
   Answer Affirmative Responses to Critical
      Negative Attacks
   Respond to Added Advantages
First Negative Rebuttal
   Extend Attacks Against the General Lines of
      Argument
   Focus the Debate on Issues the Negative Is
      Winning
   Aid the Second Negative in Coverage of
      Important Arguments

Key Terms

construction
concession
refutation
repetition
extension
prima facie case
traditional need
comparative advantage
goals criterion
plan
transition
negative position
add-on
negative block
grouping arguments

In every debate, certain expectations govern how the debate will proceed. There are many different formats for debate, but in policy debate two teams, each composed of two individuals, debate each other. An affirmative team must defend the resolution and a negative team must deny the resolution. Each individual debater must give two speeches: one constructive speech and one rebuttal speech. Conventional debate practices specify the order and time limits for these speeches. Unless indicated otherwise (classroom time limits frequently require adjustments), the order and length of the speeches is as follows.

	Time Limits	
	High School	*College*
First Affirmative Constructive	8 minutes	9 minutes
First Negative Constructive	8 minutes	9 minutes
Second Affirmative Constructive	8 minutes	9 minutes
Second Negative Constructive	8 minutes	9 minutes
First Negative Rebuttal	5 minutes	6 minutes
First Affirmative Rebuttal	5 minutes	6 minutes
Second Negative Rebuttal	5 minutes	6 minutes
Second Affirmative Rebuttal	5 minutes	6 minutes

By ordering the speeches in this manner, the affirmative team has the first and last opportunity to present its case to the judge. This structure provides competitive fairness, given that the affirmative team has the burden of proving that the resolution should be affirmed.

What distinguishes the eight speeches from each other in a debate is the combination of argumentative strategies available to you. In the most general sense, you have five options in a debate. You can construct arguments, concede arguments, refute arguments, repeat arguments, and extend arguments. Each speech in the debate is made up of a particular combination of these strategies, with some speeches requiring certain arguments and other speeches prohibiting certain arguments.

Construction involves the initiation of new claims in a debate. Both affirmative and negative debaters have an opportunity to present the arguments that they feel will win them the debate. Construction of an argument should involve a label specifying the argument, some supporting evidence to sustain the claim, and some reasoning to explain the importance of the argument within the entire debate.

Concession is failure by a member of either team to answer opposing arguments. If you fail to respond to an argument, you "drop," or concede, the argument. Sometimes, debaters concede arguments intentionally. As the previous chapter on analyzing the interaction among arguments indicated, conceding one argument can allow a team to capitalize on other arguments in the debate. At other times, debaters will concede arguments unintentionally. They may forget that the original argument existed or they may simply not have time to respond. Regardless of the reason for conceding the argument, the other team always wins the argument and can use the claim to whatever benefit they choose.

You may also respond to an argument by refuting the argument directly. **Refutation** is the process of denying the reasoning of an opponent's argument. We have explained how to analyze the validity of evidentiary support for an argument (see Chapter Five, of the core text). We have also described how to analyze the reasoning of particular claims (see Chapter Six of the core text). Finally, we have described several lines of argument for refuting the general lines of argument for policy debate (see Chapters Two through Five of this text). Refutation is an attempt to disprove your opponent's claim through these methods.

At times, debaters choose to use **repetition** of arguments previously made in a debate. If one team concedes an argument, for example, a debater from the other team might repeat the original argument and explain why winning this argument would help win the debate. Repetition of the label of an argument can alert the debate judge to which argument is under discussion. At times, however, repetition can be harmful to a debater. If a debater's opponent responds to an original argument, repetition of that argument would be equivalent to conceding the point. Debaters should not confuse repetition of an argument with answering objections offered by the opponent.

When you answer your opponent's response, you should extend your argument rather than repeat your initial argument. **Extension** elaborates on the original point by either directly clashing with arguments against the original point or by expanding the scope of the original argument.

An example will help illustrate the difference between repetition and extension in a debate. Greg might argue that drugs are harmful in the workplace. Tabitha, Greg's opponent, might respond that the harms of drugs are exaggerated because of the drug war mentality. If Greg merely repeats that drugs are harmful in the workplace, he would concede the argument to Tabitha. Yes, drugs might be harmful but those harms are greatly exaggerated. Greg could choose to extend the argument by indicating that drug harms are underestimated. Because drugs are illegal, individuals are unlikely to report drug use. Therefore, drug use is underreported. In this way, Greg extends the original argument, that drug use is harmful, by blunting Tabitha's attack, that drug use is exaggerated.

Greg can also extend the argument by elaborating on the original argument. By specifying how drugs are harmful, he could strengthen the argument that drugs are harmful. He could argue that accidents increase and productivity decreases when drugs are used in the workplace. Note, however, that Greg would still have to respond to Tabitha's argument that drug use is exaggerated. Without additional materials supporting the accuracy of the information on harm, Greg's efforts to specify problems would also be vulnerable to a claim of exaggeration. Merely repeating the original argument that drugs are harmful does not help Greg's position since Tabitha has answered the more general argument already.

We will examine how the five argumentative strategies—construction, concession, refutation, repetition, and extension—interact within each speech of the debate. In the discussion of each speech, you should become acquainted with the conventions and options for structuring your arguments.

First Affirmative Constructive

The first affirmative constructive is limited to the argumentative strategy of construction. Absent any other arguments in the debate, the first affirmative constructive must initiate entirely new arguments throughout the speech. This speech attempts to construct a **prima facie case,** that is, one that on its face presents a reasoned argument for the resolution. To structure a prima facie case, the affirmative should present the four general lines of policy debate: significance, inherency, solvency, and topicality. Ordinarily, topicality arguments can be implicit, with the proposed plan serving as an operational definition of the resolution. With the other three lines of argument, the affirmative must provide supporting evidence and reasoning to prove the need to adopt the resolution. The strategies for initiating and supporting these lines of argument have been fully discussed in earlier chapters of this volume and in your core text.

Strategically, the affirmative has numerous options for constructing the affirmative case. As Chapter Seven on analyzing interactions among arguments indicated, inclusion of certain arguments can encourage your opponent to present contradictory, irrelevant, or trivial arguments in the debate. When constructing a first affirmative speech, you should consider how you want the debate to conclude. The decision to include or exclude a given argument at this stage can improve or diminish your chances of winning the debate.

To organize the affirmative case into a persuasive case for change, the first affirmative constructive should arrange the lines of argument carefully. The affirmative team can choose how best to present the material by familiarizing themselves with the following organizational options, noting their strengths and weaknesses for the topic of the case. Then they should choose the alternative that emphasizes their strengths and minimizes their weaknesses.

Traditional Need

With a **traditional need** case, the affirmative presents a significant problem, shows why that problem will continue to exist, and demonstrates how their proposal will eliminate the problem. The affirmative debaters who use this structure frequently imply that the resolution can eradicate the significant problem that exists in the present system. An outline of a first affirmative constructive relying on the traditional need format might look like this.

I. Drugs in the workplace are harmful.
  A. Drugs cause accidents.
  B. Drugs diminish productivity.
II. In the present system, labor unions oppose mandatory drug-testing in the workplace.
   (Plan for mandating drug tests of federal employees)
III. The affirmative's plan of mandatory drug-testing would be beneficial.
  A. Drug tests would eliminate workplace drug use.

B. Eliminating drug use would remove drug-related accidents.

C. Eliminating drug use would increase worker productivity.

Looking at this particular case outline, affirmative debaters might question whether they could persuasively argue that drug tests would completely eliminate drug use in the workplace. To alleviate this problem, they might choose the second method of organizing their case structures.

Comparative Advantage

Like the traditional needs case, the four general lines of policy argument are present in the comparative advantage organizational pattern. The debater using the **comparative advantage** structure usually recognizes that the present system may be making some attempt to solve the problem but claims the affirmative proposal would offer a comparatively better approach to the problem. The drug-testing case in the comparative advantage format might look like this.

Observation I: Labor unions oppose mandatory drug-testing of federal employees.

(Plan specifying mandatory drug tests for federal workers)

Advantage I: Improved safety in the workplace

A. Drugs in the workplace cause accidents.

B. Drug tests would reduce workplace drug usage, thereby decreasing accidents.

Advantage II: Improved productivity in the workplace

A. Drugs in the workplace reduce productivity.

B. Drug tests would enhance worker productivity.

In this structure, the affirmative has specified two separate advantages for adopting a drug-testing policy. The inherency appears in an overview because labor unions are the obstacle blocking each advantage. To avoid repetition within each advantage, this affirmative outline separates the inherency from the advantage structure. This step is not essential to the comparative advantage structure. You should note that the affirmative could establish significance and solvency by winning either the safety or the productivity advantage.

Multiple advantages are commonplace in comparative advantage structures because they maximize the different options the affirmative has for meeting its burden of proof. Multiple advantages are most effective when they are independent. In the example above, the advantages, though different, are not fully independent. Both specify problems that result from drug use in the workplace. If the negative team can disprove use, then both advantages fall together. Truly independent advantages would stem from different actions proposed by the affirmative or rely on different aspects of solvency. In drug-testing, for example, the affirmative could argue, independent of any direct benefits from reducing drug use, that drug-testing on this scale would provide employment benefits for medical workers involved in the process. These benefits could in turn stimulate the U.S. economy. Such an advantage would be truly independent because it prompts entirely separate lines of argument.

Goals Criteria

With a **goals criterion** structure, the affirmative must show that present institutions are committed in theory to a certain goal, that the goal is a valuable one, that present policies undermine the chance to reach the goal, and that the affirmative proposal will meet the goal. In the solvency portion of the case, the affirmative can claim to meet the goal entirely or merely come closer to the goal than present mechanisms. The drug-testing case in a goals criteria structure might resemble the following.

I. The United States is committed to fighting the drug war.
  A. Fighting the drug war would increase safety in the workplace.
  B. Fighting the drug war would increase productivity in the workplace.
II. Labor union resistance undermines the fight against the drug war. (Plan for mandatory drug-testing of federal employees)
III. Mandatory drug-testing would help win the war on drugs.

Why would an affirmative want to use the goals criteria structure? This structure allows the affirmative to align itself with the presumptively beneficial goals and aspirations of the present system. In so doing, the affirmative can argue that it should gain presumption in the debate. The present system believes the affirmative proposal is pursuing valuable goals. However, something causes the present system to be diverted from achieving such goals. By advocating that they can better achieve the goals of the present system, the affirmative can argue that even advocates of the present system should support the proposal.

The Plan

In addition to structuring the affirmative case, the first affirmative constructive also presents the outline of the affirmative plan. The affirmative supports the resolution by presenting a plan that fulfills the requirements of the resolution. The **plan** includes the specific mandates that will be necessary to justify the resolution, the mechanism to enforce the specific mandates, the funding source for the plan, and a statement that future affirmative speeches will help clarify plan intent. Here is an example of a plan for the drug-testing case.

I. All present and future federal employees will submit to semiannual drug tests. Failure to pass the drug test will result in either treatment or dismissal for the first offense and automatic dismissal for a second offense.

II. The Drug Enforcement Agency will oversee program compliance. Failure to meet with plan mandates will result in fines and/or imprisonment.

III. Funding for the proposal will come from confiscated assets of convicted drug offenders.

IV. Affirmative speeches shall serve to answer any questions of plan intent.

The amount of specificity required in the affirmative plan is up to you. Some debaters would outline the particular drug test to be used. Others would regulate any reapplications for other federal jobs by suspended employees. You can be as specific or general as you choose. With increased specificity, the plan clearly defines the ground on which the negative must debate. With a shorter, more general plan, the affirmative has more flexibility to clarify their intent as the debate progresses.

The rationale for increased specificity is that affirmative debaters are best served by a plan that clearly defines the ground in which the negative must debate. For example, in the plan above the affirmative specifies that the plan is funded though assets confiscated from drug offenders. The affirmative plan is attempting to prevent a potential disadvantage or solvency argument indicating that funding for the plan would be unavailable or available only by sacrificing funding of a more desirable program.

The rationale for a shorter, more general plan is that it allows affirmative debaters to reveal their intent as the debate proceeds. While the plan does specify how frequently the drug test will be given (semiannually), it does not specify the type of drug test that will be used. If the affirmative specified the type of drug-screening test, the negative might point out disadvantages or solvency problems with the particular test. The affirmative does not specify the test to be used in order to retain some flexibility in answering solvency arguments and disadvantages.

Regardless of whether they choose to use a general or more specific plan, most debaters include funding and enforcement provisions. These guidelines are usually considered integral to the course of action specified by the resolution, whether or not the wording of the resolution explicitly calls for them. In many plans debaters mandate that their funding will come from the general revenues of the federal government. Other plans call for a reduction of the defense budget, a tax on luxury items, cuts in wasteful government spending, or taxes on gasoline. Debaters can choose whatever funding mechanism they desire, but they should be prepared to debate the consequences of their choice.

Plan enforcement usually involves penalties such as fines or imprisonment for a failure to comply with plan mandates. A common phrase is that penalties will result from "mis-, mal-, or nonfeasance." This language helps prevent debates about creative circumvention arguments that depend solely on skirting the letter of the plan mandates. Debaters should keep in mind that if the enforcement mechanism is too severe, they risk accusations of violating the cruel and unusual punishment provision of the Constitution. Further, they may face specific

PLANS

Some affirmative plans are highly specific. They are tailored to a specific program and have highly specific plans. Others are very general and attempt to retain flexibility for the affirmative.

In the final round of the 1988 National Debate Tournament, Shawn Martin of Dartmouth College offered a highly specific proposal terminating nuclear submarine sales to Canada. In the 1989 final round, Andrew Schrank of the University of Michigan offered a very elaborate but nonetheless general plan increasing population control services to African nations.

Specific Plan

The sale of nuclear powered submarines to Canada will not be allowed. This will be done through denial of technology, use of technical safeguard agreements, and appropriate diplomatic measures with emphasis on incentives under the Defense Production Sharing Agreement of 1959 and other U.S.–Canadian defense procurement pacts. Enforcement and funding [will be] through normal means. Affirmative speeches will clarify what we mean.

General Plan

We offer the following plan to be adopted through normal means. The United States will resume funding of agencies that allow abortions, specifically the IPPF and UNFPA, in a manner consistent with previous guidelines. The United States will increase support for African family planning and education programs in order to provide reasonable access to birth control. Programs will educate men and women in basic family planning and related health practices. Programs will utilize community-based outreach systems. The United States will monitor and oversee programs, and support for population control will be banned. Any necessary funding to be reallocated from existing development aid to Africa outside the Egypt project [will come] from within existing agency budgets. Enforcement [will be] through normal means. Relevant actors abroad, including the French, African Muslims, and Soviets shall be first consulted with an open mind toward their noncoercive suggestions or contributions. Speeches shall serve as intent.

evidence that judges will not find defendants guilty if the penalty is too harsh. As with the funding mechanism, the enforcement provision can vary depending on how the debaters feel their plan would best be implemented.

One final component of most plans is the intent plank. The intent plank reserves for the affirmative team the right to clarify vague portions of the plan. Like legislative history which helps the courts interpret the intent of Congress in passing a law, the intent plank suggests that the debate as presented by the affirmative should serve as the legislative history for the affirmative plan. Common phrasings of the intent plank include "Affirmative speeches will serve to answer questions of plan intent" or "Affirmative speeches will serve as legislative history to answer questions of plan intent." If affirmative debaters fail to include this plank, negative debaters may attempt to capitalize by redefining and potentially distorting the meaning of the plan away from what the affirmative intends.

Language and Transitions

Having the outline of the affirmative case and plan in mind, you are ready to write the first affirmative constructive. Unlike the other speeches in the debate that are given extemporaneously, the first affirmative constructive is written out word for word. As a manuscripted speech, it offers you an opportunity to present an eloquent, persuasive speech. If you word the speech precisely and persuasively, you can make a strong impression on the judge.

In wording the speech, use the most powerful language possible. Phrases that convey precise meaning are essential. Efficient use of language ensures that your points are made in the least amount of time. Because all of the speeches in a debate are timed speeches, you should attempt to use your time as efficiently as possible. The first affirmative constructive speech provides you with an excellent opportunity to present your arguments clearly and forcefully. You should use the strategies for effective delivery discussed in Chapter Seven of the core text.

Transitions are an often overlooked aspect of first affirmative constructives. **Transitions** are words or phrases that provide a logical bridge from one argument to the next, from one piece of evidence to the next, and from one argument to a piece of supporting evidence. In many weak speeches, they are included as afterthoughts, if at all. Proper transitions should (1) preview upcoming arguments or claims made in the context of supporting material, (2) connect one idea to another by indicating the speech's organizational structure, and (3) show the importance of an argument or evidentiary claim within the overall persuasive case for change. Strong transitions can present a coherent picture to a judge struggling to make sense of a myriad of arguments and evidenced claims. On a purely strategic level, they also give the judge time to take notes successfully on the arguments presented in the affirmative case.

A properly argued, strategically constructed, and well-worded first affirmative constructive can be invaluable to affirmative debaters. A strong speech can provide a reference point for all the subsequent arguments in the debate. The

First Affirmative Constructive

I. Drugs in the workplace are harmful.
   A. Drugs cause accidents.
   B. Drugs diminish productivity.

II. In the present system, labor unions oppose mandatory drug-testing in the workplace.
   (Plan for mandating drug tests of federal employees.)

III. Mandatory drug-testing is beneficial.
   A. Drug tests would eliminate workplace drug use.
   B. Eliminating drug use would remove drug-related accidents.
   C. Eliminating drug use would increase worker productivity.

Figure 8.1 Case Flowsheet after First Affirmative Constructive

speech should enable the affirmative debater to preempt some of the likely attacks by the negative and should leave no doubt that the case meets the prima facie burdens of significance, inherency, solvency, and topicality. If the speech accomplishes these goals, it will make a persuasive case for affirming the resolution.

First Negative Constructive

Like the first affirmative constructive, the first negative constructive presents new arguments in the debate. As the first speech representing the position opposed to the resolution, the first negative constructive introduces many of the arguments that makeup the negative attack. But unlike the first affirmative constructive, the first negative constructive can also concede and refute arguments in the debate. If part of the first affirmative constructive is blatantly true, the first negative may choose not to waste time arguing the point. The first negative may also have strategic reasons for conceding parts of the first affirmative constructive. (Debaters should refer to Chapter Seven of this text to identify parts of the first affirmative that are likely to create tensions with other arguments in the debate). The first negative constructive will want to refute the remaining claims of the first affirmative constructive to prevent them from becoming winning arguments for the affirmative.

To illuminate the first negative constructive, let's return to our first affirmative constructive on drug testing. This sample debate demonstrates the three conventional responsibilities of the first negative constructive.

Introduce the Negative Position

A **negative position** statement is an overview of all the negative arguments in the debate and establishes the ties between them. If the negative's plan of attack is consistent and well considered, some theme should emerge as the guiding philosophy of all negative arguments. In the debate on drug-testing, Tabitha says in the negative position statement that "all individuals should not have to pay for the crimes of a few people." This position clearly encompasses the other negative arguments presented. Claiming that the harm is exaggerated highlights the small number of citizens causing the problem. By advocating employee firings for substandard work performance, the negative lays the blame for the problem on the guilty individuals. The problem of drug user circumvention indicates that only the innocent will pay under the proposed policy. The disadvantages explore how the innocent will have to pay monetarily and with infringements on their civil rights.

A good position statement not only encompasses all of the negative arguments. It also magnifies the impact of arguments beyond what they would have been if they had been considered separately. In this case, the negative presents the judge with a choice: either support a policy that makes innocent people pay for the crimes of a few or let employers handle the problem by punishing those

First Affirmative Constructive	First Negative Constructive
	All individuals should not have to pay for the crimes of a few persons.
I. Drugs in the workplace are harmful. A. Drugs cause accidents. B. Drugs diminish productivity.	1. Harms from the drug war are exaggerated because of the drug war mentality.
II. In the present system, labor unions oppose mandatory drug-testing in the workplace. (Plan for mandating drug tests of federal employees.)	1. Employers can fire individuals that have low productivity or produce large number of accidents.
III. Mandatory drug-testing is beneficial. A. Drug tests would eliminate workplace drug use. B. Eliminating drug use would remove drug-related accidents. C. Eliminating drug use would increase worker productivity.	1. Drug users will subvert tests.

Figure 8.2 Case Flowsheet after First Negative Constructive

guilty of drug abuse. The negative, in this instance, does not have to win each separate argument, but each argument that the negative does win heightens the rationale for staying with present policies.

Refute First Affirmative Arguments

The first negative constructive should initiate arguments undermining the affirmative's significance, inherency, solvency, and topicality. (See Chapters Two through Six of this text for arguments that deny these four general lines of argument). You can choose to attack the argument, the evidence used to support the argument, or both. While an attack on each line of argument is not essential, the first negative constructive has the option of initiating arguments against each one. If you are not certain where the affirmative's case is weak, you may want to attack all parts of the case to ensure some options later in the debate. In the debate between Greg and Tabitha, Tabitha refutes the significance claim by indicating that the harms are exaggerated, refutes the inherency claim by defending the present system's firing of employees for poor performance, and refutes solvency by showing that drug addicts will circumvent the tests.

The first negative needs to remember that concession is also an option when attacking the affirmative case. The negative only has to win one of the four general lines of argument to win the debate. Consequently, it may be to your advantage to have the first negative constructive concede affirmative claims that are unwinnable, claims that force you into contradictions with other arguments in the debate, or claims that, if conceded, will enhance some or all of your arguments in the debate.

Construct Abbreviated Plan Attacks and Topicality Arguments

Up until a few years ago, the first negative constructive rarely mentioned arguments stemming from the plan. Recently, the advantage of prompting the affirmative's responses to plan attacks early in the debate have resulted in many first negatives to initiate shortened versions of these arguments. The abbreviated form is necessary because the first negative constructive has so many other important responsibilities in the debate. The abbreviated form of a disadvantage consists of a quick explanation for why the plan causes the disadvantage to occur, a reason why the plan uniquely causes the disadvantage, and a statement of the impact of the argument. Tabitha presents two disadvantages in the debate with Greg: that mandatory drug-testing will violate the privacy rights of individuals and that it will be costly.

The reasons negatives may choose to develop short versions of topicality arguments are the same reasons they may choose to develop shortened versions of plan attacks. The time pressure produced by the other responsibilities of the first negative and the need to elicit affirmative responses to topicality arguments are good reasons to place a shortened version of a topicality argument in the first negative constructive. The abbreviated topicality argument should include the

First Affirmative Constructive	First Negative Constructive
	Disadvantages: I. Drug tests violate privacy.
	II. Drug tests are costly.

Figure 8.3 Plan Flowsheet after First Negative Constructive

violation of topicality committed by the affirmative, an alternative definition of terms offered by the negative, the standard for determining if a legitimate violation exists, and the impact of the topicality argument.

By the end of the first negative constructive, the bulk of the negative's arguments should be constructed, at least in an abbreviated form. A strategic first negative presents a coherent structure that will ultimately provide a frame for assessing all the arguments in the debate.

Second Affirmative Constructive

The second affirmative constructive is the first speech in the debate that can take advantage of all five strategies for argument. The second affirmative constructive constructs new arguments that will enhance the affirmative's position in the debate, concedes negative arguments that are true or that prompt contradiction, refutes arguments that might be threatening to the affirmative position, extends original arguments to bypass the negative attack, and repeats arguments unanswered by the first negative.

Rebuild the Affirmative Case

From the first sentences of the second affirmative constructive, you must present a strong overall reason for asking the judge to affirm the resolution. Usually this involves responding to the negative's position statement, perhaps turning it to the affirmative's advantage. In the debate between Greg and Tabitha, Greg points out that while only a few individuals use drugs in the workplace, everyone suffers from the accidents and low productivity of those who do. A united effort, then, is needed to stamp out this threat in the workplace. The second affirmative constructive needs a simple statement or two to rebuild the rationale for the affirmative case. This opening statement should place the affirmative on the offensive from the beginning of the speech.

Answer the First Negative Arguments

The second affirmative constructive is responsible for answering each argument presented in the first negative constructive. The second affirmative can choose to extend, refute, or concede an argument, but failure to respond will result in the negative winning a particular argument.

Greg extends the significance, inherency, and solvency arguments outlined in the first affirmative constructive in response to the first negative refutation of these arguments. He responds to the negative claim that drug use is exaggerated by indicating why it is more likely to be underestimated: many drug-using employees are not tested. Greg responds to Tabitha's claim that employers can fire employees whose performance suffers due to drug use: employers cannot fire subpar employees because many of them have established seniority and many are veterans of military service. He agrees that drug addicts may be able to

First Affirmative Constructive	First Negative Constructive	Second Affirmative Constructive
	All individuals should not have to pay for the crimes of a few persons.	Drug using employees endanger all citizens, so all should pay.
I. Drugs in the workplace are harmful. A. Drugs cause accidents. B. Drugs diminish productivity.	1. Harms from the drug war are exaggerated because of the drug war mentality.	1. Numbers are underestimated because drug tests have not been performed on all employees.
II. In the present system, labor unions oppose mandatory drug-testing in the workplace. (Plan for mandating drug tests of federal employees.)	1. Employers can fire individuals that have low productivity or produce large number of accidents.	1. Seniority or veteran status protects weak employees from firing.
III. Mandatory drug-testing is beneficial. A. Drug tests would eliminate workplace drug use. B. Eliminating drug use would remove drug-related accidents. C. Eliminating drug use would increase worker productivity.	1. Drug users will subvert tests.	1. Test used by this plan is ninety percent accurate.

Figure 8.4 Case Flowsheet after Second Affirmative Constructive

First Affirmative Constructive	First Negative Constructive	Second Affirmative Constructive
	Disadvantages: I. Drug tests violate privacy.	1. People have a choice to go to nonfederal jobs.
		2. Results from the test will be confidential.
	II. Drug tests are costly.	1. Increased productivity will offset the cost of the plan.
		2. Money diverted from confiscated property of drug users will fund plan.
		Add-on: Affirmative plan reduces crime. I. Drug-testing will decrease drug users.
		II. Drug costs cause crime.

Figure 8.5 Plan Flowsheet after Second Affirmative Constructive

circumvent some drug tests but extends the affirmative solvency argument by pointing out that the test used in the affirmative plan has a ninety percent success rate.

Greg also refutes the disadvantages constructed in the first negative speech. He argues that the right of the individual to privacy will be acknowledged because people can choose other jobs or take the federal job and be assured that their test results will remain confidential. The costs of the plan will be offset by productivity gains from workers who are not on drugs and by profits from selling confiscated property of drug dealers.

In all the examples from the debate between Greg and Tabitha, the attacks by both the affirmative and negative debaters have focused on the claims offered by both sides. Debaters should also feel free to attack the evidence used to support the claims in a debate. (For lines of argument useful for refuting evidence, see Chapter Five of the core text.)

When refuting each argument presented by the first negative and extending important arguments offered by the first affirmative, you should work within the organizational framework of the first affirmative constructive. If you merely answer the first negative attack with no reference to the first affirmative constructive, the result would be a defensive speech that would leave the impression that the affirmative is on the run. Instead, you should repeat the label of each first affirmative contention and paraphrase the original, supporting evidence. Only then should the second affirmative constructive quickly refer to the negative's arguments related to the point and offer the affirmative response. By using this approach, you will be reminded of arguments dropped by the negative team and of possible answers to the negative arguments incorporated into the structure of the first affirmative constructive. No less important, your judge will be reminded as well.

Construct Additional Advantages

The second affirmative constructive has the option to present additional reasoning for why the judge should affirm the resolution. Because this speech is the last opportunity the affirmative will have to construct new arguments, the second affirmative constructive frequently spends some time presenting additional advantages, sometimes called **add-ons** for short. Greg offers one add-on in the debate with Tabitha. Greg maintains that mandatory drug-testing will decrease crime. If drug tests can encourage people not to use drugs, the need to buy drugs is diminished. Crimes committed to obtain money for drugs, therefore, should also decrease.

Preempt Second Negative Attacks

In some debates, negative debaters will save some of the most difficult arguments against the affirmative until the second negative constructive. The reason for this is that the affirmative speaker following the second negative constructive

First Affirmative Constructive	First Negative Constructive	Second Affirmative Constructive	Second Negative Constructive
	All individuals should not have to pay for the crimes of a few persons.	Drug using employees endanger all citizens, so all should pay.	Costs of drug-testing are a risk for some; costs of drug-testing are certain for all.
I. Drugs in the workplace are harmful. A. Drugs cause accidents. B. Drugs diminish productivity.	1. Harms from the drug war are exaggerated because of the drug war mentality.	1. Numbers are underestimated because drug tests have not been performed on all employees.	
II. In the present system, labor unions oppose mandatory drug-testing in the workplace. (Plan for mandating drug tests of federal employees.)	1. Employers can fire individuals that have low productivity or produce large number of accidents.	1. Seniority or veteran status protects weak employees from firing.	
III. Mandatory drug-testing is beneficial. A. Drug tests would eliminate workplace drug use. B. Eliminating drug use would remove drug-related accidents. C. Eliminating drug use would increase worker productivity.	1. Drug users will subvert tests.	1. Test used by this plan is ninety percent accurate.	

Figure 8.6 Case Flowsheet after Second Negative Constructive

has only approximately half the time that the second affirmative has to answer arguments. Knowing this, the second affirmative constructive may want to anticipate arguments that the negative will be making in the debate. Certainly, this strategy has the potential to backfire. You could make several arguments to an anticipated negative attack, and the negative could choose not to initiate the argument. Nevertheless, if the affirmative has a weakness that takes time to explain away, the second affirmative constructive may choose to preempt negative argumentation.

Second Negative Constructive

The second negative constructive is the only other speech in the debate in which the speaker can use all five argument development strategies. The second negative constructive is the last opportunity that the negative has to initiate new arguments. The speaker can concede, repeat, or extend arguments in the debate as they benefit the negative team. The second negative constructive should not attempt to answer all affirmative arguments in the debate. The reason for this is **the negative block**. At this point in the debate, the negative has two speeches in a row, the second negative constructive and the first negative rebuttal. If the second negative constructive attempts to answer all the arguments in the debate, the first negative rebuttal will be wasted. Strategically, the negative speakers should divide the affirmative arguments in the debate to maximize the number and quality of responses they can provide.

In our debate, Tabitha chooses to refute the add-on presented in the second affirmative constructive and the two disadvantages, leaving arguments related to the four general lines of argument to the first negative rebuttal. When structuring the second negative constructive, the speaker should consider four responsibilities.

Extend the Negative Position

Like the other speakers in the debate, the second negative constructive wants to start on the offensive. Coordinating with the first negative constructive's position statement, the second negative constructive can extend the negative's philosophy for how they plan to resolve the issues in the debate. In this debate, Tabitha extends the original position statement arguing that law-abiding citizens should not have to pay for the crimes of the few. She reconstructs the position to offer a way of weighing the arguments in the debate. She argues that while there is a risk that an individual will be affected by drugs in workplace, all individuals will bear the costs of mandatory drug-testing. Juxtaposing a certain cost against a potential one frames the negative arguments in the debate as the superior position.

Construct New Plan Attacks or Case Attacks

Ordinarily, the second negative constructive spends the bulk of the speaking time raising objections to the affirmative's plan. These can take the form of

First Negative Constructive	Second Affirmative Constructive	Second Negative Constructive
Disadvantages: I. Drug tests violate privacy.	1. People have a choice to go to nonfederal jobs.	1. Weak economy means few jobs available. 2. Privacy is still violated for those wanting federal jobs.
	2. Results from the test will be confidential.	1. Taking the test itself violates the individual's privacy. Impact: Privacy is the most fundamental right. Concede the cost disadvantage.
II. Drug tests are costly.	1. Increased productivity will offset the cost of the plan. 2. Money diverted from confiscated property of drug users.	
		Disadvantage: court backlog I. People will sue for loss of jobs. II. Overburdened system will collapse.
	Add-on: Affirmative plan reduces crime. I. Drug-testing will decrease drug use.	1. Fired employees will commit more crimes and be more violent.
	II. Drug costs cause crime.	

Figure 8.7 Plan Flowsheet after Second Negative Constructive

plan-meet-needs, plan-meet-advantages, circumvention arguments, or disadvantages. If the first negative constructive is not able or chooses not to respond to an argument that is critical to the affirmative's case, the second negative constructive is the last opportunity the negative has to respond to the point. Therefore, you must be sufficiently flexible to ensure that no major arguments by the affirmative go unanswered as you move into the rebuttal speeches.

In our debate, Tabitha constructs one additional disadvantage: that mandatory drug-testing will lead to a collapse of the criminal court system. Had a threatening affirmative argument remained unanswered, Tabitha would have had to refute the argument in the second negative constructive. She could not allow the argument to remain unanswered going into the rebuttal speeches or it would be too late. New arguments are not permissible in rebuttals. Refutation of previously unanswered arguments is equivalent to presenting a new argument and is therefore illegitimate. You must be certain that you respond to all affirmative constructive positions that were not answered by the first negative constructive by the conclusion of the second negative constructive, or recognize that the affirmative will win the arguments left unanswered.

Answer Affirmative Responses to Critical Negative Attacks

Since the second negative constructive is the longest speech remaining for the negative team, it should extend arguments critical to opposing the resolution. This requires refuting arguments the negative is losing that could cost them the debate or extending arguments that might ultimately win the debate for the negative.

In the debate between Tabitha and Greg, Tabitha responds to the affirmative answers to the two disadvantages presented in the first negative constructive. Tabitha chooses to extend the privacy disadvantage because she believes that is the most important argument for the negative in this specific debate. Determined to win the debate on the argument that drug-testing violates privacy rights, Tabitha refutes each of the affirmative answers to the disadvantage.

Tabitha refutes the affirmative answer that individuals can choose other jobs with two arguments. Choosing another job is not a viable alternative when the economy is weak, and even if the economy were strong, tests would still violate the rights of those individuals wanting to remain federal employees. Tabitha refutes Greg's claim that the results from the tests will remain confidential by indicating that the answer is irrelevant in the debate. The act of imposing the drug test violates the individual's privacy. Tabitha reasons that being forced to take a urine test without probable cause is an undue infringement on an individual's privacy.

In this debate, Tabitha clearly believes that the privacy argument is a potentially winning argument in the debate. As a good second negative constructive speaker, she extends the importance of the argument to the debate. Rather than merely moving on to the next argument, she offers support for the claim that privacy is the most fundamental individual right. By taking this step, Tabitha magnifies the issue in the context of the debate and increases the chances that the negative team will win the debate.

Tabitha also chooses to concede that the plan will be costly. The decision is a good one because the affirmative responses to the argument eliminate its impact. If profits from sales of the property of convicted drug dealers will pay for the plan, what does the cost of the plan matter? The negative, thus, concedes the issue and spends time on issues that they are more likely to win in the debate. You should make concessions when there is little to be gained from refuting or extending the argument. You will lose nothing, and you will gain time to focus on more compelling arguments.

Respond to Added Advantages

Usually, the second negative constructive has the responsibility to answer any additional advantages presented in the second affirmative constructive. Having the time allotted to a constructive speech, the second negative constructive has more time to develop the negative's responses to new advantages. The options available for answering an added advantage are identical to those appropriate for responding to the first affirmative constructive. Is the problem significant? Is it inherent? Will the plan solve the problem? Can the plan topically provide a solution to the problem? Tabitha chooses to turn the added advantage into a disadvantage. Rather than reducing crime, the affirmative plan will actually increase the number and severity of crimes. While out of work, fired employees will commit more crimes. In this way, she argues that the crime is not a significant advantage for the affirmative proposal, but it is a significant disadvantage to the affirmative plan.

Because the second negative constructive is the last constructive speech in the debate, it is your last opportunity to construct new arguments. The debater who delivers the second negative constructive must have a strong overall picture of what is occurring in the debate. Where are new responses needed to ensure a negative victory? Will constructing new negative plan attacks place a larger burden on the affirmative rebuttalists? The second negative should allocate time for presenting arguments in accordance with strategic benefits to the negative team.

First Negative Rebuttal

In the first negative rebuttal, debaters have four options for developing arguments. You can concede, repeat, or refute new arguments presented in the second affirmative constructive; refute extensions from the second affirmative constructive; or extend arguments presented in the first negative constructive. Like all the rebuttalist in the debate, the first negative rebuttalist cannot construct new arguments. New arguments are forbidden in the rebuttal speeches to ensure that the debate remains narrow enough so that the debaters can resolve existing issues. Sometimes the notion of no new arguments in the rebuttal can be confusing to beginning debaters. The key is to distinguish between new arguments and extensions or refutations. If the second affirmative initiates a new argument, the first negative rebuttalist can refute the claim. However, constructing a new plan attack or new case attack against issues introduced in the first affirmative constructive is illegitimate.

Debaters who plan to present the first negative rebuttal should remember that they need to divide the argumentative responsibilities with their partners, who are giving the second negative constructive. The debate will become very confused if both negative debaters attempt to respond to the same arguments. If you have answers that you believe your team should make and those answers respond to arguments being covered by your partner, you should explain your potential responses to your partner. Trust your partner to respond successfully to the designated arguments for the second negative constructive. Keeping the division of labor in mind, the first negative rebuttal has three argumentative responsibilities, as discussed in the following sections.

Extend Attacks Against the General Lines of Argument

The first negative rebuttal attempts to further the original attacks made against the affirmative's claims of significance, inherency, solvency, and topicality. This requires the first negative rebuttalist not only to answer the affirmative responses but to explain why the negative's claims are stronger than the affirmative's claims. As an example, Tabitha would want to extend her argument against Greg's claim of inherency: that employers can fire employees for substandard job performance. Tabitha might undermine the affirmative extension that seniority and veteran status preclude the remedy's effectiveness by showing that drug usage in the workplace tends to occur most frequently in younger employees. As a result, she could argue, employers could still check the majority of employees using drugs in the workplace. In addition to answering the affirmative response, however, Tabitha should indicate the impact of the argument on the debate. She could argue that employers could eliminate the majority of the problem, reducing the significance of the affirmative's problem.

When extending arguments made against the four general lines of argument, the first negative rebuttalist has a number of options. Throughout this volume, we have outlined arguments used to resolve significance, inherency, solvency, and topicality claims (see Chapters Two through Five). Additionally, first negative rebuttalist can indicate why the evidence they use in support of their claims is superior to that of the affirmative (see Chapter Five of the core text).

Focus the Debate on Issues the Negative Is Winning

With only a small amount of time for the rebuttal speech, you want to spend the bulk of your time extending arguments that the negative is winning. As the first negative rebuttalist, you must be able to distinguish between those arguments the negative is losing that are unimportant to the outcome of the debate and those that must be extended for the negative to be able to win the debate.

First Affirmative Constructive	First Negative Constructive	Second Affirmative Constructive	Second Negative Constructive
	All individuals should not have to pay for the crimes of a few persons.	Drug using employees endanger all citizens, so all should pay.	Costs of drug-testing are a risk for some; costs of drug-testing are certain for all.
I. Drugs in the workplace are harmful. A. Drugs cause accidents. B. Drugs diminish productivity.	1. Harms from the drug war are exaggerated because of the drug war mentality.	1. Numbers are underestimated because drug tests have not been performed on all employees.	
II. In the present system, labor unions oppose mandatory drug-testing in the workplace. (Plan for mandating drug tests of federal employees.)	1. Employers can fire individuals that have low productivity or produce large number of accidents.	1. Seniority or veteran status protects weak employees from firing.	
III. Mandatory drug-testing is beneficial. A. Drug tests would eliminate workplace drug use. B. Eliminating drug use would remove drug-related accidents. C. Eliminating drug use would increase worker productivity.	1. Drug users will subvert tests.	1. Test used by this plan is ninety percent accurate.	

Figure 8.8 Case Flowsheet after First Negative Rebuttal

1. Drug users are most
   frequently the
   younger employees
   in the workforce.
2. Employers can
   eliminate most of the
   problem without
   testing.

Figure 8.8 (Cont.)

First Negative Constructive	Second Affirmative Constructive	Second Negative Constructive
Disadvantages: I. Drug tests violate privacy.	1. People have a choice to go to nonfederal jobs.	1. Weak economy means few jobs available. 2. Privacy is still violated for those wanting federal jobs.
	2. Results from the test will be confidential.	1. Taking the test itself violates the individual's privacy. Impact: Privacy is the most fundamental right. Concede the cost disadvantage.
II. Drug tests are costly.	1. Increased productivity will offset the cost of the plan. 2. Money diverted from confiscated property of drug users.	
		Disadvantage: court backlog I. People will sue for loss of jobs. II. Overburdened system will collapse.
	Add-on: Affirmative plan reduces crime. I. Drug-testing will decrease drug use. II. Drug costs cause crime.	1. Fired employees will commit more crimes and be more violent.

Figure 8.9 Plan Flowsheet after First Negative Rebuttal

Recognizing and conceding losing issues that will not cost the negative team the debate is critical for ensuring a successful first negative rebuttal. In the debate between Greg and Tabitha, Tabitha realizes that the negative has no analytical or evidenced responses to the specific test used in the affirmative plan. She cannot answer Greg's extension that the affirmative test is ninety percent accurate. Therefore, she should concede the argument and focus attention on reducing the existence of the problem and advocating employer remedies to seek out those guilty of using drugs in the workplace.

Aid the Second Negative in Coverage of Important Arguments

At times, the second negative constructive will not succeed in initiating all of the negative team's answers to important issues in the debate. When this occurs, the first negative rebuttalist should be willing to help. If the second negative constructive has not had time to respond to the affirmative's add-on about decreased crime, for example, the first negative rebuttalist should use a portion of the speech to make sure that the argument has a sufficient response. Again, the first negative rebuttalist can answer arguments that are presented in the second affirmative constructive even if the second negative constructive does not respond, or drops, the affirmative answers. If the second negative constructive and the first negative rebuttalist fail to respond to an argument, the affirmative will win the issue. Debaters reluctant to view the entire debate as a team effort will lose debates because they do not compensate for each individual debater's weaknesses.

The first negative rebuttalist wants to place as much pressure as possible on the next speaker who must respond to both the second negative constructive and the first negative rebuttal within the time limit of a rebuttal speech. If the first negative rebuttalist can extend, rather than repeat, the original arguments from the first negative constructive, this speaker can play a key role in undermining the affirmative's chances of winning the debate.

First Affirmative Rebuttal

Like the first negative rebuttalist, the first affirmative rebuttalist can concede, refute, repeat, or extend arguments in the debate. But the argumentative responsibilities of the first affirmative rebuttalist are much broader than those of the first negative. The first affirmative rebuttalist must respond to all of the arguments that can win the debate for the negative. To achieve this monumental task, you should identify similar arguments so that they can be answered by their common weakness; this is sometimes referred to as **grouping arguments.** Additionally, you will want to deemphasize unimportant arguments, read little evidence or read efficiently phrased evidence, emphasize word economy, speak more rapidly than other speakers, and minimize the transitions used when moving from point to point. As much as possible, the first affirmative rebuttalist should attend to each of the four points described in the following sections.

First Affirmative Constructive	First Negative Constructive	Second Affirmative Constructive	Second Negative Constructive
	All individuals should not have to pay for the crimes of a few persons.	Drug using employees endanger all citizens, so all should pay.	Costs of drug-testing are a risk for some; costs of drug-testing are certain for all.
I. Drugs in the workplace are harmful. A. Drugs cause accidents. B. Drugs diminish productivity.	1. Harms from the drug war are exaggerated because of the drug war mentality.	1. Numbers are underestimated because drug tests have not been performed on all employees.	
II. In the present system, labor unions oppose mandatory drug-testing in the workplace. (Plan for mandating drug tests of federal employees.)	1. Employers can fire individuals that have low productivity or produce large number of accidents.	1. Seniority or veteran status protects weak employees from firing.	
III. Mandatory drug-testing is beneficial. A. Drug tests would eliminate workplace drug use. B. Eliminating drug use would remove drug-related accidents. C. Eliminating drug use would increase worker productivity.	1. Drug users will subvert tests.	1. Test used by this plan is ninety percent accurate.	

Figure 8.10 Case Flowsheet after First Affirmative Rebuttal

First Negative Rebuttal	First Affirmative Rebuttal
1. Drug users are most frequently the younger employees in the workforce.	1. Even if the numbers of accident and productivity losses are exaggerated, there is still some significant problem.
1. Employers can eliminate most of the problem without testing.	1. Drug tests are necessary to discover all offenders.

Figure 8.10 (Cont.)

First Negative Constructive	Second Affirmative Constructive	Second Negative Constructive
Disadvantages: I. Drug tests violate privacy.	1. People have a choice to go to nonfederal jobs.	1. Weak economy means few jobs available. 2. Privacy is still violated for those wanting federal jobs.
	2. Results from the test will be confidential.	1. Taking the test itself violates the individual's privacy.
		Impact: Privacy is the most fundamental right. Concede the cost disadvantage.
II. Drug tests are costly.	1. Increased productivity will offset the cost of the plan. 2. Money diverted from confiscated property of drug users.	
		Disadvantage: court backlog I. People will sue for loss of jobs.
		II. Overburdened system will collapse.
	Add-on: Affirmative plan reduces crime. I. Drug-testing will decrease drug use.	1. Fired employees will commit more crimes and be more violent.
	II. Drug costs cause crime.	

Figure 8.11 Plan Flowsheet after First Affirmative Rebuttal

First Negative Rebuttal	First Affirmative Rebuttal
	1. Skilled federal employees can get jobs even in weak economic times.
	2. Costs in terms of accidents and productivity losses warrant violation of having to submit to a drug test.
	1. Money from drug confiscations could be used to increase the number of courts and judges.
	2. If firings do increase crime, both the affirmative and negative would cause this effect.

Figure 8.11 (Cont.)

Refute New Arguments Made in the Second Negative Constructive

Since the affirmative has had no prior opportunity to respond to new arguments in the second negative constructive, the first affirmative rebuttalist usually answers these at the beginning of the speech. This speaker can deny the negative's claims, minimize their force in the debate, or turn them into additional reasons for why the affirmative should win the debate.

In the debate between Tabitha and Greg, Tabitha argues a new disadvantage in the second negative constructive. Since this is the first opportunity the affirmative has to respond to the argument, the affirmative can offer new responses to the disadvantage. In response to the court backlog disadvantage, the first affirmative rebuttalist should capitalize on the concessions of the second negative constructive. Earlier, the second negative conceded that the plan would have sufficient revenues to pay for the plan. In the first affirmative rebuttalist Greg argues that profits obtained through the confiscation of drug dealers' property could be used to increase the number of courts and judges. As a result, no collapse of the court system would occur. You should always be looking for ways of using conceded arguments to answer other arguments in the debate.

Extend Answers to Important Negative Arguments

In our debate, Tabitha has argued three arguments to weigh against the advantages of the affirmative proposal: crime, privacy, and court backlog. If the affirmative loses any of these arguments, they stand to lose the debate.

Having refuted the court backlog disadvantage, Greg extends the crime add-on which Tabitha has attempted to turn into a disadvantage resulting from affirmative proposal. He indicates that if firings increase crime, both affirmative and negative policies have this effect. After all, the negative is committed to having employers fire individuals caught using drugs.

Greg also needs to extend the answers to the privacy disadvantage. In response to the privacy issue, he might indicate that skilled federal employees can get other jobs even in weak economic times. The costs in terms of accidents and productivity losses warrant the small violation of having to submit to a drug test. You need to be certain to extend the answers to a disadvantage since the negative frequently relies on the disadvantage to outweigh the affirmative significance.

Extend the General Lines of Argument

In this step, the first affirmative rebuttalist must respond to negative responses to the four general lines of argument. The first affirmative rebuttalist must make sure that by the end of the speech the affirmative is winning its claims of significance, inherency, solvency, and topicality. To do this, the first affirmative rebuttalist must extend some arguments relevant to each of these claims. Concessions may be necessary because of time constraints, but the overall objective of winning each of the lines of argument must be paramount.

Greg might point out that even though the affirmative concedes the number of accidents and extent of productivity losses are exaggerated, the negative has conceded that some of the significant problem still exists. Employers might be able to fire some employees who use drugs at work, but drug tests are necessary to discover all offenders. Given that the negative has already conceded that the affirmative tests will prevent circumvention and that the negative never questioned whether the plan was topical, the first affirmative rebuttalist would be extending each argument necessary to prove the argumentative burdens of the affirmative.

Make Selective Responses to Other Negative Arguments

Once the first affirmative rebuttalist has responded to all new arguments by the second negative constructive and critical case arguments, the speaker can use the remaining time to cover issues less crucial to the ultimate decision in the debate. Additional advantages to affirming the resolution are frequently the choice of the debater with time to spare. In choosing which additional arguments should be extended, you should keep the overall goal of presenting your plan as more cost-beneficial than negative alternatives. What arguments add to the costs of remaining with the present system or other nonresolutional alternatives? What arguments add to the benefits of affirming the resolution?

Second Negative Rebuttal

Like the other rebuttalists in the debate, the second negative rebuttalist can concede, repeat, refute, or extend arguments, but he or she cannot construct new arguments. The second negative constructive is the summary speech that explains why the negative should win the debate. The second negative rebuttalist must provide the judge with a reason to believe that the individual arguments offered by the negative come together to deny the affirmative defense of the resolution.

The second negative rebuttalist must identify the strategic options available in light of the position taken by the first affirmative rebuttalist. What strategic options are available for Tabitha in our debate? Several issues stand out. First, she conceded the cost disadvantage, so that argument is not available. She also has no answer to Greg's argument against the court backlog disadvantage which claims that money diverted from confiscated drug property can fund more judges and courtrooms. Tabitha does, however, believe that the privacy disadvantage has withstood Greg's argumentation. She also believes that much of the affirmative significance is minimized by arguments indicating that drug-related accidents and lost productivity are exaggerated and that employers will fire drug users for poor performance. Believing that the affirmative significance claims are minimized and that the privacy disadvantage overwhelms the remaining

First Affirmative Constructive	First Negative Constructive	Second Affirmative Constructive	Second Negative Constructive
	All individuals should not have to pay for the crimes of a few persons.	Drug using employees endanger all citizens, so all should pay.	Costs of drug-testing are a risk for some; costs of drug-testing are certain for all.
I. Drugs in the workplace are harmful. A. Drugs cause accidents. B. Drugs diminish productivity.	1. Harms from the drug war are exaggerated because of the drug war mentality.	1. Numbers are underestimated because drug tests have not been performed on all employees.	
II. In the present system, labor unions oppose mandatory drug-testing in the workplace. (Plan for mandating drug tests of federal employees.)	1. Employers can fire individuals that have low productivity or produce large number of accidents.	1. Seniority or veteran status protects weak employees from firing.	
III. Mandatory drug-testing is beneficial. A. Drug tests would eliminate workplace drug use. B. Eliminating drug use would remove drug-related accidents. C. Eliminating drug use would increase worker productivity.	1. Drug users will subvert tests.	1. Test used by this plan is ninety percent accurate.	

Figure 8.12 Case Flowsheet after Second Negative Rebuttal

First Negative Rebuttal	First Affirmative Rebuttal	Second Negative Rebuttal	Second Affirmative Rebuttal
		An occasional accident or crime does not justify a loss of privacy for all individuals who consider working for the federal government.	
1. Drug users are most frequently the younger employees in the workforce.	1. Even if the number of accidents and productivity losses are exaggerated, there is still some significant problem.	1. The affirmative has conceded that accidents and productivity losses are exaggerated.	
1. Employers can eliminate most of the problem without testing.	1. Drug tests are necessary to discover all offenders.	1. Employers can fire the bulk of the employees responsible for the actual problems.	

Figure 8.12 (Cont.)

First Negative Constructive	Second Affirmative Constructive	Second Negative Constructive
Disadvantages: I. Drug tests violate privacy.	1. People have a choice to go to nonfederal jobs.	1. Weak economy means few jobs available. 2. Privacy is still violated for those wanting federal jobs.
	2. Results from the test will be confidential.	1. Taking the test itself violates the individual's privacy. Impact: Privacy is the most fundamental right. Concede the cost disadvantage.
II. Drug tests are costly.	1. Increased productivity will offset the cost of the plan. 2. Money diverted from confiscated property of drug users.	
		Disadvantage: court backlog I. People will sue for loss of jobs.
		II. Overburdened system will collapse.
	Add-on: Affirmative plan reduces crime. I. Drug-testing will decrease drug use. II. Drug costs cause crime.	1. Fired employees will commit more crimes and be more violent.

Figure 8.13 Plan Flowsheet after Second Negative Rebuttal

First Negative Rebuttal	First Affirmative Rebuttal	Second Negative Rebuttal
	1. Skilled federal employees can get jobs even in weak economic times. 2. Costs in terms of accidents and productivity losses warrant violation of having to submit to a drug test.	1. Privacy violations could snowball in the future, affecting more individuals. 2. Privacy as the most important issue was conceded by the affirmative; thus a risk of the disadvantage outweighs crime, accidents, or decreased productivity.
	1. Money from drug confiscations could be used to increase the number of courts and judges. 2. If firings do increase crime, both the affirmative and negative would cause this effect.	1. Crime has no impact compared to privacy, any other impact would be a new argument.

Figure 8.13 (Cont.)

Roles of the Speaker   177

significance, Tabitha can make intelligent choices of which arguments to concede, repeat, refute, and extend. The second negative rebuttalist should proceed with the following arguments.

Present the Closing Statement for the Negative

The second negative rebuttalist's opening statement should provide a concise, comprehensive perspective on the arguments in the debate. The statement should encompass the remaining issues in the debate, emphasizing why the judge should negate the resolution. Tabitha, for example, might begin by claiming that an occasional workplace accident or crime should not justify a loss of privacy for all individuals who consider working for the federal government. With such a statement, the second negative rebuttalist attempts to place the remaining arguments in a light that is favorable to the negative team.

Extend the Winning Combination of Arguments for the Negative

To do this, the second negative rebuttalist must strategically determine which set of arguments provides the negative with its best opportunity to win the debate. Then, the debater must refute any affirmative responses to the set of winning arguments. Finally, this speaker must explain why the combination of arguments ensures a negative victory.

In the debate between Greg and Tabitha, the primary reason offered by the negative to oppose drug-testing is the violation of privacy. The court backlog disadvantage is not meeting with success because of concessions made by the negative earlier in the debate. Limited to the privacy disadvantage, the second negative constructive needs to maximize the argument's impact. Tabitha would therefore want to point out that in the second negative constructive she had argued that privacy was the paramount issue. The first affirmative rebuttalist had conceded the point. Privacy, then, should outweigh any loss of productivity, any amount of crime, or any number of accidents in the workplace.

Minimize Winning Affirmative Arguments

The second negative rebuttalist is attempting to convince the judge through a cost-benefit analysis that the resolution should not be affirmed. Having maximized the impact of the negative arguments, the next step is to minimize the claims of the opposition. Tabitha would want to point out the affirmative had conceded that the number of accidents and the loss of productivity has been exaggerated. Employers would be able to fire the bulk of those responsible for any remaining problem.

These three tasks produce arguments that look very much like one another, but they have distinct roles to play nonetheless. The closing statement provides a context in which to understand the basic negative arguments. In this respect, it is very similar to the negative position statement that opened the first negative constructive. The closing statement reframes the issues in terms of the arguments that have taken place in the five intervening speeches. By extending and selecting a winning combination of arguments, the second negative rebuttalist proves the value of the position articulated in the closing statement. This is the time in the speech when the rebuttalist is most specific about individual arguments, their importance, and the inadequacy of affirmative responses. By minimizing the affirmative's remaining issues, the second negative rebuttalist covers the last base, showing that, even if a judge is leaning toward the affirmative on some issues, those considerations are minor and should not weigh against a negative decision.

Anticipate and Refute Second Affirmative Rebuttal Responses

The second negative rebuttalist must remember that the final affirmative speaker can respond to any claims made in the second negative rebuttal. Therefore, the second negative should anticipate how the affirmative will attempt to win the debate and accordingly extend arguments that answer the affirmative position and refute arguments that could enhance its position.

Looking at the entire debate between Tabitha and Greg, Tabitha can probably anticipate that Greg will be arguing that the crimes that can be prevented by drug-testing should outweigh the privacy disadvantage. Since the negative's defense of employee firings ultimately increases crime, the focus by the second affirmative rebuttalist is predictable. How could crime outweigh privacy? The second affirmative rebuttalist could argue that crime violates a citizen's privacy too. The second negative rebuttalist could preempt this argument by saying that such a claim would be a new argument which would not give the negative an opportunity to respond. Crime could affect more individuals than privacy. The second negative rebuttalist could preempt this argument by showing that erosions of privacy snowball so that future attempts to undermine privacy would likely increase. The result would be a decrease in privacy for all citizens. The second negative rebuttalist could maintain that these arguments are extensions of the claim that privacy is the most fundamental right; that is, they are merely the reasons why privacy is so fundamental.

Second Affirmative Rebuttal

The second affirmative rebuttal is the mirror speech to the second negative rebuttal. Like the previous speakers, the second affirmative rebuttalist has the option to concede arguments, to repeat arguments, to refute arguments, and to extend arguments. The second affirmative rebuttalist cannot initiate or construct new arguments in the debate. Having the opportunity to give the last speech in the debate, the second affirmative rebuttalist should present the strongest summary possible for why the affirmative is winning the debate.

How can Greg determine the strongest possible affirmative position in our debate? First, he must remember that he has to win the four general lines of argument. The negative has conceded solvency and never challenged the topicality

First Affirmative Constructive	First Negative Constructive	Second Affirmative Constructive	Second Negative Constructive
	All individuals should not have to pay for the crimes of a few persons.	Drug using employees endanger all citizens, so all should pay.	Costs of drug-testing are a risk for some; costs of drug-testing are certain for all.
I. Drugs in the workplace are harmful. A. Drugs cause accidents. B. Drugs diminish productivity.	1. Harms from the drug war are exaggerated because of the drug war mentality.	1. Numbers are underestimated because drug tests have not been performed on all employees.	
II. In the present system, labor unions oppose mandatory drug-testing in the workplace. (Plan for mandating drug tests of federal employees.)	1. Employers can fire individuals that have low productivity or produce large number of accidents.	1. Seniority or veteran status protects weak employees from firing.	
III. Mandatory drug-testing is beneficial. A. Drug tests would eliminate workplace drug use. B. Eliminating drug use would remove drug-related accidents. C. Eliminating drug use would increase worker productivity.	1. Drug users will subvert tests.	1. Test used by this plan is ninety percent accurate.	

Figure 8.14 Case Flowsheet after Second Affirmative Rebuttal

First Negative Rebuttal	First Affirmative Rebuttal	Second Negative Rebuttal	Second Affirmative Rebuttal
		An occasional accident or crime does not justify a loss of privacy for all individuals who consider working for the federal government.	The nation allows small violations of privacy on a regular basis to protect the citizenry's safety. Search warrants would never be issued if privacy truly outweighed citizen safety.
1. Drug users are most frequently the younger employees in the workforce.	1. Even if the number of accidents and productivity losses are exaggerated, there is still some significant problem.	1. The affirmative has conceded that accidents and productivity losses are exaggerated.	1. Significant problems will continue unless drug-testing is implemented. Only the affirmative policy will solve crime, accidents, and losses in productivity.
1. Employers can eliminate most of the problem without testing.	1. Drug tests are necessary to discover all offenders.	1. Employers can fire the bulk of the employees responsible for the actual problems.	

Figure 8.14 (Cont.)

First Negative Constructive	Second Affirmative Constructive	Second Negative Constructive
Disadvantages: I. Drug tests violate privacy.	1. People have a choice to go to nonfederal jobs.	1. Weak economy means few jobs available. 2. Privacy is still violated for those wanting federal jobs.
	2. Results from the test will be confidential.	1. Taking the test itself violates the individual's privacy. Impact: Privacy is the most fundamental right. Concede the cost disadvantage.
II. Drug tests are costly.	1. Increased productivity will offset the cost of the plan. 2. Money diverted from confiscated property of drug users.	
		Disadvantage: court backlog I. People will sue for loss of jobs.
		II. Overburdened system will collapse.
	Add-on: Affirmative plan reduces crime. I. Drug-testing will decrease drug use. II. Drug costs cause crime.	1. Fired employees will commit more crimes and be more violent.

Figure 8.15 Plan Flowsheet after Second Affirmative Rebuttal

First Negative Rebuttal	First Affirmative Rebuttal	Second Negative Rebuttal	Second Affirmative Rebuttal
	1. Skilled federal employees can get jobs even in weak economic times. 2. Costs in terms of accidents and productivity losses warrant violation of having to submit to a drug test.	1. Privacy violations could snowball in the future, affecting more individuals. 2. Privacy as the most important issue was conceded by the affirmative; thus a risk of the disadvantage outweighs crime, accidents, or decreased productivity.	1. The reason that balancing is important is because crime affects all of society. The privacy disadvantage only inconveniences a few federal employees.
	1. Money from drug confiscations could be used to increase the number of courts and judges. 2. If firings do increase crime, both the affirmative and negative would cause this effect.	1. Crime has no impact compared to privacy, any other impact would be a new argument.	1. Only the affirmative solves crime by decreasing drug use.

Figure 8.15 (Cont.)

of the affirmative. Greg only has to worry about winning inherency and significance. Tabitha has argued that drug-using employees will be fired for poor performance, and therefore drug tests are unnecessary. He must address this argument because firing is an alternative solution to the problems of accidents and productivity. Tabitha has argued that these problems are exaggerated and that privacy outweighs the remaining affirmative significance. Greg must be certain to address these three arguments and extend other arguments that may be useful to the affirmative position. An explanation of the affirmative position in the second affirmative rebuttal requires the following three elements.

Present the Closing Statement for the Affirmative

As in second negative rebuttal, the second affirmative rebuttalist should begin with a statement that explains the basic reason why the judge should affirm the resolution. It is to the affirmative's benefit if this statement somehow transforms the negative perspective on the debate into a nonflattering framework.

In the last speech, Tabitha argued that privacy should outweigh all other issues in the debate. Greg might want to reframe the issue by indicating that the nation allows small infringements of privacy rights on a regular basis to protect the safety of individuals. Search warrants could never be issued if privacy truly outweighed the citizenry's safety. A balance is necessary, whereby proven risks to the lives and property of individuals are worth minor inconveniences to a few employees.

Maximize the Winning Affirmative Arguments

The second affirmative rebuttalist must be conscious of the need to win each of the four general lines of argument. Within that framework, the debater should choose the arguments that are most likely to be persuasive with the judge. Having made these choices, the debater should respond to any negative arguments addressing these issues. Finally, the debater should provide reasons why these arguments should win the debate for the affirmative.

Greg could indicate that significant problems will continue unless drug-testing is implemented, namely accidents, decreased productivity, and increased crime. While the number of problems may not be as high as the affirmative originally claimed, the problems still represent a sufficient reason for choosing an alternative policy. Greg could indict the negative's counter-policy by indicating that the negative's own policy of employer firings will result in increased crime. Only drug-testing, which reduces the number of individuals on drugs, will decrease the incentive to commit crimes. Because the negative has conceded the solvency and topicality issues since the constructive speeches, Greg does not need to address them in the final rebuttal.

Minimize the Winning Negative Arguments

Second affirmative rebuttalists should realistically examine the arguments in the debate and determine the ones that the affirmative is losing. The strongest second affirmative rebuttalists can recognize when an argument is potentially troublesome and can argue persuasively that its impact is minimal.

The negative's best hope in our debate is that the disadvantage related to privacy will outweigh the affirmative's advantage. After all, the first affirmative rebuttal did concede the negative's claim that privacy is the most fundamental right. Or did it? The second affirmative rebuttalist will look at all the arguments in the debate and see if any statement by the affirmative could be used to offset the negative's defense of absolute privacy rights. Greg could argue that the affirmative's position statement in the second affirmative constructive argued that society as a whole was endangered unless a few individuals were willing to undergo drug tests. On the privacy disadvantage itself, the affirmative indicated that a balance of rights was necessary. While it would be a new argument for the second affirmative rebuttalist to show how much infringement occurred, the speaker still has the option of attempting to convince the judge that the arguments in the debate should be weighed in accordance with the number of individuals that each affects. Since crime potentially affects all individuals and the plan only inconveniences a few federal employees, the judge should affirm the resolution.

Summary and Conclusions

In debate, several rules govern how the debates will proceed. Two teams, one affirmative and one negative, always debate according to a prescribed set of time limits and a designated speaking order. While some rules govern how arguments can be developed in these speeches, the debaters are generally free to argue their strongest case in whatever form they choose.

The requirements of the first affirmative constructive are that the speaker limit the speech to constructing new arguments and that the four general lines of policy argument occur either implicitly or explicitly. When constructing the case, the first affirmative has the option to use the traditional need, comparative advantage, or goals criteria formats. When writing the plan, the debater should include mandates, enforcement mechanisms, funding provisions, and an intent plank. Debaters should word the first affirmative constructive powerfully, providing transitions that make clear the logic of their case for change.

The first negative constructive must limit the development of arguments to construction, refutation, and concession. By convention, this speaker introduces the negative position, attacks the four general lines of policy argument, and introduces abbreviated versions of plan attacks.

The second affirmative constructive can construct, concede, repeat, refute, or extend arguments in the debate. This speaker usually extends the affirmative case, refutes all attacks made in the first negative constructive, constructs additional advantages for adopting the resolution, and preempts likely second negative attacks.

The second negative constructive can also construct, concede, repeat, refute, or extend arguments in the debate. Ordinarily, this speaker extends the negative position, extends abbreviated versions of plan attacks, constructs new plan attacks or case attacks as needed, and refutes added advantages presented in the second affirmative constructive.

None of the rebuttal speeches in the debate can construct new arguments. The rebuttals serve to resolve arguments through concession, repetition, refutation, and extension of previous arguments. Given the shorter time limits of the rebuttal speech, the rebuttalists must focus on the debate arguments that will win the debate for their respective teams.

The first negative rebuttal extends attacks made against the general lines of argument, strives to focus the debate on issues that the negative is winning, aids the second negative in covering any responses to major negative issues that have not been answered, and extends any winning negative arguments not debated by the second negative. The first affirmative rebuttal covers all the issues in the debate by refuting new arguments presented in the second negative constructive, extending the general lines of argument, and making selective responses to other negative arguments.

The second negative rebuttal and the second affirmative rebuttal are the final speeches in the debate. As a result, the rebuttalists should summarize why their team is winning the debate. Ordinarily, these speakers open their rebuttal with a closing statement indicating the general reason they are winning, maximize the arguments that will help them win the debate, and minimize the winning arguments of the opposition.

In this chapter we summarized the conventions regarding placement of particular issues in the debate. The techniques for accomplishing these objectives have been described in previous chapters in the core text and this volume. The conventional placement of arguments is important to know because it generally has strategic value for the debaters. If, however, you discover that alternative placement of the issues is more beneficial, you should feel free to follow a different approach. Remember, though, that judges expect debate strategies to be fair to both sides in the debate and educational for all participants in the debate. You should be certain that any unconventional approach you take to the roles of the speakers is consistent with the principles of competitive fairness and academic integrity.

Exercises

1. Suppose you are writing a first affirmative constructive that argues that all products that contain toxic chemicals should have child-proof caps. Construct the case as a traditional need, comparative advantage, and goals criterion case. Which version appears to be most persuasive? Why?

2. Using the same topic described in the previous exercise, write an affirmative plan. Be sure to include mandates, an enforcement provision, a funding provision, and an intent plank. Try drafting a second version of the plan that would be more specific and a third version that would be more general.
3. Imagine that you are debating against a case that argues that nude dancing should be a protected form of free speech. You plan to argue that such expression has no value and is, in fact, objectionable because it degrades women. Write a negative position statement that encompasses all of your arguments.
4. Participate in a debate with three of your classmates. Designate one person the first affirmative, one the second affirmative, one the first negative, and one the second negative. Incorporate all of the speaker roles specified in this chapter. Use time limits of eight minutes for constructives and five minutes for rebuttals.
5. Watch a debate on public television or C-SPAN. Follow it until you are able to identify examples of each of the following techniques: construction, concession, refutation, repetition, and extension. Record an example of each. Make sure your examples are consistent with the definitions of the terms provided in this chapter.

9

Evaluating the Debate

Chapter Outline

Audience Analysis
Paradigms
    Stock Issues
    Policy-Making
    Hypothesis-Testing
    Critics of Argument
    Tabula Rasa
    Games Theory
Determining the Judge's Perspective
    Previous Ballots
    Networking
    Publications
    Nonverbal Feedback
Determining Your Own Perspective
Summary and Conclusions

Key Terms

audience analysis
paradigm
stock issues judge
policy-making judge
hypothesis-tester
critic of argument
tabula rasa judge
games theorist

The judges of a debate have no easy task to perform. They must be, of course, unprejudiced as to the subject. They must not forget that they are to decide on the merits of the debate, not on the merits of the question. . . . They must neither be stupefied by dull figures which may yet be pertinent, nor, on other hand, be hypnotized by brilliant rhetoric which may be but effervescent after all. They must sift, analyze, weigh, decide. It is a task but little easier than that of the debaters themselves.

William Horton Foster
Debating for Boys, 1922

In the preceding chapters we have identified the lines of argument generally available for affirming and negating a policy debate resolution. You should not conclude from these chapters that it is easy for judges to determine which side has won or lost these arguments or how these arguments interrelate. You have a responsibility as a debater to persuade the judge that your arguments are sufficient to win the debate.

Judges attempt to act as impartial observers, assessing each debate as fairly and as conscientiously as possible. However, the task of evaluating a debate is not a simple one. The complexity of arguments in any one debate can be staggering, leaving the judge with well-reasoned positions on both affirmative and negative sides of the resolution. In close debates, these critics frequently resort to their own attitudes and beliefs to resolving difficult disputes.

Audience Analysis

To enhance the persuasiveness of your arguments you should become familiar with some fundamental tenets of audience analysis. **Audience analysis** is the attempt by speakers to identify the beliefs, values, and attitudinal dispositions of their audiences. Audience analysis is a highly imperfect process. However, anytime you attempt to persuade another individual or group of individuals, it is vital in order to be effective. Lobbyists before the Congress, who are frequently engaged in recommending that members of Congress vote to adopt the very laws you are proposing in debates, engage in elaborate audience analysis. They attempt to identify the voting records of important legislators, determine a legislator's place on the political spectrum from conservative to liberal, and understand key elements of the voting constituency of a legislator to assess whether personal and political interest will sway a vote in their direction. After this analysis, lobbyists tailor their messages to appeal to the beliefs and attitudes of those congressional actors they believe are important to a successful lobbying campaign. Similarly, candidates for public office, attorneys before juries and judges, advertising executives, and media entertainers all engage in a sophisticated analysis of their audience in order to present the most appealing messages they can.

You do the same sort of thing yourself every day. If you want to go to a new restaurant with a friend who rarely has a lot of money to spend, you will probably emphasize the availability of inexpensive food rather than the fabulous cuisine. On the other hand, you might stress the restaurant's reputation for outstanding cream cheese brownies if you were speaking to a friend who likes desserts.

While debate is an academic exercise that judges try hard to evaluate with an open mind, that standard is impossible to achieve. The closer the debate, the more difficulty critics have not yielding to their own biases. Debaters need to adapt their messages to the attitudes and beliefs of their judges. Many types of bias can enter into a judge's decision making, but we believe three types tend to surface more often than others. Judges can have (1) strong political beliefs, (2) strong beliefs about the purposes of debate, and (3) strong beliefs about the role of the judge in a debate.

While debate judges as a rule make every effort to leave their political and social biases at the door, such beliefs can have important effects on the way a round is evaluated. This is particularly the case in a close round when a judge is required to think carefully about evidence and make choices between sophisticated positions. For example, critics might find evidence from sources who are consistent with their own beliefs more credible than evidence from sources with whom they disagree. Evaluators might find the reasoning process of those who agree with their own political beliefs more persuasive. If you take positions that are directly opposed to the political beliefs of your critic, you may find it difficult to win a close debate. If you must take a position which is inconsistent with their sociopolitical beliefs, you should attempt to present that position in the most positive light. You should not take positions that stress opposition to the evaluator's view. Instead, you should attempt to find areas of agreement between the position you are taking in the debate and the beliefs and attitudes of your judge.

Many critics also have personal beliefs and attitudes about the role debate should play in the life of the debater. These assumptions can have a direct influence on how they decide some arguments. All judges believe that debate should teach students some of the persuasive skills of a good public speaker. However, some critics view strong public speaking skills as the primary test of good debating. These individuals might pay less attention to the exact wording of opposing evidence. Instead, they place more emphasis on presentation. Other judges believe the primary purpose of debate should be to teach students the process of argumentation and support with less regard for the skills of public presentation. Such individuals will lean toward debaters who present the most compelling reasoning and evidence rather than those who present their arguments in the most persuasive fashion.

> Obviously the manner of the speaker has a more immediate appeal than the subject matter. However, a debate is not a declamation contest. It is a presentation of arguments for or against a proposition so arranged and related that they move to an irresistible conclusion. Certainly what the debater says is of more importance than how he says it. It would be impossible to define the relative importance of the two divisions of the subject.
>
> William Horton Foster
> *Debating for Boys*, 1922

Sometimes you will find yourself debating before judges who have little exposure to competitive academic debates. These critics could include school administrators and interested members of the community who have been asked to judge the debate. These evaluators may have little academic training in debate, but you should respect their perspective and expectations of debate. You should certainly not assume that they are unable to evaluate the debate with expertise. In fact, studies indicate that these judges are likely to vote in accordance with the decisions of more expert critics. The general lines of argument in debate are appropriate for policy debating in any format. As a debater, you should be able to communicate to the most inexperienced judge the significant need for change, the inherent inability of present policies to solve the problem, the sufficiency of resolutional policies to solve the problem, and the topical approaches of the resolution. When challenging the four general lines of argument, you should be able to communicate the failure of the affirmative to fulfill these arguments and why the failure to fulfill these arguments justifies negating the resolution. Remember, no judge is required to adapt to your ideas or style of presentation; you must adapt to your judges.

Paradigms

Judges often have personal or professional biases toward issues in the debate and the purposes of debate. Many critics also have specific conceptual frameworks for assessing debates. You can best understand these frameworks, called **paradigms,** as analogies drawn between debate and some other realm of activity in society where the participants engage in evaluation. One judge, for example, might consider debate to most closely resemble a criminal courtroom, complete with a prosecutor (the affirmative team, which makes charges against the present system), a defense attorney (the negative team, which defends the innocence of the present system), and a judge. Following this analogy, these judges would require proof beyond reasonable doubt prior to their affirmation of the resolution.

The critic's use of a paradigm in the evaluation of a debate has many advantages. First, the paradigm helps the judge determine the strength of each argument within a debate. As an example, the evaluator might want to know how much significance the affirmative team would have to prove to make a convincing case that the resolution should be affirmed. In the criminal courtroom, the requirement is proof beyond a reasonable doubt. Using another paradigm, a judge might be satisfied with the side that furnishes a preponderance of the evidence. Paradigms, then, help the critic evaluate each argument in a debate.

Second, using a paradigm is likely to produce a more consistent evaluation from one debate round to the next. Letting an analogy guide the selection of important arguments within a debate makes it easier for judges to avoid voting for debate teams merely because they like them better. The paradigm introduces an element of objectivity. The guidelines remain consistent, so the evaluation of arguments takes on a similar consistency.

Finally, a paradigm provides debaters with some forewarning about how a judge will assess a debate. Debaters can envision themselves in a role consistent with the analogy that the critic is using, thereby gaining insight into the strength and relevance of their claims.

Despite these advantages, paradigms have their drawbacks. On some occasions, judges will appear to accept a particular paradigm but ignore the implications of that paradigm for certain arguments. This situation can occur when the debater misinterprets the paradigm the judge is using or when the critic does not fully understand or accept the guidelines of a particular paradigm. Given the imprecise application of these paradigms, debaters should be prepared to initiate arguments that are persuasive across paradigms or to make claims that persuade the judge that a single argument fits into his or her specific paradigm.

In some instances, judges and debaters are completely conscious of the paradigm guiding their evaluation and the argumentative implications of that paradigm. Nevertheless, the paradigm can never offer a perfect representation of a debate round. A courtroom trial, after all, is not an academic debate, as defined in this textbook. Differences between the debate and the processes operating in the analogy are bound to emerge. When these differences arise, debaters cannot anticipate how the judge will resolve the issue based on an understanding of the paradigm alone. Critics, for example, may be forced to rely on their intuition to make the determination. To maintain maximum predictability debaters must argue actively and carefully for a favorable decision under the terms of the paradigm as they understand it.

This textbook provides debaters with an approach that allows them to minimize the negative impact of judges' paradigms. The general lines of argument for policy debate are applicable in all paradigms. If debaters can master the general lines of argument, they have the means for developing an arsenal of arguments that will allow them the flexibility to succeed regardless of the judges' preferred framework.

To maximize the strategic opportunities offered by this argumentative arsenal, debaters should understand the paradigms and their implications for evaluating arguments. An understanding of the predominant paradigms will not ensure that the debater will win all or even most of their debates. What it will do is give debaters a means for framing issues as persuasively as possible. In this chapter we outline the predominant paradigms, emphasizing their assumptions and implications for the general lines of argument for policy debate. We focus on those paradigms that many judges find useful when evaluating debates. Many other paradigms exist today and even more will emerge in the future. Debate theory is a constantly evolving academic pursuit. Debaters should be prepared to adapt to frameworks generally accepted by the bulk of the debate community or by their debate judges.

Stock Issues

> The problem of burden of proof, in common with many other specific problems of general argumentation, can best be studied by investigating its treatment in legal procedure; for it is in the law that practical reasoning has received most attention and reached its highest development. . . . If close attention were paid in argumentation outside the courtroom as well as in legal trials to such matters as burden of proof, burden of rebuttal, prima facie case, types of negative cases, etc., much confusion, disorganized bickering, and futile disputing would be avoided. These doctrines are simple to understand, easy to apply, and should be adhered to in all argumentation which has any serious purpose whatsoever.
>
> James Milton O'Neill,
> Craven Laycock, and
> Robert Leighton Scales
> *Argumentation and Debate*, 1920

Stock issues judges view debate as being similar to criminal courtroom advocacy. In a trial situation, the prosecution must meet certain stipulated burdens before a jury will find a presumptively innocent defendant guilty. Similarly, the stock issues judge presumes that the present system is "innocent," or adequate, until the affirmative meets certain burdens.

In order for the affirmative team to establish that the present system is "guilty beyond a reasonable doubt," they must win the four general lines of policy advocacy: significance, inherency, solvency, and topicality. Because the affirmative must win these four arguments, they are vulnerable to a negative defense of any one of them. If the negative can show that a significant problem does not exist, that the problem will be remedied in the foreseeable future, that the affirmative plan will not solve the problem, *or* that the affirmative plan does not fall within the boundaries of the resolution, they will succeed in creating a reasonable doubt sufficient to dismiss an affirmation of the resolution.

Since the presumption against affirming the resolution is central for stock issues judges, they tend to place a somewhat higher burden of proof for each of the four general lines of policy argument than judges following other paradigms. A stock issues judge might dismiss an affirmative's claim of significance because the problem is not important enough to justify changing existing structures. The stock issues judge generally expects the affirmative's inherency claim to show that existing attitudes or structures will preclude adoption of the affirmative plan. These judges permit the negative team substantial latitude in offering minor repairs that allow the present system to solve the affirmative's harm.

Stock issues judges also view counterplans from a traditional perspective. Since presumption rests with the "innocent" status quo, these judges expect the counterplan to fall outside the boundaries of the resolution and to be competitive with resolutional action. A negative team that chooses to offer a counterplan in front of a stock issues judge forfeits their "presumption of innocence." Because the negative has admitted that the present system is guilty of causing some significant harm, the same burdens of proof normally falling on the affirmative team become shared equally by the two teams in the debate.

Policy-Making

Whereas stock issues judges see their role as similar to that of a jurist or courtroom judge, **policy-making judges** see themselves in the position of legislators or executive decision-makers. Legislators and executives recognize that in a constantly changing world they must continually make choices between competing policies. These judges consider each debate to be between at least two competing policies: the specific plan advocated by the affirmative team and the present policy and/or counterplans supported by the negative team.

Presumption for the policy-making judge resides with the team advocating the policy of least change. Like legislators, policy-making judges believe there are risks inherent in any change; the larger the amount of change, the greater the potential risk in adopting a particular policy. In many debates, the policy-making judge assigns presumption to the negative team, since they are defending familiar policies already in operation in the present system. When the negative team chooses to advocate a counterplan, however, the judge must determine whether the plan or the counterplan causes the least change in order to assign presumption. A policymaker forced to choose between an affirmative team's offer to change the system of selecting juries because too many juries are biased against the poor and a negative team's counterplan to eliminate all trials by jury would assign presumption to the affirmative team. Changing the selection process for juries is certainly a less radical change than banning trial by jury completely. Having offered the plan of least change, the affirmative can argue that the policy-making judge should presume the affirmative plan is superior to the radical change offered by the negative team.

The process of weighing two competing policies makes the plan the focus of the debate for the policy-making judge. The resolution, as a whole, takes on a secondary importance. As long as the particular policy that the affirmative advocates falls within the scope of the resolution, it meets the expectations of the judge. Topicality is generally a jurisdictional issue, with the plan emerging as the focus of the debate if it falls within the boundaries of the general topic. The affirmative has a reduced obligation to justify each term of the resolution, explaining why each limiting word or phrase is necessary or sufficient to solve the significant problem identified by the affirmative.

Significance arguments are central to the evaluation of the debate for policy-making judges. As they analyze the costs and benefits of the two competing policies, advantages and disadvantages become the focus of the policy-maker's judgments. In this paradigm, every significance argument should be linked to the specifics of the competing policies. Arguments addressing the totality of the resolution tend not to be as persuasive. For example, if a resolution called for a ban on United States military intervention and the affirmative advocated a specific ban on intervention into the Middle East, the negative's disadvantage would be stronger if it stemmed from the consequences of banning intervention into the Middle East. More general arguments related to banning intervention worldwide would appear vague or tangential to the more specific concerns of the debate.

Likewise, the solvency claims should relate directly to the specific mandates of the affirmative plan. In the previous example, the affirmative team might be able to show that a ban on military intervention worldwide might bring stability to the Middle East, but such a claim would not be specific to the plan calling for a prohibition on intervention into only the Middle East. A policy-making judge would likely be swayed by claims that a ban on intervention into the Middle East would shift the conflict to other regions of the world with the result that there would be no net gain for peace. Thus, both the affirmative and the negative teams should be careful to show how their claims to affirm or deny solvency link to the particular plan advocated in the debate.

The policy-maker's view of inherency is largely effects-oriented. In general, the affirmative need only prove that the effect of the present system is the existence of a problem. Identifying the precise cause for the problem's continuation is less important. If the problem exists, then all that remains is to determine if the present system is solving it. Absent such a determination, the affirmative would be inherent.

If the negative determines that they cannot defend the current system's solution to the problem successfully, they may choose to offer a counterplan. Many policy-making judges consider a team that offers a counterplan to be committed to their policy. Policies conditional on winning or losing other arguments in the debate are less persuasive because such arguments dilute the direct comparison of two policies. While policymakers generally frown on conditional argumentation, these judges frequently allow the negative debater to defend a topical counterplan. As long as the affirmative and the negative proposal compete (i.e., the existence of one precludes or undermines the benefits of the other), the policy-maker is willing to choose between the two policies. Since the purpose of topicality arguments is to divide ground between the two teams, a topical counterplan fulfills that function if it merely offers a competitive alternative to the affirmative proposal.

In sum, a policy-making debate critic expects debaters to be advocates of a policy that has fewer costs and more benefits compared to other competing policies. To overcome the inherent risks of change, the debaters need to frame their significance, inherency, solvency, and topicality arguments as stemming directly from the specifics of the policies defended in the debate.

Hypothesis-Testing

While stock issues judges make decisions like jurists and policymakers decide like legislators, **hypothesis-testers** view themselves more as scientific theorists. Like the scientist, the hypothesis-tester attempts to test the probable truth or falsity of a claim. In debate, this claim is the resolution, and the hypothesis-tester seeks to understand if the claim in its entirety is probably a true statement.

Presumption for the hypothesis-tester always rests against the resolution. The reason lies in the analogy to science. When scientists seek to understand some relationship, they use the null hypothesis. The null hypothesis assumes that no relationship exists. As an example, a scientist attempting to discover whether saccharin causes cancer would test the null hypothesis that saccharin does not cause cancer. By testing the relationship in this manner, scientists can rule out alternative causes that might result in cancer. In a debate, the hypothesis-tester works according to the same logic. By assuming that the resolution is false, the hypothesis-tester always grants presumption to the negative team, regardless of the amount of change proposed in the counterplan.

When assessing significance claims, hypothesis-testers focus their attention on the entirety of the resolution. Unlike policymakers, who only consider issues directly linked to specific affirmative plan mandates, the hypothesis-tester wants to determine if the resolution as a whole is probably true. Generic arguments, that is, those linked to the entire resolution, serve as the most comprehensive resolutional test. As a result, the hypothesis-tester allows the affirmative to claim advantages from any aspect of the resolution. Likewise, the negative team can successfully undermine the probable truth of a resolution by presenting disadvantages resulting from the imagined adoption of the resolution regardless of the specific components of the affirmative plan.

Inherency for the hypothesis-tester tends to be cause-oriented. This is because in order to understand probable truth, the scientist must understand not only that something occurs but why it occurs as well. Affirmative teams need to demonstrate why, absent the resolution, the problem will continue. If they fail to do so, the hypothesis-tester would consider the resolution unnecessary to solve the problem. Negative teams need to demonstrate that nonresolutional alternatives are sufficient to solve the problem.

When negatives present alternatives to the resolution, whether minor repairs or counterplans, they may do so conditionally for the hypothesis-testing judge. These judges do not limit themselves to a direct comparison of two policy alternatives. Instead, they imagine what the world would be like if the affirmative took the action specified in the resolution. In this process, the judges can consider the myriad options offered by both the affirmative and negative, each viewed as an experiment that tests the probable truth of the resolution. For some hypothesis-testers these alternatives can even be contradictory as long as the judge can imagine that both possibilities might exist.

If the negative chooses to offer a counterplan as an alternative to the resolution, the argument must be nontopical. A topical counterplan would merely be more support for the probable truth of the resolution. If the negative proves advantages to a topical counterplan, the judge would likely use these advantages to warrant a vote for the affirmative, the team designated to defend the probable truth of the resolution. Thus, to be successful, negatives should show that their counterplan is nontopical and competitive and thus could prove the resolution is probably false.

The hypothesis-tester also insists that the affirmative prove the resolution is sufficient to solve the problem. If the resolution by itself cannot reduce or eliminate the significant problem cited by the affirmative, it should not be adopted. Thus, the negative should carefully examine whether extratopical actions, those falling beyond the bounds of the resolution, are required to gain the affirmative's advantage.

In summary, the hypothesis-tester expects the affirmative to support the resolution and the negative team to negate it. There is no other expectation regarding consistency. At the end of the debate, the judge asks, did the affirmative team overcome the inherent doubt about the probable truth of the resolution? This provides a striking contrast to the policymaker who asks, between the two competing policies advocated by the affirmative and the negative, which is the superior alternative?

The remaining paradigms in policy debate lack the level of development that the stock issues, policy-making, and hypothesis-testing models offer. Rather than provide guidance concerning each of the four general lines of argument, they work from a basic assumption that determines how the judge evaluates each argument. While we will treat each of these three paradigms individually, debaters should be aware that many judges combine the assumptions of these paradigms with other basic assumptions about how to evaluate debates.

Critics of Argument

> The other possibility . . . is a critic's vote, or expert's vote, giving expert opinion as to the comparative excellence of the debating done.
>
> O'Neill, Laycock, and Scales
> *Argumentation and Debate*, 1920

Judges who consider themselves to be **critics of argument** assume that the debaters must master a certain quality of argument to be persuasive. The standards for what constitutes a good argument vary from judge to judge but generally include analytical reasoning, evidentiary support, and assessment of the argument's impact within the context of the whole debate. If a debater fails to provide evidence or reasoning to bolster a given claim, the critic of argument will likely ignore the issue altogether. Weak arguments, even if the opposing team does not refute them, are seldom voting issues in the context of the debate. Critics of argument generally do not allow their predispositions about the importance of particular types of debate arguments, such as conditional arguments, topical counterplans, or standards for topicality, to influence their evaluation of the debate. Instead, they rely on the strength of the debaters' evidence and reasoning to assess all lines of argument in the debate.

Tabula Rasa

In many ways, the **tabula rasa judge** is the antithesis of the critic of argument. This judging philosophy views the judge's mind as a "blank slate" which debaters "write upon" when they debate. The judge minimizes the use of personal preferences or arbitrary requirements in evaluating the debate. Complete open-mindedness is the goal of judges using this paradigm. As a result, they place a premium on the debaters' ability to evaluate and summarize the issues within a debate. Arguments that opposing teams fail to refute frequently become deciding issues. Standards for what constitutes a good argument are left to the debaters to dispute during the debate. The basic expectations or argumentative burdens discussed throughout this book are open to debate for the tabula rasa judge. If an affirmative team argues that they should not have to show why a problem is inherent and the negative team cannot articulate why the affirmative should have to demonstrate inherency, this general line of argument would not enter into the judge's evaluation.

Some tabula rasa judges recognize that taking this philosophy to its extreme could lead to absurd evaluations of debates. If one team insists that each team must tell a joke every twenty seconds to win and the opposing team fails to explain why this standard should not exist, should the first team win the debate? The modified tabula rasa judge intervenes in the debate only long enough to reject a blatantly flawed or silly argument, whether it is refuted or not. All other arguments, however, remain for the debaters to resolve in the context of the debate.

Games Theory

> The custom has grown in recent years of referring to contest debating as a sport
> or game. . . . This conception helps us to decide on proper grounds, and frees us
> from much cant and hypocrisy.
>
> O'Neill, Laycock, and Scales
> *Argumentation and Debate*, 1920

Games theorists do not view debate as a mock courtroom, a clash of policies, as a test of a hypothesis, or as an argumentative exercise. Rather, they view debate as a competitive contest in which each side must have an equal opportunity to win. The governing standard for evaluating any argument in this paradigm is fairness. While the notion of fairness varies from one debate judge to another, all game theorists expect the debaters to explain any stances on the theoretical issues that affect the competitive fairness of debate. Theoretical issues in a debate are the rules by which the debaters play the game. Who gets the right to define the terms of the resolution? Does a counterplan have to be competitive? What standard of evidence is appropriate for establishing the case for adopting a particular policy? Debaters must resolve these issues and others like them so that each team retains an equal opportunity to win. Arguments indicating that one team receives a competitive advantage as a result of a particular theoretical issue have a strong persuasive effect on the games theorist.

Some debate judges view games theory as the umbrella paradigm that encompasses all other paradigms and their attendant rules. These judges feel that the issue of fairness is of such paramount importance that issues of how a legislator would act or how a scientist might proceed are secondary. Regardless of which role the judge assumes, these individuals consider fairness to be a primary concern.

Determining the Judge's Perspective

Up to this point, we have assumed that the you can identify what influences a judge's perspective. In many instances, however, you may not know the judge well enough to know his or her sociopolitical beliefs, attitudes toward debate students, or beliefs about the role of debate. Since a debater's success can frequently turn on knowing the framework within which a critic is operating, the remainder of the chapter offers some suggestions for identifying a judge's perspective.

Previous Ballots

Debaters have an opportunity to learn about a judge's thinking by carefully considering his or her written comments in previous rounds. The ballot may reveal that the judge finds some sources of evidence or arguments with a liberal or conservative twist more persuasive than others. Comments on style and presentation on the ballot may expose the critic's view of the function of debate in the student's education. The ballot may indicate that the judge finds a disadvantage too generic to be persuasive, that the debaters failed to provide sufficient reasoning to sustain their arguments, or that the judge considers conditional argumentation to be an ineffective strategy. Comments like these, coupled with an understanding of the assumptions of different paradigms, allow the debater to predict how that same judge is likely to evaluate other issues in future debates.

Networking

Debaters should speak with former colleagues, former and current debaters, and current debate coaches from the judge's region of the country to discover a judge's perspective. Be sure to speak to more than one source when gathering information about a judge's preferences and tendencies. Consulting a variety of sources will improve your chances of finding valuable information as well as provide you with a more balanced view.

Publications

Debaters should be aware that many debate judges publish articles and books in which they outline how debates should be evaluated. *Argumentation and Advocacy* (formerly *The Journal of the American Forensics Association*), *Rostrum*, and *Speaker and Gavel* are three journals that feature many articles of debate evaluation. Argumentation conferences, such as the Alta Conference, publish proceedings that record many judge's interpretations of judging philosophies. Debate handbooks may contain articles by prominent debate judges, and debate textbooks may offer insights as well. By keeping up-to-date on what members of the debate community are publishing, debaters will extend their knowledge of the argumentative preferences of their judges.

Nonverbal Feedback

Frequently, despite your best efforts, you will be unable to find out anything about your judge before a round. That does not mean, however, that you have exhausted your options for learning about your judges' probable reactions. During an actual debate, debaters will often receive nonverbal responses concerning the quality of their arguments. The judge may nod along with a winning argument, frown during an argument that is less appealing, or even wave a debater past uninteresting issues. Debaters should take heed of these comments on the types of arguments they are initiating and use them to understand the perspective from which the judge is operating.

While it is important to use a variety of sources to try to determine your judge's preferences, you should be careful not to stereotype judges. The differences between your expectations and the judge's actual preferences can sometimes be shocking, and the failure to respect an individual because you categorize their beliefs based on appearance or background can also be terribly insulting. Polling surveys, for example, indicate that in political elections African-Americans vote a liberal ticket approximately ninety percent of the time. However, you would be foolish to assume that all African-Americans are liberals. Many very prominent African-Americans scoff at the notion of liberal politics. Supreme Court Justice Clarence Thomas is an example of a prominent conservative African-American. Many Jewish voters tend to support pro-Israeli congressional and senatorial candidates. However, many Jewish voters would rather see Israel seek an accommodation with the Palestinians and its neighboring Arab states. Stereotyping can lead you to false conclusions and offensive behavior.

Even if you learn your judge has certain very strong biases, you should not sound as if you are pandering to these preferences. By overemphasizing expected biases, you may risk insulting or alienating judges who do not like to be categorized. You should respect the cognitive ability of your audience. If you act as though your critics are unable to listen to all sides of an issue, because of their sociopolitical beliefs, their views of what debate should mean for the student who participates, or their normal judging paradigm, you run the risk of insulting them. Judges strive for intellectual honesty and expect debaters to address the issues without pandering to their personal beliefs.

> At least occasionally visit with them, always be cognizant of their proceedings, and let their reports be given to you for this purpose. Thus you will have provided for them a most profitable as well as most exciting exercise. Young men will find that its invitations are stronger than the saloon and frivolous society, and all will, in after life, cherish it as their most valuable school-work. It may cost you an effort, it may tax your ingenuity, it may sometimes weary your patience;

but what attainments do we have that do no require our best energies? Surely none.

O. P. Kinsley
The Normal Debater, 1876

Determining Your Own Perspective

Up to this point, we have described debate evaluation in terms of the judge exclusively, but how you evaluate debate is important too. You can use the same basic principles of evaluation to assess your own perspective on participating in debate.

Ask yourself the following questions: What am I doing when I debate? Am I learning to test the truth of arguments? Am I determining the course of public policy? Am I discovering how to prove guilt beyond a reasonable doubt? Am I learning to evaluate public arguments? Am I playing games? Your purposes in engaging in policy debate will guide your approach to the activity. Debate is an educational activity in which you can establish personal objectives. Explore and establish your own goals and objectives, and seek the advice of instructors to help determine the viability of those objectives and the best avenues for achieving them.

The different paradigms for viewing debate can help you determine what is important and what is unimportant in the activity. Being aware of your perspective allows you to identify modern conventions of debate that do not further your own goals. It also permits you to focus your energies on the debate process better. By exploring differing perspectives on the dynamic activity of debate, you can better understand how debate functions as a competitive and educational activity.

By exploring different perspectives on debate, you can also further your understanding of other activities you engage in. The perspectives we discuss in debate are borrowed from other fields of study: public policy, science, law, and other academic disciplines. Do these fields of discourse affect your views in other areas of your life? By moving from one field of study to another, comparing the processes within and between fields, and exploring the interrelationships between fields, you can expand your perspective on many interests in your life.

> To be a poor debater at first is not proof that you cannot ultimately succeed.
> Some of the most celebrated debaters of history were woefully weak in oratory,
> but attained well-deserved eminence by persevering, against all discouragements,
> in their determination to conquer every obstacle.

A. H. Craig
Pros and Cons, 1897

You might also come to find that your explorations of perspective will lead you to change the way you view debate. Different perspectives might capture your attention or interests at different times. This is also a healthy practice. Changing times alter how we think. When you sense a change of perspective, ask yourself: why am I leaning toward a different perspective and what is the purpose of this new perspective? As we grow and find new ways of looking at things, it helps us to compare our new perspective to where we have been. What caused the change in my point of view, and why is the new perspective compelling? The views we discover in the practice of debate can have great influence on the views we have of the world.

Throughout this book, you have been asked to examine the process of debate through a lines of argument perspective. The place to begin your critical assessment is here. If you discover that the lines of argument approach is useful to you, begin to ask why. Would the approach be applicable to other aspects of your life? What are the strengths and weaknesses of the perspective? What do you gain and what is left for you to explore?

Summary and Conclusions

Despite strong efforts to remain impartial when evaluating debates, judges must rely on their personal frameworks for assessing the complexity of many debates. These frameworks may be based on a judge's sociopolitical beliefs, interpretation of the purpose of debate, and interpretation of the role of the debate critic. The frameworks that describe the role of the judge are called paradigms. They are analogies drawn between debate and other aspects of society that involve some sort of evaluation. All judges, implicitly or explicitly, adhere to some paradigm which guides their evaluation of debates.

Paradigms have both advantages and disadvantages. On the positive side, a paradigm provides guidance to the judge in determining the relative merit of particular arguments in the debate, offers a consistent method of debate evaluation, and allows debaters some ability to predict how an individual critic will view a particular argument within the context of a debate. The drawbacks of paradigms arise from inconsistent application, incompleteness of analogy, or rigid application.

Judges who adhere to the stock issues paradigm view debate as if it were a courtroom trial, with the affirmative team prosecuting the present system and the negative team defending the ''innocence'' of the status quo. Presumption rests with the negative team as long as they are defending present policies. Once the negative commits to a counterplan, presumption shifts to the team that can show that its proposal most closely resembles present policies. Stock issues judges tend to impose a greater burden of proof on the four general lines of policy argument.

Policymakers view their role in judging a debate to be akin to that of a legislator or executive decision maker. Recognizing the world's dynamic nature, they seek to compare two competing policies. Presumption rests with the policy that poses the least amount of change from present policies. Disadvantages and solvency claims need to link directly to the specifics of the affirmative plan. Inherency evaluations tend to be effects-oriented. Topical counterplans are acceptable as long as they compete with the affirmative proposal. Topicality is viewed as a jurisdictional issue, with justification and conditional arguments generally considered nonpersuasive.

Hypothesis-testers consider their role as debate evaluator as similar to that of a scientist in search of probable truth. Presumption is always against the resolution. Significance and solvency claims can link to either the specifics of the plan or the entirety of the resolution. Evaluation of inherency arguments tends to be cause-oriented. Counterplans should be nontopical, competitive, and advantageous. Conditional and justification arguments tend to be more persuasive to the hypothesis-tester.

The critic of argument establishes standards for good argument, usually stressing the need for analytical reasoning, evidential support, and impact in relation to the other arguments in the debate. Tabula rasa judges assume that the debate judge should be completely impartial, bringing no predetermined standards to bear on a debate. The games theorist treats debate as a competitive contest in which both teams should have an equal opportunity to win.

To determine the paradigm that is either implicitly or explicitly guiding a particular judge's evaluation procedure, debaters have several options. They can carefully assess the written comments provided by judges on previous ballots, they can network with colleagues and debaters familiar with a given judge, they can keep abreast of debate publications that indicate the preferences of some debate judges, and they can react to the nonverbal feedback that occurs in a debate.

While understanding the evaluation process of the judge is useful, debaters should also examine evaluation from a personal perspective. The various analogies discussed in this chapter can help debaters ask, what am I doing when I debate. The answer to this most important question can provide debaters with a means of judging their participation not only in debate but in other life activities as well.

Exercises

1. Assume you are watching a debate in which one team is clearly the stronger of the two. The stronger team has better speaking skills, they have superior evidence, and they win every argument in the debate—except one. They do not respond to an argument by their opponents that the plan will not solve the problem because the public would never accept the plan. Who wins the debate? Evaluate the debate according to the various paradigms.

2. Assume you are in a debate in which the negative team establishes that the affirmative plan is not topical. In the same debate, the affirmative team proves that the negative's counterplan is topical. Both the plan and the counterplan achieve the exact same amount of advantages. Who wins the debate? Explore how different paradigms would decide this debate.

3. Assume you are watching a debate in which the negative team argues that the present system is solving the affirmative's harm. At the same time, the negative argues that solving the problem would have undesirable consequences. The affirmative claims that both arguments should be ignored because the contradiction proves that the negative has failed to advocate a consistent position in the debate. The negative responds that both arguments prove that the resolution is not true, so either one justifies a vote against the resolution. Who wins the debate? Would the different paradigms resolve the debate differently?

4. Suppose you are debating against an affirmative plan that bans the right to an abortion. The judge assigned to your debate has a reputation for being a strong pro-life advocate. How can you convince the judge to vote against the affirmative? What arguments might be persuasive? How could you phrase these arguments so they would not alienate the judge? How would these arguments change if your judge were pro-choice?

Glossary

A

add-on additional advantages to adopting the resolution usually presented in the second affirmative constructive and frequently independent of other affirmative advantages.

affirmative the side in a debate charged with defending the debate resolution.

agent of change the authority designated in the resolution to carry out resolutional action.

attitudinal inherency oppositional forces that allow problems to continue presently.

attitudinal plan-meet-need the predisposition of existing agents that will undermine the effectiveness of the affirmative proposal.

audience analysis the attempt by a speaker to identify the beliefs, values, and attitudes of an audience.

B

better definition a topicality standard that indicates the better definition read in the debate should be used to interpret the resolution.

brief an essentially complete argumentive chain of reasoning that you expect to use in a debate.

brink the point at which the impact of an argument becomes inevitable.

burden of proof (1) the requirement that sufficient evidence or reasoning to prove an argument be presented. (2) when applied to the affirmative, the requirement that those affirming changes in the course of action must demonstrate significance, inherency, solvency, and topicality.

C

case argumentation representing the rationale for the resolution, referring to both affirmative and negative arguments over significance, inherency, solvency, and topicality.

circumvention a solvency argument that indicates that those with selfish or perverse motives will attempt to avoid the mandates of the plan.

citation specific information on the source of evidence including publication, date of publication, page excerpt,

author's name, and author's qualifications.

comparative advantage the line of argument positing that a plan would reduce a problem or prevent expected increases of the problem in the future to a greater degree than possible in the present system.

competitiveness (1) the line of argument holding that a counterplan could not, should not, or would not exist with the affirmative proposal. (2) the aspects of a counterplan that make the policy a reason to reject the affirmative proposal.

complementary argument an argument that supports the reasoning of another claim in a debate.

concession granting an argument to an opponent, either by direct reference or by the failure to answer opposing arguments.

conditional argument argument that depends on a set of specified circumstances. Such an argument can be conceded without detrimental effect on a team's other arguments in the debate.

construction the initiation of new claims into a debate.

contention (1) a major point advanced in the debate. (2) a subdivision of an affirmative case.

context (1) a standard for evaluating topicality arguments to determine if the definitions offered in the debate are consistent with the meaning of other words in the resolution. (2) the relationship of the evidence read in the debate to the original source material.

contradictory argument an argument that disproves the assumptions or claims made previously by the same side in a debate.

cost-benefit analysis a means of resolving significance arguments by weighing the benefits of affirming the resolution against the costs of doing so.

counterplan an alternative proposal by the negative for solving the harms perpetuated by current policies.

critic of argument an evaluator who believes the debaters must master a certain quality of argument to be persuasive.

cross-application when an argument is applied to more than one position.

cross-examination a specified period of time reserved in the debate for each side to ask questions of the other speaker, usually between the constructive speeches.

D

debatability a topicality standard that argues that as long as a definition provides fair grounds for debate it should be accepted.

degree of reparability a standard for assessing the impact of an argument based on projections of the degree to which society can recover from certain effects.

disadvantage a deleterious or undesirable consequence of affirming the resolution (sometimes referred to as "D.A." or "Disad"). To prove a disadvantage, the negative must prove that the disadvantage is caused by the affirmative proposal (link), that the disadvantage can only be caused by the affirmative proposal (uniqueness), and that the disadvantage's impact is significant enough to outweigh the affirmative significance claims.

dropping an argument failure to respond to an opponent's argument.

E

existential inherency the line of argument that the existence of the problem is sufficient proof that it will continue.

extension a line of argument that elaborates on the original point by either directly clashing with the argument against the original point or expanding the scope of the original argument.

extratopical term describing the portions of the affirmative plan that fall outside the boundaries of the resolution (sometimes referred to as an extratopicality argument).

F

fiat the assumption that the particular policy advocated by the affirmative would be put in place.

flowcharting note-taking in debates.

funding plank the part of the plan that identifies the sources of money which will pay for the plan to be carried out.

G

games theorist an evaluator who views debate as a competitive contest in which each side must have an equal chance to win.

goals criteria a defense of the resolution that indicates that present institutions are committed in theory to a certain goal, that the goal is a valuable one, that present policies undermine the chance of achieving the goal, and that the affirmative proposal will meet the goal.

grammatical context the topicality standard that holds that the grammatical function of a word within a sentence should help govern the word's meaning.

grouping arguments tying multiple arguments to each other for a single response or set of responses.

H

hypothesis-testers an evaluator who views the judge's role as testing the probable truth or falsity of the resolution.

I

impact turn the line of argument that holds that the impact of a disadvantage is positive.

implicit definition a situation in which debaters present their plan as an operational definition of the resolution.

incrementalism the process of gradually working toward

the elimination of a problem, constantly evaluating each step of the process.

independent argument a claim that relies on no other claim in the debate to serve as a reason to affirm or negate the resolution.

inherency the line of argument that posits that the problem will continue unless the actions specified in the resolution are adopted.

irrelevant argument an argument that does not relate to the final outcome of a debate.

J

judge the person who evaluates the debate and is empowered to declare the winner.

L

linearity a line of argument that establishes for every incremental increase in cause there is an inevitable incremental increase in effect.

link the argument that posits that the affirmative policy will cause a disadvantage to occur.

link turn the argument that instead of causing a disadvantage, the affirmative policy prevents it from occurring.

M

magnitude a type of significance argument concerning the degree to which individuals are adversely affected by the current policy.

minor repair a small adjustment of the current policy designed to reduce the significance of an existing problem.

moral imperative a type of significance argument that

identifies ethical responsibilities that are fundamental to the human order.

mutual exclusivity the competitiveness argument that indicates that a counterplan could not exist simultaneously with the affirmative plan, usually because legal or physical impediments preclude mutual coexistence.

N

negative the debate team charged with denying the resolution.

negative position a statement that encompasses all the negative arguments in a debate and establishes argumentative ties between them.

net benefits the competitiveness argument that argues that adoption of the counterplan or the plan will be less advantageous than adopting both plans simultaneously.

P

paradigm an analogy drawn between debate and another activity that involves the process of evaluation.

permutation a creative process of testing the compatibility of two policies through plan or counterplan alterations.

pilot project a program designed and implemented to test the implications of potential policies.

plan the proposal advocated by the affirmative to solve a significant problem.

plan mandates the specific directives of the plan designed to achieve solutions to the significant problem.

plan-meet-advantage a solvency challenge raised against claims that the affirmative policies will be allegedly advantageous compared to the present system.

plan-meet-need a solvency challenge raised against claims that the affirmative will eliminate a problem.

policy debate the process of advocating competing courses of action.

policy-making judge an evaluator who views the judge as like a legislator or executive decision maker who compares at least two policy options.

presumption (1) the assumption that the current course of action is justified until we are convinced otherwise. (2) the assumption that the resolution is assumed to be false until convinced otherwise. (3) the assumed importance of fundamental values.

prima facie case a series of arguments presented by the affirmative that on their face presents a reasoned argument for the resolution.

probability the likelihood that something is true. In causal reasoning this would include the likelihood that one thing will cause another. In prediction this would include the likelihood that something is going to occur.

R

reasonability a topicality standard that requires the affirmative to offer a definition that is not overly broad.

rebuttal a speech in which the debaters resolve competing claims that have already been initiated.

redundancy the competitiveness argument positing that the action called for by the resolution is not necessary to solve the problem because a nonresolutional alternative can solve it equally well.

refutation the process of denying the reasoning of an opponent's arguments.

repetition the repeating of an argument for emphasis.

resolution the central issue under discussion that the affirmative must defend and the negative must deny.

S

scope a type of significance argument in which debaters describe the number of victims of the current policy.

should-would argument a line of argument that confuses the issue of whether a plan should exist with whether or not it would exist.

significance the line of argument that identifies the problem occurring under existing policies.

social significance a type of significance argument implying that a problem affects the entire society.

solvency the line of argument maintaining that the problem can be reduced or eliminated by new policies.

status quo the situation under the present system.

stock issues the four general lines of policy debate: significance, inherency, solvency, and topicality.

stock issues judge an evaluator who views debate

as similar to criminal courtroom advocacy, thus presuming that the present system is "innocent" until the affirmative proves the four general lines of policy argument.

structural inherency a structural problem such as a shortage of resources, bureaucratic or statutory limitations, or legal obstacles preventing the present system from solving the affirmative's harm.

structural plan-meet-need a codified characteristic of the present system that impedes the affirmative's ability to solve the problem.

T

tabula rasa judge an evaluator who believes the judge's mind should be a blank slate which debater should write on during a debate. These judges attempt to minimize their use of their personal preferences or arbitrary standards when evaluating debates.

threshold the point at which the impact of an argument becomes inevitable.

time-frame the line of argument that posits when an event will occur.

topical the quality of fulfilling the requirements of the resolution.

topicality the line of argument about whether or not the policies advocated are the policies recommended by a given debate resolution.

topicality standards criteria used to resolve conflicts between competing interpretations of the resolution.

traditional needs a defense of the resolution that presents a significant problem, shows why that problem will continue to exist, and demonstrates how a new proposal will eliminate the problem.

traditional significance a type of significance argument holding that some of the conventions of nations, cultures, and communities are valuable historically.

transition a word or phrase that provides a logical bridge from one argument to the next.

trivializing the process of reducing the impact of a specific argument in the context of an entire debate.

turnaround an argument used to answer a disadvantage indicating that the plan solves the disadvantage (link turn) or that the impact of the disadvantage is actually good (impact turn).

U

uniqueness the argument positing that a given cause and only a given cause will result in a particular effect. It is frequently applied to address the question of whether or not the affirmative proposal alone would cause the disadvantage to occur.

V

voting issue an argument that independently of all other arguments in the debate, justifies voting for one side over the other.

Index